Communication

The Ultimate Guide to Being Great at Conversations, Boosting Your Social Skills, Mastering Small Talk and Becoming Skillful at Reading Body Language

© Copyright 2019

All Rights Reserved. No part of this book may be reproduced in any form without permission in writing from the author. Reviewers may quote brief passages in reviews.

Disclaimer: No part of this publication may be reproduced or transmitted in any form or by any means, mechanical or electronic, including photocopying or recording, or by any information storage and retrieval system, or transmitted by email without permission in writing from the publisher.

While all attempts have been made to verify the information provided in this publication, neither the author nor the publisher assumes any responsibility for errors, omissions or contrary interpretations of the subject matter herein.

This book is for entertainment purposes only. The views expressed are those of the author alone, and should not be taken as expert instruction or commands. The reader is responsible for his or her own actions.

Adherence to all applicable laws and regulations, including international, federal, state and local laws governing professional licensing, business practices, advertising and all other aspects of doing business in the US, Canada, UK or any other jurisdiction is the sole responsibility of the purchaser or reader.

Neither the author nor the publisher assumes any responsibility or liability whatsoever on the behalf of the purchaser or reader of these materials. Any perceived slight of any individual or organization is purely unintentional

Contents

PART 1: CONVERSATION SKILLS 0

INTRODUCTION 1

CHAPTER 1: INTROVERTS VS. EXTROVERTS 3
  INTROVERSION VS. EXTROVERSION SELF-ASSESSMENT 6
  CASE STUDIES 7

CHAPTER 2: UNDERSTANDING PEOPLE 8
  INTROVERSION VS. EXTROVERSION 9
  GENDER DIFFERENCES 10
  EMOTIONAL STATES 11
  CULTURAL DIFFERENCES 12
  PERSONALITY TYPES 12
  CASE STUDIES 13

CHAPTER 3: COMMUNICATION REALLY DOES MATTER 14
  COMMUNICATION MATTERS 15
  BENEFITS OF IMPROVING YOUR COMMUNICATION SKILLS 16
    Just for Introverts 16
    For Anyone 16
  CASE STUDIES 17

CHAPTER 4: SOCIAL ANXIETY 18
  THE SHY INTROVERT 18
  THE ANXIOUS INTROVERT 18
  THE EASIEST WAY FOR INTROVERTS TO REDUCE ANXIETY 19
  WHAT ELSE YOU CAN DO 19

CASE STUDIES..21

CHAPTER 5: COMMUNICATION FUNDAMENTALS 22
SLICING UP THE COMMUNICATIONS PIE 22
10/40/50 24
LISTENING SKILLS 26
Active Listening..26
QUESTIONING...28
The Difference Between Open and Closed Questions 28
Are Closed Questions Bad?...29
Open Questions 30
From Closed to Open - Exercise 31
LEADING QUESTIONS 34
From Leading to Open - Exercise 35
CASE STUDIES..37
THE INTROVERT'S SURVIVAL GUIDE TO ACTIVE LISTENING 37
THE INTROVERT'S SURVIVAL GUIDE TO ASKING QUESTIONS 38

CHAPTER 6: NON-VERBAL COMMUNICATION 40
WHY BODY LANGUAGE MATTERS..42
BODY LANGUAGE FOR INTROVERTS 43
Open Body Stance 43
CULTURAL DIFFERENCES 48
Eye Contact 48
Personal Space..48
Gestures...49
CONTEXT IS EVERYTHING 51
A Meeting with Marty..51
Fred's Meeting with Norman 51
The Monday Meeting...51
The RRR Rodeo Team Meeting..52
The President Speaks...52
The Family Business..52
A Meeting with Marty – Angelina's perspective...............................53
Fred's Meeting with Norman – Fred's perspective..........................53
The Monday Meeting – Melinda's perspective.................................53
The RRR Rodeo Team Meeting – Ruth's perspective 54
The President Speaks – Nancy's perspective....................................54
The Family Business – Jack's perspective 55
MESSAGE MISMATCH 55
Personal Safety and De-escalating Situations..................................56
THOSE DARN SMARTPHONES 57
CASE STUDIES..59
THE INTROVERT'S SURVIVAL GUIDE TO NON-VERBAL COMMUNICATION 60
THE INTROVERT'S SURVIVAL GUIDE TO SMARTPHONES...............................61

CHAPTER 7: ADAPTING TO TYPE 63
PERSONALITY TYPE MODELS..66

ADAPTING TO TYPE 68
    Choice of Topic *70*
    Word Choice *70*
    Vary Your Tone *70*
    Mirror Body Language *70*
    Mood Match *71*
CASE STUDIES 76
THE INTROVERT'S SURVIVAL GUIDE TO ADAPTING TO TYPE 77

CHAPTER 8: MEETING STRANGERS 79

BEING APPROACHABLE 79
CONVERSATION OPENERS 79
CONVERSATION TIPS 80
CHATTING IN CLUSTERS 81
ENDING A CONVERSATION 81
50 CONVERSATION STARTERS 81
CASE STUDIES 84
THE INTROVERT'S SURVIVAL GUIDE TO MEETING STRANGERS 84

CHAPTER 9: GETTING PEOPLE TO TALK 86

GETTING OTHER PEOPLE TO TALK 89
YOUR MAGIC CONVERSATION STARTERS 89
BONUS: 100 MORE CONVERSATION STARTERS 90
CASE STUDIES 94
THE INTROVERT'S SURVIVAL GUIDE TO GETTING PEOPLE TO TALK 95

CHAPTER 10: INCREASING YOUR LIKABILITY 96

THE CHARISMA MYTH 96
BEING LIKEABLE 97
CASE STUDIES 98
THE INTROVERT'S SURVIVAL GUIDE TO LIKEABILITY 98

CHAPTER 11: FINDING YOUR VOICE 100

TONE OF VOICE 100
METAPHORICALLY SPEAKING 102
STORYTELLING 103
CASE STUDIES 104

CHAPTER 12: NETWORKING 101 105

WALLFLOWERS, MINGLERS, AND ACES 106
    Wallflowers *106*
    Minglers *106*
    Aces *106*
NETWORKING SKILLS SELF-ASSESSMENT 106
NETWORKING FOR INTROVERTS 108
MASTERING SMALL TALK 109
THE TRANSFORMATION FROM WALLFLOWER TO MINGLER 110
3-PART NETWORKING STRATEGY 111

    1. Have a goal *111*
    2. Take a leap *112*
    3. Act with intention *112*
  CASE STUDIES 113
  THE INTROVERT'S SURVIVAL GUIDE TO SMALL TALK 113
  THE INTROVERT'S GUIDE TO 7 DIFFERENT TYPES OF NETWORKING
  OPPORTUNITIES 114
  THE INTROVERT'S GUIDE TO NETWORKING–AT NETWORKING EVENTS 115
  THE INTROVERT'S GUIDE TO NETWORKING–AT LECTURE-STYLE
  PRESENTATIONS 116
  THE INTROVERT'S GUIDE TO NETWORKING–AT WORKSHOPS AND CLASSES ... 117
  THE INTROVERT'S GUIDE TO NETWORKING–AT LUNCHEONS 118
  THE INTROVERT'S GUIDE TO NETWORKING–AT DINNERS 119
  THE INTROVERT'S GUIDE TO NETWORKING–AT CONFERENCES 120
  THE INTROVERT'S GUIDE TO NETWORKING–AT TRADE SHOWS 121

CHAPTER 13: SPECIAL SITUATIONS **123**
  CASE STUDIES 123
  THE INTROVERT'S GUIDE TO 5 SPECIAL SITUATIONS 124
  THE INTROVERT'S SURVIVAL GUIDE TO INTERVIEWS 124
  THE INTROVERT'S SURVIVAL GUIDE TO BUSINESS MEETINGS 125
  THE INTROVERT'S SURVIVAL GUIDE TO THE OFFICE COMMUNICATIONS 126
  THE INTROVERT'S SURVIVAL GUIDE TO OFFICE PARTIES 127
  THE INTROVERT'S SURVIVAL GUIDE TO VOLUNTEERING 128

CHAPTER 14: EMERGENCIES **129**
  HANDLING EMERGENCIES – THE 5 R'S 131
    Retreat *131*
    Reach Out *131*
    Reflect *131*
    Rest *131*
    Rebound *132*
  CASE STUDIES 134
  THE INTROVERT'S SURVIVAL GUIDE TO TRIUMPHING OVER SOCIAL
  EMERGENCIES 135

CHAPTER 15: WRITTEN COMMUNICATIONS **136**
  WRITE TO CONTRIBUTE 137
  CASE STUDIES 137
  THE INTROVERT'S SURVIVAL GUIDE TO E-MAIL 138

CHAPTER 16: SELF-CARE FOR INTROVERTS **139**
  SELF-CARE – 4 ESSENTIALS 139
  OTHER POSSIBILITIES 140
  CASE STUDIES 141
  THE INTROVERT'S SURVIVAL GUIDE TO SELF-CARE 142

CONCLUSION **143**

PART 2: SOCIAL SKILLS 145

INTRODUCTION 146

CHAPTER 1: HOW TO DEAL WITH SOCIAL ANXIETY 148

CHAPTER 2: THE IMPORTANCE OF SOCIAL SKILLS 153

CHAPTER 3: INTROVERT TRAITS 159

CHAPTER 4: GOALS 164

CHAPTER 5: ANALYZING PEOPLE 169

CHAPTER 6: BODY LANGUAGE 175

CHAPTER 7: FACE READING 181

CHAPTER 8: THE FOUR PERSONALITY TYPES 186
- CHOLERIC 187
- SANGUINE 188
- PHLEGMATIC 189
- MELANCHOLIC 190

CHAPTER 9: HOW TO DETECT A LIAR 192

CHAPTER 10: MAKE BODY LANGUAGE YOUR SUPERPOWER 198

CHAPTER 11: HANDLING SMALL TALK AS AN INTROVERT 204
- WHY IS SMALL TALK DIFFICULT AND DESIRABLE FOR INTROVERTS? 205

CHAPTER 12: INTROVERT PROBLEMS AND RELATIONSHIPS 209

CHAPTER 13: INTROVERT PROBLEMS IN AN OPEN WORKPLACE 215

CHAPTER 14: INTROVERT PROBLEMS AT SOCIAL GATHERINGS, EVENTS, AND PARTIES 221

CHAPTER 15: EMOTIONAL INTELLIGENCE 226
- WHAT IS THE IMPORTANCE OF EMOTIONAL INTELLIGENCE, PARTICULARLY FOR YOU? 228

CHAPTER 16: PRACTICAL COMMUNICATION TIPS (ADDITIONAL TIPS) 232

CHAPTER 17: INSPIRING INDIVIDUALS 237

CONCLUSION 241

PART 3: SMALL TALK 243

INTRODUCTION 244

CHAPTER 1: WHAT IS SMALL TALK? 246

CHAPTER 2: UNDERSTANDING THE INTROVERT AND HOW THEY INTERACT WITH THE WORLD 251

CHAPTER 3: ARE THERE ANY ADVANTAGES TO BEING SHY? 258

CHAPTER 4: WHAT IS THE DIFFERENCE BETWEEN BEING SHY AND BEING AN INTROVERT? 264

CHAPTER 5: SOCIAL ANXIETY IS HOLDING YOU BACK AND HOW TO LEAVE IT IN THE DUST 268

CHAPTER 6: GOOD LISTENING SKILLS CAN MAKE SMALL TALK EASIER 274

CHAPTER 7: TIPS TO START A CONVERSATION AND KEEP IT GOING 282

CHAPTER 8: CAN I MAKE FRIENDS AS AN INTROVERT? 288

CHAPTER 9: SIMPLE THINGS YOU CAN DO TO BE MORE LIKEABLE 293

CHAPTER 10: HOW TO START AND BUILD UP RELATIONSHIPS AS AN INTROVERT 298

CHAPTER 11: OTHER WAYS TO INCREASE YOUR COMMUNICATION SKILLS 307

CHAPTER 12: TIPS TO HELP YOU DEVELOP YOUR SOCIAL SKILLS 317

CONCLUSION 325

PART 4: BODY LANGUAGE 327

INTRODUCTION 328

CHAPTER 1: WHAT IS AN "ALPHA" AND WHY ARE THEY WINNERS? 329

CHAPTER 2: THE ALPHA MALE: HOW TO SPOT ONE 337

CHAPTER 3: THE ALPHA FEMALE: HOW TO SPOT ONE 343

CHAPTER 4: BODY LANGUAGE IN SOCIAL SITUATIONS: HOW TO CHARM 350

CHAPTER 5: BODY LANGUAGE IN DATING: HOW TO IMPRESS WITH CHARISMA 356

CHAPTER 6: BODY LANGUAGE AT WORK: HOW TO BE MEMORABLE 361

CONCLUSION 367

Part 1: Conversation Skills

Secrets for Introverts on How to Analyze People, Handle Small Talk with Confidence, Overcome Social Anxiety and Highly Effective Communication Tips for Networking with People

Introduction

The following chapters will discuss why communication matters, conversation fundamentals, connecting with people and social survival.

Let me introduce you to four people who will be your case studies throughout this book: Rebecca, Larry, Chris and Kelly.

- Rebecca is an introvert who is finding it challenging to contribute to discussions at work. Rebecca's goal is to share her ideas with her team– and be heard!
- Larry is an introvert, but he has adapted well in an extrovert's world at work. Larry's goal is to improve his networking skills through better conversation skills.
- Chris is an introvert, tends to be anxious and, embarrassingly for her, has been called terribly shy. Chris' goal is to be less stressed at work.
- Kelly is not an introvert, but still wants to improve his conversation skills. Kelly's goal is to understand what makes his introvert friends tick.

As you progress through this book, you'll learn more about each case study's unique challenges and ultimately, how they achieved their goals by applying the principles in this book.

I suggest you read with a notebook at hand, so that you can complete the self-assessment, make note of key learnings, and jot ideas.

There is a seemingly unending supply of books on communication skills, so thank you again for choosing this one!

I hope you will find the information in this book as practical as I intended. It is my hope that you will find useful skills along with a few inspiring gems to help you move toward your own goals.

Enjoy!

Chapter 1: Introverts vs. Extroverts

"Extroverts organize their thoughts by talking and gain more energy by seeking outside stimuli. Introverts on the other hand, store information, reflect first, and then speak afterwards. They feel most rested and rejuvenated after they spend time alone, thinking or reading."

Marti Olsen Lany

We hear a lot about how extroverts rule the world, but is that really true?

The truth is that there are a lot of assumptions made about introverts and what makes them tick. And you may be surprised to learn who is an introvert.

Exercise: Reflect on famous people that you think may be introverts. Next, Google famous introverts to see who shows up. Were you right? Are you surprised by any names on the lists?

It is a common assumption that introverts are lacking in confidence and hate public speaking. While some may fit this profile, this is a broad generalization that is far from true. Conversely, some think that people who are confident when speaking in public must be extroverts. This is not necessarily so.

Have a look at the following summary of the characteristics of introverts and extroverts.

Characteristics of introverts:

- Restore their energy with time alone
- Prefer smaller gatherings
- Find large gatherings exhausting
- Get overwhelmed in noisy settings with multiple conversations going on
- Internal thinkers
- Need time to reflect to generate ideas and to do their best work
- Tend not to like change

Characteristics of extroverts:

- Restore their energy by being around people
- Enjoy large gatherings
- Find small gatherings boring
- Get into the spirit of meeting people, especially at a big event
- Are the only ones who will say, "The more the merrier!"
- Think out loud by talking
- Come up with ideas seemingly instantly, on the spot
- Love change

As you can see, a key difference between introverts and extroverts is how they restore their energy.

Exercise: The next time you attend any conference or other big event, observe what happens when the formal sessions are over. Look in the bar and you will find the extroverts, restoring their energy by talking with other people. The introverts, for the most part, will be in their rooms, or out for a walk, restoring their energy by spending time alone.

Consider these common myths about introverts:

- Introverts are shy: It is an assumption that someone who is not talking is shy when, in fact, they may be deep in thought, reflecting on the subject at hand.
- Introverts don't have anything to contribute: Just because someone doesn't immediately jump into a conversation doesn't mean they have nothing to say. Perhaps they are inclined to wait until asked, or for a pause before they speak up (which may never happen) or need time to reflect.
- Introverts have social anxiety: Maybe yes or maybe no. While it is not uncommon for an introvert to experience social anxiety, not all do, and the degree certainly varies by person and situation.

You may be asking yourself, is introversion a bad thing? No, absolutely not. It is just one of the ways in which humans are different. We will look at other ways people differ in the next chapter. We are simply calling out introversion first, as this book is written to benefit introverts by offering conversation strategies specific to their unique needs.

As we wrap up this chapter, here are a few helpful caveats to keep in mind:

- While our society seemingly places a high value on extroverts, keep in mind that introverts contribute just as much to the world, if not more.
- Neither introversion nor extroversion is inherently right or wrong–these are just two different ways of being in the world.
- Learn to value what makes you tick as an introvert and carve out time to do what you need to do to take care of yourself. If that means you need half an hour of silence to restore your energy while your extrovert co-workers are at the bar, that's fine.
- Trust your gut.
- Focus on your strengths and build on them.

What do you think? Are you an introvert?

Introversion vs. Extroversion Self-Assessment

Take a few minutes to reflect on whether you are an introvert or an extrovert.

1. What restores your energy:
a) being with people
b) time alone
2. What do you prefer:
    a) a big party
    b) a quiet dinner with a friend
3. How do you do your best thinking:
    a) out loud
    b) internally
4. How do you problem solve:
a) verbally (sharing possibilities with others)
b) internally (reflecting on possibilities as you refine them)
5. Do your best ideas:
a) come to you right away
b) come to you after you have had time to reflect
6. If you are at a gathering with multiple conversations going on at the same time, are you:
a) energized by the buzz
b) overwhelmed by the noise
7. If you are attending a conference, do you tend to:
a) mingle with and meet lots of people
b) keep to yourself
8. What best describes your ability to concentrate? Are you:
a) easily distracted
b) able to concentrate for long stretches of time
9. Do you share personal information about yourself with:
    a) just about anyone
    b) just close family and friends
10. What best describes how you feel about change. Do you:

a) love it
b) resist it

If you answered the first option (a) more than the second option (b), you are probably an extrovert. That's ok. While this book isn't written specifically for you, you'll probably find you still get plenty of ideas from it.

If you answered the second option (b) more than the first option (a), you are probably an introvert. Great, this book is written for you!

Case Studies

- Rebecca never really thought of herself as an introvert, but that changed after she learned that introverts need time alone to restore their energy. That'd be her!
- Larry has always thought of himself as outgoing, but supposes he is an introvert because he likes lots of time alone and is very analytic.
- Chris knows she is definitely an introvert. There's no hiding it!
- Kelly knows he is an extrovert and he is ok with that.

Chapter 2: Understanding People

"The most important thing in communication is hearing what isn't said."

-Peter F. Drucker

We've touched on introversion versus extroversion already.

Now we will explore other ways in which people differ.

When you are aware of the many ways in which people differ, you will be better equipped to understand what makes them tick, allowing you to adapt your approach in order to have better communications.

The Gender Gap - Exercise

Which gender would you associate the following with?

Men/women:
- Use communication to create connections
- Use communication to achieve tangible outcomes
- Aim to build understanding
- Want to feel needed, appreciated and admired
- Have an underlying desire to establish dominance
- See the purpose of conversation as a means to share ideas

and feelings
- See conversations as an opportunity to offer advice
- Tend to be more expressive
- Value differences
- Are less likely to interrupt
- Tend to be more rational
- Are driven to avoid failure
- Seek to impress listeners
- May offer solutions simply to avoid further discussions
- In conflict situations, will seek empathy and understanding
- Deal with stress by withdrawing

Were the answers obvious to you? Or not?

Keep your thoughts on this in mind, as we will return to gender differences shortly.

Introversion vs. Extroversion

Here is a summary of the key differences between introverts and extroverts outlined in Chapter 1.

Introverts:
- Restore their energy with time alone.
- Prefer smaller gatherings over large ones.
- Are internal thinkers and need time to reflect.

Extroverts:
- Restore their energy by being around people.
- Enjoy the stimulation of large gatherings.
- Think out loud and can come up with new ideas on the spot.

An awareness of whether you are dealing with an introvert or extrovert will allow you to adapt your approach. For example, you won't be surprised if an extrovert wants to share their ideas all at once, whereas you should allow an introvert time to reflect before answering.

Gender Differences

Women and men differ in many ways, including differences in needs, goals and values.

The following are generalizations about how each gender communicates.

You may find the gender differences feel obvious to you or you may find you resist the categorization between the sexes. This is natural. Few people are entirely one way or the other. Consider the growing acceptance of variances along the gender scale.

Regardless, an awareness of tendencies that are both innate and those developed as a result of societal norms can help you in your communications with others.

Generally speaking, women:

- Aim to build understanding and avoid isolation.
- Are relationship-oriented.
- Are synergistic (having common goals).
- Prefer equality and symmetry.
- Value the cooperation, similarities, closeness and the communications process itself.
- Want to feel cherished and respected.
- Seek understanding.
- Use communication to create connections and establish relationships.
- See the purpose of conversation to build intimacy and as a means to share ideas and feelings.
- Tend to be more expressive, talkative, polite, tentative, emotional and social than men.
- Are less likely to interrupt and swear than men.
- Deal with stress by talking about the source of stress.

- In conflict situations, seek empathy and understanding.

In general, men:
- Aim to establish dominance, impress others, be seen as a leader and avoid failure.
- Are goal- and results-oriented.
- Are adversarial (having conflicting goals).
- Prefer inequality and asymmetry.
- Value independence and differences.
- Want to feel needed, appreciated and admired.
- Seek control.
- Use communication to exert dominance and achieve tangible outcomes.
- See the purpose of conversation as a means to transmit information and offer advice.
- Tend to be more rational, unemotional, assertive and power hungry than women.
- Are more likely to interrupt or swear than women.
- Are more likely to offer solutions simply to avoid further discussion than women.
- Deal with stress by withdrawing.
- In conflict situations, will offer solutions for quick resolution.

Emotional States

Our emotional state impacts how we communicate in the moment.

Think of yourself for a moment: if you are generally easy going in your communications, might you respond differently when under a lot of stress?

Here are some emotional states to be aware of:
- People think and respond differently when they are under stress. The greater the stress, the shorter the attention span. Patience and tolerance for others slip.

- Someone who is sick or is sleep-deprived will not be at their best.
- A person who is angry isn't able to think rationally. When we are angry, our fight or flight instincts are activated. In this state, blood rushes to our extremities, far away from our brains, leaving us unequipped mentally. Expecting someone to make good decisions or communicate well when angry is foolish.
- Grief can cause someone to lose their grounding, impacting their ability to think clearly, plan, work productively and communicate with others. People grieve differently over a long time, so take personal losses into consideration.
- Other emotional states to consider include sadness, trauma or even extreme joy.

All can impact one's ability to communicate and interact with others.

Cultural Differences

People from different cultural backgrounds have many differences, ranging from beliefs, upbringing, cultural norms, life experiences, and communication skills.

Chapter 6: Non-Verbal Communications will explore cultural differences that are communicated non-verbally.

Personality Types

We are not all the same. Aside from the differences already mentioned, you know this instinctively.

Two people brought up the same, in similar circumstances, may vary in how they think and act. One person is laid back, while another never sits still. One person is casual about deadlines, while another is deadline-driven. One person coasts through life, happy with their circumstances, while another pursues their goals with dedication. None are right, and none are wrong; they are just personality differences. That said, to be effective you need to adapt your approach with each type to get your message across.

Chapter 7: Adapting to Type will provide strategies for different personality types.

As we wrap up this chapter, here are a few helpful caveats to keep in mind:

- Be open to the reality that gender differences may play.
- Make allowances for the fact that we don't know what is going on with others in any given moment.
- Look for highly emotional states and steer clear or leave lots of room for misunderstandings and reworking.
- Do not try to rationalize with an angry person.
- Be aware of possible cultural differences (more on this in Chapter 6. Non-Verbal Communications).
- It is important to adapt your approach to different types of people (more on this in Chapter 7: Adapting to Type).

What do you think? Do you have a pretty good sense of how people differ? Or are those differences a mystery to you?

Case Studies

- Rebecca finds it challenging to communicate ideas on the spot with others who are concise and fast thinkers. She needs time to reflect.
- Kelly does not know how to respond to people in heightened emotional states (upset, angry) in the workplace.
- Chris is troubled by her boss who is very task-oriented. The situation had been causing Chris to become flustered.
- Kelly is curious about how gender differences impact conversations.

Chapter 3: Communication Really Does Matter

Consider this story: Peggy was at an international conference and made time to visit the newcomer's reception, as she wanted to meet a few new people. The room was pretty busy, and most people were chatting, so she busied herself getting a nibble. With a glass of wine in her right hand, she examined the table of snacks. As soon as she had a few slices of cheese wrapped in a napkin in her left hand, another participant approached the table and introduced himself, 'Oh, this cheese selection looks fantastic, mind if I join you? I'm Mo.' Not really thinking, Peggy stuck the cheese packet into her right hand, which was already balancing her glass of wine, laughed, and reached out her left hand in response. 'Sorry, wrong hand, but all the cheese got me excited too! Nice to meet you, Mo. I'm Peggy.' She was a little surprised by the look that overcame her new friend's face and wondered why he faltered before speaking again. Peggy had been unaware that in some parts of the world, the left hand was only used for bodily functions, and never for food or touching others. By presenting her left hand, she had made an offensive gesture.

Faux Pas - Exercise

Take a moment to reflect on Peggy's story.

How could Peggy have avoided this faux pas, or embarrassing social blunder?

Communication is central to our lives.

Whether verbal or non-verbal, spoken or electronic, sighted or blind, no matter how you do it, communication is at the heart of our lives and how we interact with the world.

Communication is such a broad topic that it can be hard to narrow it down to just a few points to begin an exploration, so let's pause to look at why communication matters.

Communication Matters

Communication really does matter.

Here are some of the ways communication matters in day to day life.

Communication helps you:
- Get your ideas across
- Provide and receive feedback
- Feel heard
- Connect with people
- Contribute to your community

Faux Pas - Possibilities

Let's return to Peggy's story.

If Peggy had an awareness of cultural differences in non-verbal communication, she may have been able to avoid her blunder.

Granted, you can't be expected to know every cultural difference around the world, at least in your day-to-day work, however Peggy *was* going to an international conference. Had Peggy learned about cultural differences and refreshed herself on variances in what non-verbal cues mean, she could have avoided this embarrassing moment for herself and for the person she met.

This is a great example of how improving your communication skills can benefit you.

Benefits of Improving Your Communication Skills

Just for Introverts

While everyone can benefit from improving their communication skills, there are some very specific ways that this can help you as an introvert:

- As an introvert, you are already adept at reading a room and picking up on non-verbal cues. With a little knowledge on what to look for, you can be a powerhouse.
- Similarly, introverts are naturally great listeners. When you intentionally apply yourself to learning active listening skills, you will take your natural abilities to a higher level.
- Writing is another common strength of introverts. If you add a bit of structure, by learning how to hone your writing skills, and apply them regularly, you will contribute a lot to those around you. You'll also feel more fulfilled.

For Anyone

There are many more benefits that anyone can realize by enhancing their communication skills. Here are just a few.

Improving your communication skills can help you:

- Be more confident
- Achieve better results
- Have more influence
- Understand others
- Collaborate with others
- Achieve your goals
- Feel empowered
- Avoid embarrassing moments
- Reduce anxiety
- Increase overall life satisfaction

- Deepen your connections
- Become more compassionate
- Help others
- Make a difference in your community

As we wrap up this chapter, here are a few helpful caveats to keep in mind:

- You already have numerous strengths–celebrate what you do well!
- You'll have many ideas about how you can improve your communication skills. Jot them down but pick just a few to work on first. Don't overwhelm yourself.
- Celebrate your victories, big and small!

What do you think? Do you see how your communication skills are impacting your work, relationships and your life? Can you see benefits to improving your skills?

Case Studies

- Rebecca is disappointed that she isn't able to share her ideas or doesn't feel heard when she does. As she wants to advance her career, she is looking for solutions.
- Larry knows he is on the cusp of being really great at his job but is aware that he does not always communicate effectively. His goal this year is to converse with ease in networking situations.
- Chris feels she has a lot to contribute, but her environment is not allowing her to be heard. She wants to figure out a way to share her ideas and figures conversation skills are a good place to start.
- Kelly believes he would be more effective and a better friend if he better understand his introverted friends and colleagues.

Chapter 4: Social Anxiety

"Shy people fear negative judgment, while introverts simply prefer less stimulation; shyness is inherently painful, and introversion is not. But in a society that prizes the bold and the outspoken, both are perceived as disadvantages."

Susan Cain

The Shy Introvert

As this chapter's opening quote says so well, being shy is not the same as being an introvert.

You might be a shy introvert, but you might not be shy at all. You just may keep to yourself.

Let the label go and be yourself.

The Anxious Introvert

Introverts have social anxiety?

Maybe yes, or maybe no.

While it is not uncommon for an introvert to experience social anxiety, not all do, and the degree certainly varies by person and situation.

There is a tendency for anxiety to build up over time. An introvert experiencing social anxiety may cause others, or even themselves, to begin to think of these to be one and the same, but it does not have to be this way.

The Easiest Way for Introverts to Reduce Anxiety

This one may surprise you, but it is good news.

As an introvert, you may find that your greatest stresses are the result of trying to live your life according to what extroverts like.

Workplaces, meetings and social settings can be loud, lack privacy and leave no time to think. The things that introverts need to survive and thrive (e.g. quiet, time to reflect and time alone) are often missing from these environments.

If you create quiet, privacy and time alone each day, you may find yourself less anxious.

Yes, it can be as simple as that.

If it sounds too simple, try it.

If you need more, that's ok, but it's a foundation.

Expecting yourself, as an introvert, to not experience stress in loud places where you get no time to think, let alone to be alone, is unreasonable.

What Else You Can Do

Here are a few other things you can do that may help you reduce your anxiety:

- Get enough sleep.
- Eat well and avoid too much caffeine.
- Arrive early at events.
- Have an exit plan.

- Give yourself permission to leave.
- Take a time out.
- Remind yourself to breathe.
- Focus outward on someone else, versus inward on yourself.
- Find one person that you can talk to and ask them a great question that will keep them talking.

Butterflies - Exercise

How do you make your butterflies fly in formation?

Take a few minutes to write down the things you currently do to reduce your anxiety.

Put big ★ stars ★ next to the ones that make the biggest difference.

Draw some butterflies if you wish.

Now add to your list the suggestions from this chapter that you would like to try.

Draw some caterpillars if you wish.

These are your future butterflies, and you *can* teach them to fly in formation.

As we wrap up this chapter, here are a few helpful caveats to keep in mind:

- Give yourself permission to take a break or step away from any situation that causes you to feel anxiety.
- Planning ahead by preparing yourself for events and activities can help to decrease your anxiety.
- If you continue to experience social anxiety that is not manageable, consider a support group, therapist or life coach for assistance.
- Chapter 14: Emergencies has tips on what to do if you have an emergency such as becoming overwhelmed or having a panic attack in a social setting.
- Chapter 16: Self-Care for Introverts has tips for taking care

of oneself as an introvert, many of which will also be supportive if you are experiencing social anxiety.

• When you give yourself what you need as an introvert, your anxiety may naturally decrease, as you won't be pushing yourself into uncomfortable zones.

What do you think? Do you experience a high level of social anxiety? Do you experience anxiety in all situations or just a few? Is your anxiety extreme or manageable? How would relieving some of your anxiety benefit you?

Case Studies

• Rebecca's social anxiety is a major factor preventing her from contributing to discussions at work. She is determined to turn the situation around.

• Larry's social anxiety mainly comes into play in business networking situations, where he gets tongue-tied. He'd like to become more skilled so that he could reach higher sales targets.

• Chris experiences occasional bouts of extreme anxiety at work, interspersed with mild anxiety. She'd like to lower her stress level without changing jobs.

• Kelly doesn't experience anxiety, per se, but occasionally finds his confidence waning. He'd like to understand what is going on when that happens and work it out.

Chapter 5: Communication Fundamentals

"Introverts are naturally adept when it comes to actively listening. We tend to be the friend or colleague you can call on when you're upset, or you have good news to share. We're going to be able to listen and be with you in that, without turning it around and making it about us."

Beth Buelow

We all know communication is important. Why else would you have bought this book? In this chapter, we will look at communication fundamentals–the core aspects of effective communications.

Let's begin by breaking down the elements of communication.

Slicing Up the Communications Pie

Here's some food for thought to start.

Consider the following and try to fill in the percentages:

What percentage of a message is conveyed by:

- The words spoken: ___%
- Tone of voice: ___%

- Body language: ___%

Jot down your best guesses and keep them in mind as we progress. We'll reveal the answer shortly.

Let's start our discussion on the communication fundamentals by 'listening in' on a few business leaders in their day-to-day worlds, speaking to their employees.

The Leaders Share Strategy

What do you imagine about what each speaker feels about the message they are conveying?

Gerry is speaking about the new direction for the company. His voice is upbeat. His body stance is relaxed as he speaks to the audience.

Geraldine is making a presentation about the company's new business strategy. Her voice is strained. She is seated with her arms crossed as she is speaking to the audience.

Gerhard is sharing the company's new mission statement. He is speaking clearly but sternly. His back is to the audience as he is reading the slides.

Gloria is unveiling the company's new product line. She is speaking cheerfully and clearly. She stands and holds each new product up in front of her as she discusses its features.

Grace is announcing the company's new overtime policy. Her voice is even but a bit quiet. Her head is down as she is reading the details aloud.

With the small amount of information provided, what do you imagine each speaker feels about the message they are conveying? Would you feel more confident in your response if you could hear the speaker's voice? What if you were actually in the room?

10/40/50

Here is the breakdown of roughly what percentage of a message is conveyed by the words, tone of voice, and body language.

Messages are conveyed by:

- The words spoken: 10%
- Tone of voice: 40%
- Body language: 50%

More specifically:

- About 10 % of a message is conveyed by the words spoken. While spoken words are extremely important, their meaning can be distorted if the other elements communicate a contrary message.
- About 40% of a message is conveyed by tone of voice. A voice tone that is loud, quiet, stern, cheerful, low, high, fast or slow will affect what the listener hears from the speaker.
- About 50% of a message is conveyed by body language. Body language that conveys openness (uncrossed arms, eye contact, smiling) will cause a listener to take in a different message than the same words spoken with closed body language (arms crossed, no eye contact, frown).

You may have seen studies with slightly different percentages, perhaps from famous studies in the 1960s, but the principles are essentially the same: words matter, but tone of voice and body language can distort the message if they are not aligned.

Are you surprised at all by these numbers?

Think for a moment about a time when you walked into a room in which someone later communicated a negative message. Did you pick up on anything in the person's body language that told you that something was wrong?

Think about a time when your boss had to give you negative news, either you were being laid off, or there was a performance concern.

Were there cues in your boss's body language, in how he or she was standing or sitting? What about their facial expression? When they began to speak, was it clear to you that this wasn't going to be good news? What told you that, even if they were just greeting you? More than likely, their tone of voice foretold a bit of what was to come.

The words, of course, told the full story, but in these situations rarely is the fact that it's not good news a surprise by the time the speaker gets down to the message itself.

The 10/40/50 percentages carry these lessons when communicating a message to others:

- Words are important, but they count less than you might think IF you send a different message non-verbally.
- Body language is very powerful and can dominate a message.
- If body language carries a message contrary to the words you use, then the intent of your message may not be believed or may not even be heard.
- Tone of voice is worth paying attention to.
- It is important to be congruent, as in your words, tone of voice and body language need to send the same message.

On the other hand, the 10/40/50 percentages offer clues when interpreting messages from others:

- If you are discomforted by a message, try to notice what signals you are picking up on: the words, the tone of voice or the speaker's body language.
- Be aware that the speaker may not even be aware that they are sending conflicting messages.
- Remember that you may respond instinctively to voice tone and body language, and not even be aware of it.
- If you notice that the message is not congruent, you have an opportunity to ask questions or otherwise determine what the real message is.

- In most cases, you do not need to act in the moment, but should reflect on what you believe the whole message to have been.

We will delve more into non-verbal communication skills in the next chapter.

In this chapter, we will focus on listening and questioning skills.

Listening Skills

The best conversationalists put as much effort into how they listen as to what they say.

The best conversationalists:

- Listen actively to the speaker.
- Make eye contact.
- Use non-verbal communication to signal understanding (nodding).
- Ask open questions.
- Respectfully allow the other person to finish.

Active Listening

As introduced earlier, as an introvert, you are naturally a good listener. When you apply yourself to learning active listening skills, you will be well positioned to take your natural abilities to a higher level.

Active listening refers to consciously paying attention to the speaker.

With active listening:

- You give the speaker your full attention.
- You concentrate on the speaker's words.
- You pay attention to non-verbal cues.
- You make a point of not allowing yourself to be distracted.
- You do NOT think about your response.
- You do NOT guess what the person means.

- You do NOT interrupt.
- You do NOT offer contrary information
- If the person says something you believe is incorrect, or you do not understand, you WAIT until they have finished speaking.

Afterward, before responding, you ensure that you understand all of what the person has said. To do this:

- You ask clarifying questions.
- You summarize to confirm understanding.

If you feel you would like to take notes, at the beginning of the conversation you can say, "I hope you don't mind if I take a few notes. I don't want to forget anything you are saying." Then just take brief notes, as needed.

The benefits of active listening are:

- There are fewer misunderstandings.
- The speaker feels heard.
- You are more likely to be listened to afterward.
- Conflict is avoided.

The opposite of Active Listening is lazy listening, in which you pay little attention to what the other person is saying, think about what you will say in response, interrupt, don't pay attention to non-verbal communication or otherwise ignore the larger context. Lazy listening is ineffective! Ask yourself: Are you a Lazy Listener?

Your Last Vacation - Exercise

Ask a person to tell you about their last vacation. Use active listening skills as they respond.

As you listen:

- Don't allow yourself to interrupt.
- Ask questions only when the other person has stopped speaking.
- STAY CURIOUS – keep asking more questions until you

really have the whole story.
- Don't interrupt to share your experiences.
- Keep going until you have learned 5 things about the person and/or their vacation.

How did you do? Did you find yourself thinking ahead or wanting to interrupt?

Questioning

Have a look at these questions. What do you notice?

"Is this your first time here?"

"Do you like raisins?"

"Have you eaten rice cakes before?"

"What is that outside the window?"

"What type of cake do you prefer?"

"What's your favorite type of pasta?"

Need a hint?

What do you notice about the first three questions as opposed to the last three questions?

The first three questions are what are referred to as "closed questions".

The last three questions are what are referred to as "open questions".

What differentiates them is the type of answer they will solicit.

The Difference Between Open and Closed Questions

Closed questions invite one-word responses, which tends to 'close' down discussion.

Open questions, on the other hand, invite the listener to respond freely, which will naturally 'open' up discussion. Open questions open the door to dialog.

To enhance your conversation skills, you need to ask more open questions than closed questions.

EXERCISE:

Identify which of the following questions are closed vs. open questions:

"Do you like Italian food?"

"What are your boys doing for the summer?"

"Are your children boys or girls, or some of each?"

"Have you been to one of these networking events before?"

"What do you like best about this type of networking event?"

"Do you have anything to add to the discussion?"

"What do you have to add to the discussion?"

"Did you like this morning's speaker?"

"What did you think of this morning's speaker?"

Are Closed Questions Bad?

Closed questions are those that can be answered with "Yes", "No" or a single word answer, such as "Boys", "Three", "Tomorrow".

Are closed questions bad?

No, not necessarily, but they have their place.

Closed questions can be handy for getting quick answers to simple questions or for collecting information quickly. For example:

"Can you hear me at the back?"

"Can you see over me?"

"Do you want coffee or tea?"

"What day is your dental appointment?"

"Will you be in tomorrow?"

What other situations can you think of where closed questions might be most appropriate?

Create your own list but remember, to become an effective conversationalist, you need to master open questions.

Open Questions

An open question is any question that elicits an answer of longer than a single word.

The reason that open questions are preferred over closed questions is that open questions engage the other person and begin a dialogue.

EXERCISE:

You are at a conference and are waiting in line to get a coffee after a morning of speakers. What are three open questions you could ask your fellow delegates?

1.

2.

3.

Tip: *You will probably quickly see how easy it is to fall into the trap of asking a closed question rather than an open one.*

As open questions really can be your SECRET WEAPON though, it's worth spending time mastering this skill.

Open questions are a BIG ADVANTAGE that introverts can have over extroverts when meeting people.

Why?

Most introverts:

- Prefer one-on-one conversations over speaking with groups.
- Would rather have a nice long chat with one person

than make a lot of small talk with many people.
- Like interesting people.

As a result, mastering open questions can truly be the key to lowering your anxiety and having engaging discussions with the people you meet.

Yes, extroverts can ask open questions too, but they may very well have already flitted onto the next person, not concerned about how deeply they have connected with the person they just met. While they are off looking for the party, you can be having meaningful conversations.

And people WILL want to talk to you.

When you ask questions that engage others, they will want to share with you.

People love to talk about themselves, so if you present yourself with confidence, have a great greeting and ask open questions of the people you meet, you will find yourself engaged in conversation.

For this reason, mastering open questions can be your SECRET KEY to getting people to talk.

From Closed to Open - Exercise

Rewrite these closed questions as open questions.

For example:

"Do you want to go for lunch today?" – closed question

"Where do you want to go for lunch today?" – open question

"Did you like this morning's speaker?"

"Are you going away for Christmas?"

"Do you play a musical instrument?"

"Are you just visiting?"

"Do you have any ideas to add?"

"Are there any questions?"

"Do you like kayaking?"

"Did you have a good vacation?"

"Do you like to travel?"

"Did you enjoy college?"

"Do you want me to phone you?"

"Do you like sunny days?"

"Do you like to go for long drives?"

"Do you like juice?"

"You've met Sally before, right?"

Possible Responses

How did you make out?

Here are some examples of how these closed questions can be transformed into open questions:

"Did you like this morning's speaker?"

"What did you think of this morning's speaker?"

"How did you like this morning's speaker?"

"What did you like best about this morning's speaker?"

"Are you going away for Christmas?"

"Where are you going for Christmas?"

"What are you doing for Christmas?"

"Do you play a musical instrument?"

"What musical instruments do you play?"

"Are you just visiting?"

"Where are you visiting from?"

"Do you have any ideas to add?"

"What ideas do you have to add?"

"Are there any questions?"

"What questions do you have?"

"What questions are there?"

"Do you like kayaking?"

"What do you like about kayaking?"

"What water sports do you like?"

"Did you have a good vacation?"

"What was the best part about your vacation?"

"Tell me about your vacation."

"Do you like to travel?"

"What types of travel do you like to do?"

"Tell me about your travel experiences."

"Did you enjoy college?"

"What did you enjoy about college?"

"What was college like for you?"

"Do you want me to phone you?"

"How do you want me to follow up with you?"

"Do you like sunny days?"

"What do you like to do on sunny days?"

"Do you like to go for long drives?"

"If you had time today for a long drive, where would you go?"

"Do you like juice?"

"What is your favorite type of juice?"

"You've met Sally before, right?"

"When and how did you meet Sally?"

Leading Questions

Have a look at this next set of questions and see what you notice?

"Do you want to go for lunch today?"

"Do you want to go to Ben's Burger's for lunch?"

"Where do you want to go for lunch today?"

You will probably have recognized the first and second questions as being closed questions, and the last question as being an open question. But what is different about the second question?

Clue: What do you think the questioner wants to hear in response?

The second question is what is referred to as a 'leading' question

"Do you want to go for lunch today?" – closed question

"Do you want to go to Ben's Burger's for lunch?" – leading question

"Where do you want to go for lunch today?" – open question

A leading question is any question in which you 'telegraph' your desired response.

For example:

"You like working at this office, right?"

"We had a great time at the party, didn't we?"

"What are the worst parts of working Saturdays?"

The reason that leading questions are not desirable is that they are not getting at what the other person thinks. They are actually manipulative, though generally without malicious intent. And they aren't going to help you become an accomplished conversationalist.

From Leading to Open - Exercise

Rewrite these leading questions into non-leading open questions.

"Do you have conflicts with your supervisor?"

"How fast was the Mercedes going before it hit the BMW?"

"Don't you hate flying?"

"Well, that was a great seminar, wasn't it?"

"How much time will the new process save you?"

"Did you have a good day at school?"

"How was your awesome vacation?"

"Did you like our new styles?"

"Did you enjoy the team-building activity?"

"You have a great boss, don't you?"

"Wasn't that movie exciting?"

"What parts of the new software are the hardest to adapt to?"

Possible Responses

How did you make out with these questions?

Here are some possibilities of how these leading questions can be transformed into open questions:

"Do you have conflict with your supervisor?"

"What is your relationship like with your supervisor?"

"How fast was the Mercedes going before it hit the BMW?"

"How fast was each car going before they collided?"

"Don't you hate flying?"

"How you do you find flying?"

"Well, that was a great seminar, wasn't it?"

"What did you think of the seminar?"

"How much time will the new process save you?"

"How will the new processes affect your productivity?"

"Did you have a good day at school?"

"What was your day at school like today?"

"How was your awesome vacation?"

"How was your vacation?"

"What was the highlight of your vacation?"

"Did you like our new styles?"

"What was your reaction to our new styles?"

"Did you enjoy the team-building activity?"

"What did you think of the team-building activity?"

"You have a great boss, don't you?"

"What's your boss like?"

"Wasn't that movie exciting?"

"What did you think of that movie?"

"What parts of the new software are the hardest to adapt to?"

"What has your experience been adapting to the new software?"

As we wrap up this chapter, here are a few helpful caveats to keep in mind:

- As an introvert, you are naturally a good listener. As you apply yourself to learning active listening skills, you will be beginning to take your natural abilities to a higher level.
- Messages are conveyed by the words spoken (10%), tone of voice (40%) and body language (50%).
- Use active listening by giving the speaker your full

attention.
- Ask more open questions than closed questions.
- Avoid leading questions that 'telegraph' the desired answer.
- Non-verbal communication carries a powerful message (more on this next in Chapter 6).
- Voice tone also matters (more on this in Chapter 11).

What do you think? After learning about the fundamentals, what do you think your strengths are? Where are your biggest opportunities for improvement?

Case Studies

- Rebecca found the techniques of clarifying and summarizing to be most helpful. Not only did she find she understood more when she took time to clarify, but summarizing conversations led to her being asked to summarize meetings, which allowed her to structure opportunities for her own input to be heard.
- Larry found the active listening to be a particularly helpful skill, not only at work but at home as well. Forcing himself to put down his phone, and stop thinking ahead immediately resulted in more revealing conversations and deeper connections with loved ones.
- Chris was delighted to learn that she could substitute open questions for closed questions and keep the other person talking longer!
- Kelly was astounded at how many leading questions he used to ask. When he stopped using them, he noticed people shared a lot more with him.

The Introvert's Survival Guide to Active Listening

Active listening is the key to people feeling heard and to you getting the full story from a person.

Here are a few do's and don'ts to keep in mind:

Do's

DO listen to what the other person is saying.

DO pay attention to their words, their tone of voice and their body language.

DO give cues that you are listening (eye contact, nodding).

DO ask clarifying questions.

DO summarize to check understanding.

Don'ts

DON'T think about your response while the other person is speaking.

DON'T interrupt the person you are listening to.

DON'T have an agenda.

3 Keys to Remember

KEY 1: Use active listening.

KEY 2: Don't think about your response.

KEY 3: Pay attention to the whole message.

The Introvert's Survival Guide to Asking Questions

Your ability to ask thoughtful open questions is your best tool for getting people to open up to you.

Here are a few do's and don'ts to keep in mind:

Do's

DO ask open questions.

DO think ahead about the questions you will ask.

DO ask follow-up questions.

DO use active listening.

DO take a few notes, if needed.

Don'ts

DON'T ask closed questions.

DON'T 'telegraph' the answer you are seeking by asking leading questions.

3 Keys to Remember

KEY 1: Use open questions and avoid closed or leading questions.

KEY 2: Listen actively to the answers.

KEY 3: If in doubt, ask another question.

Chapter 6: Non-Verbal Communication

"The typical introvert uses his or her observant nature to read the room. They're more likely to notice people's body language and facial expressions, which makes them better at interpersonal communication."

Dr. Jennifer Kahnweiler

In the last chapter, we learned that messages are conveyed by the words spoken (10%), the tone of voice (40%) and body language (50%).

In this chapter, we will look at the body language aspect of this equation, also referred to as non-verbal communication skills.

As mentioned earlier, as an introvert, you are already adept at reading a room and picking up on non-verbal cues. With just a little more knowledge on what to look for, you truly can be a powerhouse.

Non-Verbal Communication Cues

What do you think the following might mean? If you can think of more than one possibility, write them all down.

Arms crossed

Legs crossed

Knee bouncing

Body turned away

Making eye contact

Not making eye contact

Rolling eyes

Eyes wandering

Eyes closed

Looking toward the door

Looking at the floor

Looking at a watch

Chewing on a pen

Fingers tapping rhythmically

Tapping a single finger

Pointing a finger

Clenched fists

Standing up

Pacing

Slumping in a chair

Leaning back in a chair

Pounding the table

Standing at a distance

Standing very close

Pushing

We will return to the list later, but in the meantime, keep these in mind as you read this chapter.

Gestures

What do you the following gestures mean to you? Are you aware of alternate meanings in other cultures? Are there any you would avoid?

Thumbs up

Palm up and forward

Hand up with fingers spread

Finger and thumb together, forming a circle

Single finger curled towards you, beckoning

Index and baby finger up, middle fingers down

Fist with thumb poking out between the index and second finger

Snapping fingers

We will return to cultural differences later, and these gestures in particular. In the meantime, if more possible meanings come to you, jot them down.

Why Body Language Matters

About 50% of the message one hears is the from the speaker's non-verbal messages. These include eye contact (or lack thereof), arms crossed, chair pushed back, head down, looking away, rolling eyes, rigid back, laid back in the chair, legs crossed (or uncrossed), standing, or sitting.

Some are considered universal (e.g. arms crossed, lack of eye contact), whereas others are particular to the individual (e.g. a person who usually sits stands, or sitting upright when usually laid back).

You have to consider the situation (could the person with their arms crossed simply be cold?) and how well you know the person.

As a general rule, however, these non-verbal cues may not come to you consciously, at least not at first. Your body may react to non-verbal signals before you've even had a chance to think about them.

The same applies to the speaker's tone of voice, which accounts for 40% of the message conveyed. More often than not, your psyche will respond to any tension in the speaker's tone of voice before you have even had a chance to think about it. You may find yourself feeling guarded before you've even heard the essence of the spoken message.

Of course, words are important, but at 10%, you don't want to ignore the power of what you communicate non-verbally at 50%, and the message sent by the tone of your voice, at 40%, as factors in how your entire message comes across.

Body Language for Introverts

Beyond reading the body language of others, there are numerous benefits to monitoring to your own body language.

Paying attention to your body language will help you:

- Appear more confident
- Feel more confident
- Reduce your anxiety
- Boost your testosterone

This is especially good news for introverts.

When your anxiety is reduced, your focus will turn outward. And when your attention is directed outside of yourself, you will break the anxiety spiral.

Take a breath and enjoy the experience, as in this improved state you will find yourself having more enriching conversations with others.

Open Body Stance

The key is to adopt an open body stance with an erect posture, standing tall, with your head up, shoulders back and elbows out.

This posture is referred to as 'open' as, in a primitive context, your body is more exposed. In a battle, you would be more vulnerable.

A few hints:

- Keep your arms uncrossed. If your arms are crossed, you will begin to feel more anxious. Uncrossing your arms will actually reduce your anxiety.
- Plant your feet firmly on the ground, far enough apart to secure your balance. Resist the temptation to balance on one foot or lean against something.
- Hold your elbows out from your body. Take up as much room as possible. If you are holding a wine glass, practice holding it away from your body.
- Use hand gestures while you are speaking.
- When you are talking with someone, nod your head to indicate interest. A 'triple nod' when someone stops speaking will be a signal that you'd like them to continue (try it, it works).
- Resist the temptation to check your phone, as you will immediately take on a closed stance, and repel people from you (more on this later in the chapter).

The result of standing with your elbows out and using hand gestures is that your body will physically take up more space. The more space your body takes up, the more confidence you will exude.

You may recognize this posture in speakers and other people with significant personal power. This is what is referred to as a power position, but it doesn't necessarily mean you are seeking power. Rather, you appear confident.

Now let's return to what messages our body language sends to others.

Non-Verbal Communication Cues – A Few Possibilities

Earlier in the chapter, you guessed what a number of non-verbal communication cues might mean. Get out your notes and compare your ideas with the possibilities below.

Arms crossed – might mean:
- Defensive
- Closed to listening
- Cold and trying to warm oneself

Legs crossed – might mean:
- Relaxed
- Defensive
- Physical discomfort

Knee bouncing – might mean:
- Impatience
- Nervous energy
- Excitement

Body turned away crossed – might mean:
- Disinterested
- Closed to ideas
- Desire to flee

Making eye contact – might mean:
- Open
- Challenging (staring)
- Listening

Not making eye contact – might mean:
- Closed
- Avoiding
- Distracted
- Shame

Rolling eyes – might mean:
- Fed up
- Disagreeable

Eyes wandering – might mean:
- Distracted
- Disinterested
- Listening

Eyes closed – might mean:
- Listening
- Thinking
- Concentrating
- Avoidance
- Sleeping

Looking towards the door – might mean:
- Desire to flee
- Distracted

Looking at the floor – might mean:
- Thoughtful
- Distracted
- Shame

Looking at watch – might mean:
- Tight for time
- Distracted
- Desire to leave

Chewing on a pen – might mean:
- Listening
- Thoughtful

Fingers tapping rhythmically – might mean:
- Impatient
- Nervous habit
- Excited

Tapping a single finger – might mean:
- Trying to make a point

- Dominating
- Aggression

Pointing a finger – might mean:

- Accusing
- Authoritarian gesture
- Look there (if pointed away)

Clenched fists – might mean:

- Frustration
- Anger
- Impatience

Standing up – might mean:

- Ready to leave
- Deep in thought
- Physical discomfort

Pacing – might mean:

- Deep in thought
- Worried
- Impatience

Slumping in a chair – might mean:

- Relaxed
- Defeated
- Tired

Leaning back in a chair – might mean:

- Relaxed
- Listening
- Disinterested

Pounding the table – might mean:

- Feeling unheard
- Emphasis
- Anger

Standing at a distance – might mean:
- Disengaged
- Respectful
- Aloof

Standing very close – might mean:
- Intimidating
- Disrespectful
- Assertive

Pushing – might mean:
- Assertive
- Disrespectful
- Crowd behavior

Cultural Differences

As we have discussed, people from different cultural backgrounds can vary greatly in terms of beliefs, cultural norms and communication styles.

This is perhaps most evident in non-verbal communications.

Eye Contact

In the west, eye contact is not only common; it is expected. If someone does not make eye contact, we think they are hiding something. In other cultures, direct eye contact is seen as rude and confrontational, and avoiding eye contact is a sign of respect.

Personal Space

In the west, we expect a fair amount of personal space around us physically. If someone gets too close, we feel our personal space has been invaded, and we become uncomfortable. If there is incidental touch, we consider the offender to be rude and inconsiderate. Yet, in other cultures, such as highly populated countries, holding back and not asserting yourself physically can be considered a weakness.

Gestures

Gestures have completely different meanings depending upon the part of the world you come from.

If you were traveling, you would probably study the countries and the region you were traveling to in order to learn what gestures are and are not acceptable.

Living in a multicultural society, however, you could unintentionally insult someone you are speaking with by using a gesture that has a completely different meaning in their homeland.

Here are a few examples:

- Standing with your hands on your hips conveys confidence and pride and is considered to be a power position in the west, however this stance can be interpreted as challenging or anger.
- While winking might mean 'We share a secret,' or a romantic interest in the west, it is considered rude in some cultures. It can also be a signal for children to leave the room.
- Slouching may just be seen as lazy or relaxed in the west, but in some cultures, it is a sign of disrespect.
- Crossing one's legs, with the bottom of one foot exposed, may be meaningless in the west, but it is considered dirty and rude elsewhere in the world.
- Even nodding has different meanings. In the west, nodding your head up and down means yes, and shaking your side-to-side means no, but there are cultures where these meanings are reversed.

Let's return to the list of gestures from earlier in this chapter.

Gestures – Different Cultural Meanings

How many of these were familiar to you? Did you know that any could be considered to be rude or insulting?

Thumbs up – in various cultures, this gesture can mean:

- That's ok
- Up yours

Palm up and forward – in various cultures, this gesture can mean:
- Stop
- Settle down
- Call a waiter

Hand up with fingers spread – in various cultures, this gesture can mean:
- Greeting
- Eat shit

Finger and thumb together, forming a circle – in various cultures, this gesture can mean:
- OK sign
- Your anus
- Zero

Single finger curled towards you, beckoning – in various cultures, this gesture can mean:
- Come here
- Rude, only used for dogs
- Death

Index and baby finger up, middle fingers down – in various cultures, this gesture can mean:
- Positive
- Sign of the devil

Fist with thumb poking out between the index and second finger – in various cultures, this gesture can mean:
- Good luck
- Fertility
- Female genitalia
- Screw you

Snapping fingers – in various cultures, this gesture can mean:
- I have an idea
- Hurry up
- Offensive

While you no one can be expected to know what every gesture might mean worldwide, it can only help your interpersonal interactions if you can avoid some common pitfalls.

Context is Everything

Of course, you can't know for sure what is going on with someone without asking them, and that is not always appropriate. So consider the signals you pick up on to be clues, not definitive answers.

On the other hand, if you know the person, you have the extra advantage of knowing what is unusual for them. In a word, you have context. Often it is your knowledge of the person that allows you to become aware of changes in body language that others would miss.

Here are a few scenarios that illustrate this point.

In each situation, what do you think might be going on? Are there any non-verbal cues that a bystander would realize are significant?

A Meeting with Marty

Angelina walked into her boss, Marty's, office. He had a big grin on his face. He was on the phone, so signaled for her to sit, covering the mouthpiece to whisper that he would only be a minute.

Fred's Meeting with Norman

Fred checked his watch and slipped into his boss, Norman's, office. Norman was on the phone, but he signaled for him to sit down. Aside from this, he did not make eye contact.

The Monday Meeting

Melinda worked remotely but called in weekly to a team meeting with her department at home office. Her colleague, Martin, answered, said they were waiting for Maria, and put Melinda on speakerphone. When she heard the project manager, Maria's, voice, apologizing for being late, Melinda put down her pen to listen. Maria cleared her throat and began the meeting. Keith reported on last week's numbers, but then before anyone else could speak Maria said, "Before we get into today's agenda…"

The RRR Rodeo Team Meeting

Ruth, Ralph, Reggie and the rest of the RRR Rodeo team gathered in the Roundup Meeting Room. When their boss, Rudy, arrived a few minutes late, he didn't say much and shuffled his papers. There were traces of a grin on Rudy's face.

The President Speaks

Nancy slipped into the meeting room late and the President was already speaking. Everyone else was quiet. There were arms crossed and pushed-back chairs.

The Family Business

Jack was part of a business founded by his father, Leo, who now left day-to-day operations to Jack, his brother, Mack, and their sister, Missy. When he got a text to return to the office for a meeting, he didn't think much about it. When he opened the conference room door, Missy, Mack and Mr. Clifton, the family's lawyer, were already seated.

Any guesses? There isn't much to go on, is there? What additional cues might someone familiar with the individuals notice?

In situations where you already know the person (versus meeting a stranger), you have the added advantage of noticing changes in behavior. For example, a co-worker whose expressive eyes you enjoy when they speak is avoiding eye contact. Or a manager who is usually very chatty in welcoming people to meetings today has his head buried in papers as everyone arrives.

Let's return to our scenarios, this time from the perspective of the participants.

In each of these scenarios, there are signals telling the listener something about what was to come. Before a word was spoken, they had a sense of what was going to happen. This time, you have the advantage of this context.

A Meeting with Marty – Angelina's perspective

Angelina walked into her boss, Marty's, office and laughed when she saw the great big grin on his face. He was like a little kid sometimes, she thought. He was on the phone, so signaled for her to sit, covering the mouthpiece to whisper that he would only be a minute. Angelina waited with anticipation, wondering what was up.

- Interpretation: Angelina figured good news was coming.
- Non-Verbal Cues: the grin on Marty's face, his body language as he signaled for Angelina to sit down.

Fred's Meeting with Norman – Fred's perspective

Fred checked his watch, slipped into his boss, Norman's, office, and took a seat. As usual, Norman was on the phone, but he signaled for him to sit down. Fred immediately felt tense, as he noticed that Norman wasn't making eye contact with him. The two had worked together for years, and Fred instinctively picked up on a change in pattern.

- Interpretation: Norman was going to tell Fred something he wasn't going to like.
- Non-Verbal Cues: Lack of usual eye contact.

The Monday Meeting – Melinda's perspective

Melinda worked remotely but called in weekly to a team meeting with her department at home office. Her colleague, Martin, picked up the phone when it rang, said "Maria's late, we're just waiting," and put Melinda on speakerphone. It was the usual Monday morning banter, which Melinda half listened to as she made her notes for the meeting. It wasn't quite the same as being there in person, but that was ok; she was used to it. When she heard the project manager, Maria's voice, apologizing for being late, Melina put down her pen to listen. The room was largely quiet as they waited for Maria to start, which she eventually did, by clearing her throat. With a more serious tone than usual, Maria began the meeting. As usual, she had Keith report on last week's numbers, then Maria jumped in before anyone could comment, and said, "Before we get into today's agenda…" Melinda was immediately alert to the seriousness in Maria's voice and held her breath.

- Interpretation: Something's up and it's not good news.
- Non-Verbal Cues: Maria clearing her throat, the way Maria jumped in before anyone could say anything, Maria's tone of voice.

The RRR Rodeo Team Meeting – Ruth's perspective

Ruth, Ralph, Reggie and the rest of RRR Rodeo team gathered in the Roundup Meeting Room, where they had been beckoned by their boss, Rudy. When Rudy arrived, a few minutes late, he didn't say much (unusual for him) and shuffled his papers, but Ruth could see the traces of a grin playing at the side of his mouth. She wondered what was up.

- Interpretation: Ruth suspected good news or some sort of surprise.
- Non-Verbal Cues: A change in behavior, and traces of a grin.

The President Speaks – Nancy's perspective

When Nancy slipped into the meeting room late, she couldn't catch the thread of the conversation, but she noticed that the President's tone of voice – usually cheery – was restrained. As she found a seat, she looked around at her colleagues and noticed a lot of crossed arms and pushed-back chairs. Uh oh, she thought, I wonder what's up.

- Interpretation: There is bad news afoot, and the others already know it.
- Non-Verbal Cues: President's tone of voice, and the body language of her colleagues.

The Family Business – Jack's perspective

Jack was part of a family-run business, founded by his father, Leo. For the most part today, Leo played a behind the scenes role and left day-to-day operations to Jack, his brother, Mack, and their sister, Missy. When he got the text to return to the office for an important meeting, he didn't think much about it. When he opened the conference room door, however, and saw Missy and Mack sitting, with stunned expressions, across from Mr. Clifton, the family's lawyer, he knew it wasn't good news.

- Interpretation: Something has happened to dad.
- Non-Verbal Cues: The stunned expressions on Missy and Mack's faces, and the presence of Mr. Clifton.

Can you now see the signals that the participants, who were familiar with the players involved, were able to notice?

This doesn't mean that you won't notice non-verbal signals from strangers. You can, but you might not always know for sure what is going on.

It's always wise to withhold judgment, but spend some time observing body language in the meetings you attend and see what you can pick up on.

Message Mismatch

What do you do if you are faced with a disconnect between what someone says and what their body language and/or tone of voice is conveying?

Take a minute to reflect.

If you notice a mismatch between what a person is saying and the other signals you are receiving, your options are either to:

- Do nothing at the moment.
- Ask a question.
- Reflect on the interaction afterward.
- Have a follow-up discussion.
- Still do nothing.

In terms of asking a question, you could ask a specific question about the mismatch or simply mirror back what you observed. Here is some wording that might work:

- "I notice you looking at your watch. Do you have another meeting? Would you like to reschedule for when you have more time?"
- "I'm interested in your feedback on what I have said so far."
- "That's what happened, from my perspective. I'd like to hear what happened from your perspective."
- "I'm picking up that you may be uncomfortable with what I am saying. Would you like to share what's on your mind?"
- "I know you are saying that you are happy with my work on the project, but you are not smiling. Is there something that is concerning you?"

A disconnect between words and non-verbal cues could be a signal that your approach is off, so reflect on the conversation afterward.

For example: If your "Here's how I saw it unfold," brought downcast eyes or crossed arms, perhaps try a different approach next time. For example, "I'd like to share what I observed first, then I'd like to hear what happened from your perspective," may bring a different reaction.

Personal Safety and De-escalating Situations

Sometimes non-verbal cues can tell you that something is seriously off. If someone is acting aggressively–such as yelling, pointing a finger at you–you may need to extricate yourself from the situation for your own safety.

It's also good to know some tricks for de-escalating a situation.

Listening is the most important thing you can do. Ask the other person for their perspective and use your active listening skills until you fully understand things from their angle. Don't disagree or try to solve the problem at this time. Just keep probing until they feel heard. When people feel heard, they are less likely to act with hostility or shut down or refuse to listen.

You might feel like you are the only one steering the boat, but that's ok.

Those Darn Smartphones

Our discussion on non-verbal communication would not be complete without a discussion on the ubiquitous cell phone.

Scrolling or typing on a Smartphone may seem rude to you, but it actually might not be.

In today's culture, many people are so attached to their devices that they can't imagine putting them down. They may believe that they can listen just as well if they are busy on their phone versus not, but not quite. But don't take this alone to be a sign of rudeness.

That said, having your nose stuck in your Smartphone is not going to help your conversation skills. The very act will shut down any possibility of meeting new people, let alone starting new conversations.

Think about what happens when we are engaged with these devices:

- What non-verbal signals do you send when you are using your device?
- What non-verbal messages have you picked up from others?
- If you are somewhere now where people are using their

devices, have a look around. What do you notice about their body language?

- If you are alone right now, try this exercise when you are next out and about in the world. Look around you and observe the non-verbal messages being sent by those who are busy on their devices.
- Next time you go to a meeting or a gathering, observe the other people as they arrive. Who ends up in a conversation first--someone with their head stuck in their phone or the rare person who is waiting patiently for the meeting to begin?

Yes, if you'd rather be left alone, then you could consider your phone to be your best friend, but as you have purchased this book on conversation skills, this is probably not your goal. It may be your instinct, but it will not help you interact.

Here's what happens when you are looking at the screen on your Smartphone:

- Your head is tilted down.
- Your shoulders are naturally pulled in.
- Your attention is diverted.
- Your body language is closed.
- The signal you are sending is 'Stay away'.
- It is not possible for someone to even catch your eye.
- In a word, you are unapproachable.

By the way, any hope you might have that occupying yourself with your phone might suggest that you are very busy, have urgent messages or are otherwise more important than anyone else, is dead. Everyone knows what you are doing because they have done it themselves.

A few final tips about Smartphones:

- If you want to meet people, put your phone down. Put it away. Turn it off or put it in silent mode.
- When you find yourself alone at an event with no one to

talk to, resist the temptation to look at your phone.

- If you need to check your phone, step aside and do it, then put it away.

Finally, don't let your phone become a crutch. It's far too easy to cover awkward silences by retreating into your device but resist the temptation. You just might find someone interesting to talk to!

As we wrap up this chapter, here are a few helpful caveats to keep in mind:

- As an introvert, you are already adept at picking up on non-verbal cues; keep on learning–you are on your way to becoming a powerhouse.
- Keep in mind that a person could have their arms crossed because they are cold, but it could mean something else too.
- Reading body language is looking for clues but is not definitive.
- Trust your gut. If you get a strong feeling something is amiss, it probably is.
- Context is everything. If you know the person and/or the surrounding circumstances, take this into account when interpreting body language.
- Consider your own body language.
- Body language can mean different things in different cultures.
- Voice tone also matters (more on this in Chapter 11).

What do you think? Do you notice other people's non-verbal communications? Since reading this chapter, have you started noticing your own reactions to the non-verbal signals others send out? Do you notice anything you do that sends an unintended message contrary to what you intend?

Case Studies

- Rebecca knew she wore her feelings on her sleeve; there

was no hiding how she felt! With a greater understanding of non-verbal communication, she was able to be intentional with her body language, so as to not be so overtly emotional in non-critical situations.

- Larry was sometimes accused of being defensive, when he didn't think he was. After learning about non-verbal communication, he was able to consciously uncross his arms and make better eye contact. Coupled with his new active listening skills, he stopped hearing this feedback.
- Chris didn't understand why everyone thought she was intimidated by others. As she gained an understanding of her body language and the signals she sent out, she was able to make some minor adjustments to appear more confident: not bowing her head, making more eye contact and nodding while listening.
- Non-verbal communication was not something Kelly had paid much attention to in the past. Initially, he became fascinated by the non-verbal messages others sent, analyzing people in all sorts of situations. Ultimately, he was able to identify that his habit of throwing down his pen when he was fed up was putting people off. Now he laid his pen down gently.

The Introvert's Survival Guide to Non-Verbal Communication

Your ability to convey open body language and read the non-verbal cues of others can go a long way to improving the effectiveness of your communications.

Here are a few do's and don'ts to keep in mind:

Do's

DO observe the body language of others.

DO be aware of your own body language.

DO use an open body stance (stand tall, shoulders apart).

DO plant your feet firmly on the ground.

DO smile.

DO make eye contact.

DO ask a question.

Don'ts

DON'T cross your arms.

DON'T beat yourself up if you fumble.

DON'T problem-solve if you are angry.

DON'T expect everyone to respond the same.

3 Keys to Remember

KEY 1: Adopt an open body stance.

KEY 2: Stay off your phone.

KEY 3: Communicate that you are approachable.

The Introvert's Survival Guide to Smartphones

Put it away. Just put it away. You don't need your Smartphone to interact with people in person.

Here are a few do's and don'ts to keep in mind:

Do's

DO put your phone away.

DO be the one person in the room who is not on a device.

Don'ts

DON'T hide behind your phone.

DON'T cover awkward pauses by pulling out your phone.

DON'T assume others on their phones are being rude.

3 Keys to Remember

KEY 1: To meet people, put your phone away.

KEY 2: Deal with any urgent matter, then put your device away.

KEY 3: Don't use your phone as a crutch.

Chapter 7: Adapting to Type

As introduced in Chapter 2: Understanding People, there are many ways in which people differ including:

- Introversion vs. extroversion
- Gender
- Emotions
- Culture
- Personality

Next, we will explore how you can adapt your approach to different types of people.

To begin, pause to think for a moment about your friends.

My Friends – Exercise

Which of your friends, family members and co-workers you would describe as being primarily results-oriented and which you would describe as laid back?

Results-oriented friends (lots of goals, achievement-focused, driven):

1.

2.

3.

4.

5.

Laid-back friends (easy going, live in the moment, tend to go with the flow)

1.

2.

3.

4.

5.

The Proposal – Exercise

You need to get four different people in your company to review and approve a proposal you are making to fund a new training program. All four senior managers are quite different from one another.

Your proposal is 16 pages long, including a 1-page executive summary, a 10-page synopsis, 1 page of measurements and 3 pages of charts showing how the new training process fit in with other aspects of the business. There is also a financial summary at the end.

In general terms, you plan to email your proposal to each of the managers then make appointments to meet with each to answer questions and get their sign-off.

Before doing so, you spend some time thinking about the four managers and how you might adapt your approach to each.

Irene is a senior manager in the purchasing department. Extremely busy and extremely bright, there are many demands on her time. Once you had her attention though, Irene would always hear you out, listening to your ideas, and giving them careful consideration. Irene has a high need for measurements and financial details and will want time to analyze the details before committing. Sitting in her office, piled high with files, you never felt rushed; the big challenge was getting enough time in her schedule to get her input.

Randy is a senior manager in the sales department. On the rare occasions when he is not away working with sales reps in the field, client meetings, and sales conferences, Randy has office days. If you wanted to see Randy, you needed to book an appointment. If you were lucky, he would be free when you got there. He'd always see you next if you'd booked an appointment, but at times there would quite literally be a lineup outside. You always felt like you were jumping the queue if he ushered you past others waiting. And there was always the possibility of an interruption, or a meeting cut short due to a client crisis of one sort or another. As a result, you always felt a bit jittery when you had a meeting with Randy.

James was a senior manager in human resources. While not quite as busy as the other managers, meeting with James was no piece of cake. He'd generously give you more time than you asked for and would be genuinely interested in your ideas, but you'd better know your stuff. James would have read every word in your proposal and would have prepared a list of questions. If your proposal was solid, you'd walk away feeling great, though the price to pay was a 10-minute chat about your career and professional goals. Those weren't hard discussions, but if you hadn't done anything towards those goals since your last little chat, you'd feel like a dolt, hence causing you to think you should research night-school classes first.

Marjorie was a senior manager in quality control. She was a key player in the company, serving on more project teams than anyone else. Plus, she had the President's ear. Other managers would frequently ask, "Has Marjorie seen this yet?", so she was well respected. You could always book time with Marjorie, and she was open to multiple meetings if you needed her input. Marjorie's office walls were covered with charts, including the systems your proposal will need to fit in with. She wasn't going to approve anything that didn't align with the quality management system and the organization's business strategy though, so you needed to be on your game.

How would you adapt your approach to each? What does each need, and how will you provide it?

Irene in Purchasing
- Needs:
- Has little time for:
- Key to getting her approval:

Randy in Sales
- Needs:
- Has little time for:
- Key to getting his approval:

James in Human Resources
- Needs:
- Has little time for:
- Key to getting his approval:

Marjorie in Quality Control
- Needs:
- Has little time for:
- Key to getting her approval:

Give some thought to these and jot some notes in your notebook. Keep Irene, Randy, James, and Marjorie in mind as we go through this chapter.

Personality Type Models

In terms of personality type, there are many models that seek to explain how we differ.

These models:

- Strive to break down the range of types, so that we can understand what makes others tick.
- Help individuals understand themselves better so they can

get their needs met in a range of situations.

- Provide insight as to why someone may behave in a certain way, so that you can adapt your communication in such a way that the person is most likely to hear you and engage with you.
- Are particularly valuable to teams, as when a model is embraced, team members are better able to understand each other, allowing them to get the most out of their interactions and effectively work together to maximize results.

Return to the exercise you just did, where you reflected on your friends and identified which of them are result- oriented and which are more laid-back. The former is often referred to as Type A, while the latter is referred to as Type B. This is just one example of type.

Carl Jung, who identified the functions of how we perceive (sensing and intuition) and how we judge (thinking and feeling), also looked at these psychological aspects in relationship to introversion and extroversion.

From these roots, a number of popular models have evolved, including DISC, Myers Briggs and more.

These are just a few of the many ways our differences as people are organized into models that help us understand each other.

Among the other ways of differentiating people, there are models that include our:

- Psychological attitudes (introversion versus extroversion)
- Psychological types (how we perceive and judge)
- Personality types (action-oriented versus laid-back)
- Personality traits (how anxious, open, agreeable and pragmatic people are)
- Temperaments (logical, tactical, idealistic, strategic temperaments)
- Thinking styles (analyzers, organizers, innovators, and spiritual thinkers)

- Learning styles (visual, auditory and kinesthetic learners)
- Strengths (thinkers, doers, influencers and relationship-builders)

The models are as often identified by their creator's names as they are by theory names or acronyms.

How many aspects each model is broken into is influenced by the underlying concepts as well as how to make them memorable (thirds, quadrants, fifths, and sixteenths are common), and all have their catchy titles.

Is there a 'best' model?

Perhaps--it depends on who you ask.

None of these models is inherently right or wrong; each just emphasizes different aspects of personality, providing fresh ways to think about types of people.

Rather than prescribing how you should adapt to people based on a particular type model, we'll show you how to adapt to people regardless of how they may or may not be categorized.

Tip: You may already be familiar with a personality type model. If so, pull it out and use what you already know alongside the following suggestions.

Adapting to Type

Adapting to type is really a two-part process:

- The first part is to notice the unique qualities of a person.
- The second part is to adapt your approach based on what you have observed.

The intent here is not to psychoanalyze others.

Rather, the intent is to be aware of differences, notice cues and uncover interests that will best allow you to adjust your approach to the type of person you are dealing with.

When you can adapt your approach to what people need, and what they are and are not interested in, you increase your likelihood of being heard and will make stronger connections.

In a sense, you can be a chameleon.

Adapting to What People Respond To - Exercise

Reflect on these different personality types and what will and will not interest them. If you aren't familiar with any of the types, make your best guess.

What do you think each of these 15 types of people will be interested in?

- An analytical person
- A people person
- A person who cares about values
- An ideas person
- A creative person
- A task-oriented person
- A person who cares about fun
- A person who cares about everyone getting along
- A person who cares about connecting people
- A person who cares about finances
- A person who enjoys problem-solving
- A very logical person
- A person who is a strong leader
- A person who cares about the community
- A person who gets things done

Conversely, what type of information would cause these same 15 types of people to tune out?

- An analytical person
- A people person
- A person who cares about values
- An ideas person

- A creative person
- A task-oriented person
- A person who cares about fun
- A person who cares about everyone getting along
- A person who cares about connecting people
- A person who cares about finances
- A person who enjoys problem-solving
- A very logical person
- A person who is a strong leader
- A person who cares about the community
- A person who gets things done

Here are some of the ways you can adapt your approach:

Choice of Topic

Focus on what would be of most interest to the person. You might have to guess but reading their personality type can help you avoid talking about things that would cause them to tune you out.

Word Choice

Adapt the words you use. Use technical terms when speaking to someone with a higher education level, or who you have heard using longer words in conversation. For others, stick to shorter words that get to the point. Avoid terminology unless you are amongst those of the same profession.

Vary Your Tone

It can be useful to vary your tone of voice, and the speed of your speech to what you are hearing from the other person. If someone is speaking quietly and slowly, mirror their tone. Avoid speaking fast or loudly.

Mirror Body Language

As long as it is subtle, mirroring the other person's body language can make the person more receptive to you. If you are seated at a table, and the other person is leaning forward, do the same. If the other person is leaning back, adopt a relaxed posture.

Mood Match

If the other person is laughing and smiling, by all means, do the same. If the other person is very serious, or even stern, take their cue and use moderate facial expressions. Watch for cues as the conversation wraps up: if they become more expressive when business is done, do the same.

Adapting to What People Respond To - Possibilities

Earlier you identified what would and would not appeal to 15 different types of people. Get out your notes and compare your thoughts with the following. There are no right, and wrong answers here, just pay attention to themes.

An analytical person:

- Will be interested in details
- Will tune out if you talk about emotions

A people person:

- Will be interested in how people feel
- Will tune out if you talk about minute details

A person who cares about values:

- Will be interested in hearing about the meaning of things
- Will tune out if you talk about facts

An ideas person:

- Will be interested in hearing about possibilities
- Will tune out if you talk about timelines

A creative person:

- Will be interested in hearing about how something was created

- Will tune out if you talk about what people think about something

A task-oriented person:

- Will be interested in hearing about goals and timelines
- Will tune out if you talk about how you will gather feedback

A person who cares about fun:

- Will be interested in hearing about how accomplishments will be celebrated
- Will tune out if you talk about quality control

A person who cares about everyone getting along:

- Will be interested in hearing about how people collaborate
- Will tune out if you talk about market research

A person who cares about connecting people:

- Will be interested in hearing about who is involved
- Will tune out if you talk about milestones and deadlines

A person who cares about finances:

- Will be interested in hearing about budgets and contingency plans
- Will tune out if you talk about how you gathered feedback

A person who enjoys problem-solving:

- Will be interested in hearing about SWOT analysis (Strengths, Weaknesses, Opportunities, Threats)
- Will tune out if you talk about implementation plans

A very logical person:

- Will be interested in hearing about detailed implementation plans
- Will tune out if you talk about who came up with an idea

A person who is a strong leader:

> - Will be interested in hearing about key messages
> - Will tune out if you talk about project plans

A person who cares about the community:

> - Will be interested in hearing about involving community members
> - Will tune out if you talk about research archives

A person who gets things done:

> - Will be interested in hearing about project milestones
> - Will tune out if you talk about who came up with the plan

While you can never know for sure, if you pay attention to what type of person you are dealing with–or your best guess–you should be able to avoid topics that cause the person to lose interest.

If you notice that someone is tuning out (breaking eye contact, looking around, bored expression), try focusing on another aspect of the matter you are discussing or better yet, change the topic. This would be a good time to ask an open question that would invite the other person to talk about a topic of interest.

The Proposal – Possible Adaptations

Let's return to Irene, Randy, James, and Marjorie. Pull out your notes on how you might adapt your approach with each as you seek approval for your hypothetical proposal.

Did any additional ideas come to you as you read this chapter? If so, take a moment to jot them down.

When you are ready, here are some possible approaches to consider:

Irene in Purchasing:

> - Needs: Measurements, financial detail, time for analysis.
> - Has little time for: Lengthy explanations.

- Key to getting her approval: Be brief.
- Suggestions: Request two meetings with Irene, both short. Plan to review your proposal during the first one and return for questions and approval in a second meeting, if required. Bring an extra copy of the executive summary, measurements page, and financial details to the meeting.
- Greeting tip: Prepare a greeting that communicates how much you value her limited time, "Thanks for seeing me, Irene. I'm hoping you can help me by reviewing the measurements and financials in my training proposal. It's ready for sign-off…"
- Conversation tip: Make a comment that validates both her limited time and attention to detail, such as, "I've scheduled a second meeting next week, if needed, in case you'd like more time to analyze the details than we have today…"

Randy in Sales:

- Needs: Impacts on his sales team, how much training time will be needed.
- Has little time for: Fluff.
- Key to getting his approval: Make it easy for him to quickly grasp the program, the benefits, and what you need from him.
- Suggestions: Bring an extra copy of the executive summary to your meeting, state what you need at the beginning of the meeting. Be ready to get in and get out quickly, if needed.
- Greeting tip: Prepare a greeting that communicates that you respect his limited time, such as, "Good morning Randy. Today I am seeking your approval on the rebranding training proposal. It shouldn't take more than 5 minutes. Here is the summary…"
- Conversation tips: Be ready to give a 30-60 second summary such as, "There are three parts to the program, all of which support the rebranding strategy. The cost is $10K.

Unless you have concerns about delivery, your approval today will mean completion this quarter."

James in Human Resources:

- Needs: Impacts on the people.
- Has little time for: Extraneous financial details.
- Key to getting his approval: A complete proposal with all bases covered.
- Suggestions: Prepare a couple of stories about what the lack of the program is causing. Bring an extra copy of the executive summary, just in case.
- Greeting tip: Prepare a greeting that sets the stage for his interests, such as, "Hi James. I'm excited to talk with you today about how the new rebranding training will benefit our employees…"
- Conversation tips: Prepare a few open questions that will allow him to identify the impacts, such as, "How do you see this program benefiting our employees?" or "What do you see as the biggest win from this program?"

Marjorie in Quality Management:

- Needs: How the program integrates with existing programs.
- Has little time for: Details on the reasons behind the program.
- Key to getting her approval: How easily the program can be integrated with the quality management system.
- Suggestions: Bring an extra copy of the executive summary and enlarged copies of the 3 charts. Use a highlighter to show where the program would integrate with the quality program.
- Greeting tip: Prepare a greeting that validates her interests, such as, "Hi Marjorie, I've been looking forward to this meeting. I think I have all the ways the new training rebranding will integrate with the quality system but need your input…"

- Conversation tips: Prepare open questions, such as, "How well do you think this program integrates with the quality program? Do you see any gaps?"
- Bonus tip: Prepare a question that will secure her support, such as, "It would mean a lot if you would champion this program. It wouldn't take a lot of time but having your name behind it would help smooth implementation."

While there is no definitive right or wrong way to handle these situations, hopefully, these examples will help you see the range of possibilities.

As we wrap up this chapter, here are a few helpful caveats to keep in mind:

- Pay attention to the cues people give about their personality type and communication style.
- Adapt your approach to the person you are communicating with to help you connect and get your message across.
- If someone is in a heightened emotional state, it may not be the best time to try to engage them in conversation.
- Be sensitive to possible cultural differences.
- Don't forget that gender differences could be at play.

Tip: If you find you are interested in learning more about personality types, do an internet search as a starting point. You will find a world of resources that will allow you to dig deeper if you wish.

What do you think? Do you recognize different types in your workplace or your personal life? How can you adapt your approach to be more effective when dealing with different types of people?

Case Studies

- By adapting to type, Rebecca learned to be more concise. This in turn helped her to communicate more clearly with those who needed specific details. This was especially helpful with Anthony in accounting, as he was always asking for details without the fluff.

- Larry learned a new respect for his boss, Ernie. As he liked to involve everyone, wanted everyone to see the big picture, Ernie needed a lot of time to do this. Larry became more patient, no longer just focused on important details, and learned a few things too.
- Chris learned to adapt to what her boss, Ingrid, needed by getting to the point, not being put off by her demands. She realized that Ingrid wasn't disinterested in Chris' view, but she just needed the highlights pulled out.
- Kelly found the practice of thinking about who he would be dealing with and adapting to their style helped him get results. He found this particularly helpful in responding to people who tended to share their feelings and adapting to internal thinkers.

The Introvert's Survival Guide to Adapting to Type

Adapting your approach to what people need and what they are and are not interested in will increase your likelihood of being heard and will make stronger connections. In a word, be a chameleon.

Here are a few do's and don'ts to keep in mind:

Do's

DO adapt your approach to different types of people.

DO adapt your choice words to the person.

DO mirror the other person's body language.

DO match the other person's mood.

DO vary your tone to match the other person.

Don'ts

DON'T try to psychoanalyze others.

DON'T talk about things that will cause the other person to tune out.

DON'T overdo it with mirroring.

3 Keys to Remember

KEY 1: Be a chameleon.

KEY 2: Choose a topic of interest to the other person.

KEY 3: Avoid topics that will cause the other person to tune out.

Chapter 8: Meeting Strangers

"Strangers are only strangers until you meet them. Then they are new friends."

Unknown.

Being Approachable

Before you can meet people, you need to be approachable.

If you don't signal that you are interested in someone, they won't know. For this reason, don't just wait for someone to approach you.

Begin by outwardly demonstrating that you are open and interested in meeting people.

Instead of burying your head in your phone, adopt an open body stance, put a smile on your face and look around the room.

Stand somewhere where people are sure to walk by (near the bar always works). Simply saying hello to more people makes you more approachable.

Conversation Openers

Have a simple opening line, such as "Hello, how are you?"

Compliments always work. "What a great bag you have. Where did you get it?"

Look out for similarities and highlight these. If you see someone drinking the same type of beer, there's an opener.

As you are chatting with someone or a group of people, and someone mentions they like or dislike something you feel the same about, highlight the similarity. For example, "I know! I am so addicted to that show, too!"

If you want to talk to someone, don't overthink it. Just smile, make eye contact and say hello.

Conversation Tips

A few more tips when meeting people for the first time:

- Use your hands. Not only is this expressive, but showing your hands is considered more trustworthy.
- When you make eye contact, gaze deeply enough into the other person's eyes to notice their eye color. Just for a moment though, as you don't want to be perceived as creepy!
- Embrace your imperfections–it makes you relatable.
- It's ok to use self-deprecating humor, just don't go overboard.
- Asking 'why' is a great way to keep the conversation going.
- Say, "That reminds me of..." as a way to steer the conversation in a new direction.
- You can repeat back the last few words a person said, mirroring them, to encourage them to say more.
- Avoid using slang.

- Look for conversation sparks–if you see a person raise an eyebrow, that's a sign that they are interested in what you just said.

Chatting in Clusters

Depending on where you are, you may find yourself conversing in small clusters of people.

If you are joining a cluster, ask a question, or build a bridge. "How do you all know each other?" works well.

When you are introducing someone, a little gushing is ok, "This is Mary, and she is the most amazing Project Manager I have ever had!"

Tip: If you see two people in conversation, and their feet are pivoted in, this is a cue that they are engaged in a conversation that they don't want interrupted. This is a natural stance.

If you are chatting with someone, and you are open to others joining the conversation, consciously pivot your feet outwards. This will signal others that you are approachable.

Ending a Conversation

If you are having a great conversation, by all means, continue.

But if you are ready to move on, it's handy to have a strategy to wrap up a conversation.

You can do this by asking a question about future plans, such as what the person is doing later, this weekend, or on their vacation.

This creates the opportunity for you to make a graceful exit, such as, "It was great meeting you today. Best of luck during your upcoming move."

50 Conversation Starters

Sometimes all you need is a good question to get someone talking.

Browse the list below and pick out half a dozen questions that you could picture yourself asking. Next, rewrite them into your own words – and turn any closed questions into open questions.

1. How do you unwind from work?
2. What is your favorite pastime?
3. What are your hobbies?
4. What's your secret to stress relief?
5. What are you are you obsessed about?
6. Who is your favorite band? Why?
7. Who is your favorite singer? Why?
8. Who is your favorite singer-songwriter? Why?
9. Who is your favorite comedian? Why?
10. Who is your favorite actor? Why?
11. Who is your favorite actress? Why?
12. If something breaks, do you try to fix it, or do you just get a new one?
13. Tell me about your pets.
14. What's the best thing about your job?
15. What do you like most about your boss?
16. What subject did you like best in school?
17. Where did you go to university? What did you study?
18. What was your hobby as a child?
19. How would you describe yourself in a nutshell?
20. What is your favorite gadget?
21. What technology changed your life?
22. What do you still have and use that is really old?
23. If you were to put your name on a business, what kind of business would it be?
24. What would your motto for your business be?
25. What is your personal motto?
26. Where would you put yourself on the organized/disorganized scale?
27. What do you do to get yourself organized? How do you stay organized?
28. Do you still keep a paper calendar, or are you strictly online? Or a blend?
29. Have you ever done public speaking? What was the biggest audience? What was your topic?

30. Have you ever sung in public? What was your largest audience?
31. Have you ever done stand-up comedy? What was it like?
32. Who influenced your life the most?
33. Who did you randomly meet in your life who ended up being very important in some way?
34. What was the strangest coincidence in your life?
35. Have you experienced déjà vu?
36. What triggers your memories?
37. What is your comfort food?
38. Do you often run into people you know? Or not? Do you ever wonder about that?
39. How much sleep do you need? How much do you get?
40. Do you like napping? Why?
41. Do you ever stay up all night?
42. What is your favorite time of the year?
43. Do you like spring or fall better? Summer or winter?
44. What can't you live without?
45. What was the worst airport layover you ever experienced?
46. What was the best airport layover you ever had?
47. Where do you like to sit on a plane?
48. What do you always carry when traveling?
49. Do you experience jet lag? If not, what's your secret?
50. What kind of stuff gets on your nerves?

As we wrap up this chapter, here are a few helpful caveats to keep in mind:

- Remember that the other people you are meeting might be a bit nervous too.
- Always be ready with an open question or two.
- Have a game plan going in.

What do you think? Are you feeling a bit more comfortable about meeting strangers? Can you see how these techniques will help you be more at ease when meeting new people? What are the three or four things you will do differently?

Case Studies

- Rebecca found the strategies for meeting strangers helped her get over her anxiety by having a place to start. Now confident that she would have something to say and something interesting to ask, meant that she forgets about herself and just get curious about who she will meet.
- Larry quickly found he was meeting more people at events simply by using the conversation starters. He was even having fun, trying out the different starters, to see which worked best for him.
- Chris learned how not to be totally intimidated when meeting strangers. It was still a stretch, but the two conversation starters she memorized saved the day more than once.
- Kelly had always been pretty good at meeting people but found the conversation starters gave him new ways to steer things in a different direction.

The Introvert's Survival Guide to Meeting Strangers

You are equipped with all you need to meet strangers.

Here are a few do's and don'ts to keep in mind:

Do's

DO signal that you are approachable.

DO look for similarities.

DO be generous with compliments.

Don'ts

DON'T try to talk to two people chatting if their feet are pivoted towards each other.

DON'T try to be perfect.

DON'T hide your hands.

3 Keys to Remember

KEY 1: Be approachable.

KEY 2: Build bridges.

KEY 3: Be authentic.

Chapter 9: Getting People to Talk

Before we get started, take a blank page in your notebook and write the following. It will be used for a 2-part exercise.

Tip: You may want lots of room to write, so spread this over a few pages if you prefer.

ONE.

1:

2:

3:

TWO.

1:

2:

3:

Continue in this manner until you have room for 13 items in your notebook, like this:

THIRTEEN.

1:

2:

3:

What Would Get You to Talk? – Exercise Part 1

What are a dozen things about you that, if you were asked the right question, would give you a lot to talk about?

Hint: think about places you have traveled, famous people you have met, unusual hobbies, unique accomplishments (have you written a book? Do you have a blog? Did you once lose something important? Have a strange coincidence? Have one of the most memorable experiences in your life because of a fluke? Have an artist that you follow? Have a kitchen disaster story? Been stranded somewhere? Think, think, think...!).

In your notebook, pull out the worksheet you just created and jot a note about each story next to the numbers in capitals (ONE, TWO, THREE....), like this:

ONE. ← Put your first story here

1:

2:

3:

TWO. ← Put your second story here

1:

2:

3:

And so on. Yes, there is even room for 13 stories on your worksheet, in case you think of one more and want to make it a baker's dozen!

You don't need to write out each story in any detail–just a few words to jog your memory will suffice.

What Would Get You to Talk? – Exercise Part 2

Now, return to your list. What are a couple of questions that someone could ask that would cause you to bring up each of your stories in response?

Just in case you are wondering what the point is, this exercise is designed to help you craft conversation starters of your own that just might turn up magic with the people you meet. Play along... it can only benefit you!

YOUR STORY ONE.

1: ← Put your first question here

2: ← Put your second question here

3: ← Put your third question here

And so on.

Your goal is to come up with 2-3 questions per story.

Getting Other People to Talk

Remember that people love to talk about themselves, so if you have a warm and friendly greeting and ask open questions, you will find yourself engaged in conversation.

Don't forget that mastering open questions is your SECRET KEY t0 getting people to talk with you.

When you ask people questions about themselves and are genuinely curious, they will want to share with you.

Don't forget about nodding your head. As introduced earlier, a 'triple nod' when someone stops speaking will signal that you are waiting for them to continue.

Your Magic Conversation Starters

Refer back to the stories you identified about yourself and the questions you came up with that would draw them out of you.

From your list, pick 3-5 questions that you think would be particularly helpful in getting other people to talk about their experiences.

Write these on a fresh page, so that they are easy to find and read for future reference.

1.

2.

3.

4.

5.

Next time you are going to an event, review your Magic Conversation Starters and pick one or two you plan to use.

Tip: print your Magic Conversation Starters out and slip them into your wallet – or take a picture with your Smartphone.

Bonus: 100 More Conversation Starters

Have fun looking over this list of 100 more conversation starters. It's important to make them 'yours,' so adapt these to your interests and jot down others that come to you.

Tip: watch for closed questions below and challenge yourself to rewrite them into open questions that sound natural for you.

1. What's a trend you miss?
2. What surprising thing do you keep in your wallet or purse?
3. What famous person have you met? Tell me the story.
4. What famous person do you wish you'd met?
5. What famous person did you almost meet?
6. Have you ever experienced something you can't explain?
7. How do you get yourself out of a funk?
8. Do you prefer time with others or time alone?
9. Do you pack light or take as much as you can?
10. Do you like beach vacations? Why?
11. How many books are by your bed? What are they?
12. Do you carry reading material with you?
13. You are 10 minutes early to a meeting. How do you spend your time?
14. What is a charity you have been involved with?
15. What product was discontinued that you wish they'd bring back?

16. What invention do you wish you'd come up with?
17. What kind of thing lifts your spirits? Why?
18. What movie surprised you? Why?
19. What was the worst movie you ever saw? Why?
20. What was the best movie you ever saw? Why?
21. What documentary do you recommend?
22. What is your special talent?
23. What is your greatest indulgence?
24. Have you ever been stuck in an elevator?
25. Do you take transit? How do you like it?
26. What's your strangest transit story?
27. Do you buy lottery tickets? Have you ever won?
28. Do you still have cable TV?
29. Do you still have a landline? Why?
30. What's the best gift anyone ever gave you?
31. What's the gift you were most excited to give?
32. Do you like to plan ahead when you travel, or do you prefer to just let things unfold?
33. Do you drive a standard or an automatic? If both, which do you prefer?
34. Do you have a car? Do you own it or lease it?
35. What was your favorite car?
36. What was your first car?
37. Have you ever participated in any kind of car co-op or other car sharing service?
38. In your experience, what was the best cartoon ever made?
39. Are you a reader? What's your favorite genre?
40. What are you reading right now?
41. Do you prefer to read 'real' physical books over other formats??
42. Have you ever read an eBook? What do you like about eBooks?
43. Do you listen to audiobooks? Do you enjoy them the same or differently from physical books?
44. If you read physical books, do you buy them new? Used?

Or do you get them from the library?

45. You have an hour free. There is a coffee shop and a library? Which do you gravitate towards?

46. How many books do you read a week/month/year?

47. What's the best book you've read in the past year?

48. Did you have your own room as a child, or did you share?

49. Have you ever lived alone? What's the longest you've lived alone?

50. What news stories are you watching these days?

51. What was the most interesting trip you've ever taken?

52. Do you do any art? Do you paint or draw?

53. Are you an art fan? Who are your favorite artists?

54. Do you visit art galleries and museums when you travel?

55. What's the best museum you have ever visited?

56. Have you ever been to New York? When and what did you like about it?

57. Do you like Broadway-style shows? What's the best one you've ever seen?

58. Do you ever go to plays? What's the most memorable play you ever saw?

59. Have you ever done any acting? What about in school?

60. Do you ever find yourself quoting Seinfeld?

61. Do you have a favorite movie you like to re-watch every once in a while?

62. Are you a person who answers your cell phone all the time? Or do you just use it for outgoing calls?

63. Have you ever cruised? What did you like about it?

64. What's the best beach you have ever been to?

65. Have you ever been to a professional sports game?

66. Have you ever been to the Olympics? What was the experience like?

67. Do you watch the Olympics? Which do you prefer: The Summer Olympics or Winter Olympics?

68. Do you follow the Paralympics?

69. Have you ever been to Expo? If so, what year?
70. Who inspires you?
71. Do you ever go "off grid"?
72. What do you prefer, baths or showers?
73. Coke or Pepsi?
74. What type of hotel do you like to stay in?
75. When you travel, do you prefer a small town or a big city?
76. When you travel, do you plan ahead for the restaurants you are going to dine at? Or do you just taking things as they go?
77. What do you like most about large cities?
78. What do you like least about large cities?
79. Have you ever planned a trip just to see an exhibit at a museum? Tell me about it.
80. Have you ever planned a trip just to see a play or theatre production? What was it?
81. Have you ever planned a trip just to go to a concert? What was that like?
82. Would you ever plan a trip just to see a sporting event?
83. Do you run marathons?
84. Have you ever planned a trip around a marathon or other event you have competed in?
85. Have you ever attended an international conference? Where was it? What was particularly interesting about it?
86. Hawaiian pizza. Yes or no?
87. Do you have a favorite charity that you support?
88. What's the most embarrassing thing that has ever happened to you?
89. Are you a practical joker? Do you play pranks? What's the best prank you ever pulled off?
90. What's the best practical joke anyone has ever played on you?
91. Have you ever been fooled on April Fool's Day?
92. Have you ever fooled someone else on April Fool's Day?

93. What professional associations do you belong to?
94. What are your career aspirations?
95. What are your retirement plans?
96. Do you prefer to start your day with tea or coffee?
97. Have you ever taken an online course? What was it, and what was it like?
98. Is your primary computer a PC or a Mac?
99. Do you have GPS in your car?
100. Have you ever lost your car in a parking lot?

As we wrap up this chapter, here are a few helpful caveats to keep in mind:

- Remember that great questions are the key to getting people to talk.
- Try the triple nod to keep them talking!

What do you think? Do you see how human nature works when you ask people to talk about themselves? Are you inspired to try?

Case Studies

- Rebecca noticed a big improvement once she started asking people more about themselves. No longer were things lapsing into silence when conversation ran out upon meeting someone new.
- Larry began enjoying his new abilities to have more enriching discussions at networking events.
- Chris learned ways to get others to talk more and take the focus off herself. She'd met some pretty interesting people, too.
- Kelly honed his skills to get more out of business interactions.

The Introvert's Survival Guide to Getting People to Talk

Be ready to get the people you meet to talk with you by planning ahead.

Here are a few do's and don'ts to keep in mind:

Do's

DO ask open questions

DO prepare questions that will entice people to open up.

DO ask questions designed to have people share their stories.

DO use the triple nod.

Don'ts

DON'T ask a question that is commonly asked.

DON'T ask closed questions.

3 Keys to Remember

KEY 1: Have your Magic Conversation Starter questions ready.

KEY 2: Adopt your open body stance.

KEY 3: Listen actively.

Chapter 10: Increasing Your Likability

"The deepest urge in human nature is the desire to be important."

John Dewey

The Desire to Be Important - Exercise

We began this chapter with a quote from John Dewey, the American psychologist and philosopher:

Take a few minutes to contemplate Dewey's words, and ask yourself how you can use this sentiment to succeed in conversation.

Make a few notes, and we'll return to this later in the chapter.

The Charisma Myth

Forget Hollywood and what you thought you learned about charisma. The most charismatic people *aren't* the ones that go on and on about themselves. So don't be a conversational narcissist!

People really aren't that interested in hearing you talk about yourself. What they are most interested in is talking about themselves!

Being Likeable

The most important thing is to think about how you can get the other person to talk.

It should go without saying, but don't insult the other person and don't act creepy (avoid personal questions and staring).

Don't make yourself superior. Don't boast. Don't brag. Better yet, don't talk about yourself.

Finally, don't gossip, speak ill of others or 'overhead gaze' to see who might be more interesting to talk to (!).

The Desire to Be Important - Possibilities

"The deepest urge in human nature is the desire to be important."

John Dewey

Earlier in the chapter, you reflected on the above quote from John Dewey, and how this sentiment can be used to succeed in conversation.

Perhaps you thought of the following:

> - If you ask someone about themselves, they may open up to you.
> - If you express a genuine interest in someone, they may share their unique story with you.
> - If you continue to demonstrate your interest, by your body language and follow-up questions, they will feel the glow of importance that Dewey is referring to.
> - When you are interested in another in this way, they will like you.
> - Therefore, asking people about themselves in conversation, is the key to likeability.

As we wrap up this chapter, here are a few helpful caveats to keep in mind:

- It's always better to be the one asking the questions.
- To genuinely demonstrate interest in another person, use your body language, eye contact, and follow-up questions.
- Like yourself–people are far more likely to like someone who likes themselves and has high self-esteem.

What do you think? What do you think about the impact of likeability on your interactions? Do you think you can increase your likeability? How can you do so while staying true to yourself?

Case Studies

- A bit ambivalent, as she wasn't that worried whether people liked her or not, Rebecca came around when she realized likeability would help her improve her communications and results.
- Larry had never thought about likeability before. Eyes opened, he found he liked analyzing other's likability.
- Chris learned she was more likable than she thought.
- Kelly thought this was mostly a lark, but then realized he responded differently to those that presented as likable.

The Introvert's Survival Guide to Likeability

Now that we've crushed the Hollywood myth about charisma and identified that the thing people are most interested in talking about is themselves, the door is open for you to increase your likeability.

Here are a few do's and don'ts to keep in mind:

Do's

DO express a genuine interest in others.

DO ask a question that invites someone to share their story with you.

Don'ts

DON'T be a conversational narcissist!

DON'T gossip.

DON'T speak ill of others.

DON'T 'overhead gaze' to find someone more interesting to talk to.

DON'T forget: you can't please everybody.

3 Keys to Remember

KEY 1: If you make a person feel important, they will like you.

KEY 2: We like people who like us.

KEY 3: Be authentic.

Chapter 11: Finding Your Voice

This chapter will explore finding your voice on three different fronts:

- Literally, in terms of voice tone, volume, speed, inflection, and so on.
- Metaphorically, as in the confidence to speak with authenticity.
- In the power of storytelling.

As these are broad topics and the latter two beyond the scope of this book, these are mainly starting points for you to begin your own exploration.

Tone of Voice

As was introduced in Chapter 6: Non-Verbal Communication, a speaker's tone of voice can have a huge impact on the message the listener hears.

As you will recall, messages are conveyed by:

- The words spoken: 10%
- Tone of voice: 40%
- Body language: 50%

So, roughly 40% of a message is conveyed by the speaker's tone of voice.

A voice tone that is loud, quiet, stern, cheerful, low, high, fast or slow will affect what the listener hears from the speaker.

The News of the Day – Exercise

Refer to today's news. If you have a newspaper, great. If not, go online to find a news story of interest to you. Pick a story that isn't overly negative or positive. Perhaps a human-interest story or a play review.

Once you have picked out a story, read it aloud eight (8) times, and observe how your tone changes the message.

Tip: if you have someone at home or at work that can do this exercise with you, you will find it more enlightening. Even a friend can do it over the phone with you.

Make notes about what different meaning you noticed when you read the story:

Loudly

Softly/quietly

Sternly

Cheerfully

With a low voice tone

With a high voice tone

Quickly

Slowly

The Full Range - Exercise

What do you think these variations in voice may mean?

Talking fast

Talking slowly

Talking loudly

Talking quietly

Yelling

Screaming

Whispering

Fluctuating voice volume

Fading out

Stuttering

Speaking haltingly

Singing

Speaking emphatically (stressing words)

Mumbling

Using a harsh tone of voice

Using an accusing tone of voice

Using a gentle tone of voice

Using a friendly tone of voice

Using an unfriendly tone of voice

Using a sarcastic tone of voice

As these are open to interpretation, and so much varies based on the message, the speaker and the listener, there are no definitive answers. The purpose here is to be aware of the very many ways a message can be altered by the way in which it is spoken.

Metaphorically Speaking

In literature, you will find many references to when one 'finds one's own voice'.

This typically refers to when someone advances in their own personal development to have confidence in what they believe and are at a place where they can speak with authenticity about these beliefs. When these come together, we say that a person has found their voice.

Finding Your Voice - Exercise

Where are you on the journey of finding your voice? How confident are you in your beliefs? When you speak about these things, do you find yourself speaking with authenticity? Or do you still have a way to go on this journey? You may find that you have found your voice in one aspect of your life, but not in another.

Set aside some time to journal about these questions.

Tip: You may find that you return to the theme of finding your voice over time as your beliefs evolve.

Storytelling

You only need to look around yourself virtually to find references to stories and storytelling today. It is like the old art of the storyteller has been resurrected in modern times.

You'll find deep examples of storytelling in memoirs, blogs, podcasts and in your community.

You'll find less deep, but not necessarily less meaningful, examples of storytelling in your social media feed.

Regardless of format, chances are that introverts are behind many or most of these stories, as introverts are our writers and those who connect the dots for the rest of us.

Storytelling in Your Life – Exercise

Pick one of the storytelling methods listed above to explore or another of your choosing.

Spend some time reading and listening to the stories you encounter.

As you do, reflect on how you can bring storytelling into your life, either to learn more about others or to share your story.

Enjoy the journey.

As we wrap up this chapter, here are a few helpful caveats to keep in mind:

- Voice can mean different things to different people in different contexts.
- If you are interested in learning more about voice tone in particular, you may find YouTube videos a great resource, as you can actually hear the speaker.

What do you think? Does your voice impact the message you send? Do you need to work with your voice to come across more effectively? How? Do you need to talk louder, softer, with more inflection? How can you apply these skills when telling stories?

Case Studies

- Rebecca truly found her voice and learned how to influence process so that there was an opportunity to contribute her ideas. This relieved huge stress, and she found herself being more open to others and their ideas.
- Larry never really thought he needed to 'find his voice' but had in fact made big strides at networking events, big and small. He became much more comfortable in larger groups.
- This was a huge growth area for Chris, as she found ways to ensure she was heard and got the satisfaction of having her input taken seriously. Chris was quickly able to see a major positive change at work as a result of her input.
- Having already found his voice, Kelly used the tips to hone his storytelling skills.

Chapter 12: Networking 101

Natalie and Nettie went to a silent auction together. As they both were introverts and were trying to get better about these things, they decided to split up so they could meet different people.

Natalie, "It was ok, but the small talk kills me. I was so bored."

Nettie, "Really? I had a blast. But then again, I'm a rebel. One guy asked me a question about the weather, so I pretended he asked me about the last time I lost my car in a parking lot, which was last week, and I answered that instead. Turns out he's done it twice. We had a good chuckle, then had a good conversation about cars."

A good place to start our discussion on networking is to think about your friends and colleagues that you have seen in networking situations. What are your observations? Do they seem to be enjoying themselves? Are they meeting new people? Or are they just hanging out with the usual gang?

Now think about strangers you have observed at events, apparently networking with ease. What specifically have you noticed about these people? What makes you think they are at ease?

It is easy to assume that everyone else at a networking event is having an easy time but comfort yourself with the knowledge that you have no idea who else is faking it.

Wallflowers, Minglers, and Aces

It can be helpful to divide those at networking events into three rough categories:

Wallflowers

If you are reading this book, you probably don't need much of an explanation of the Wallflowers.

Minglers

These are those people who are managing in the middle, and it's not a bad place to be. For the most part, Minglers are able to calmly arrive at an event, introduce themselves to others with relative ease, and move in and out of conversations as the need arises. This is your goal.

Aces

These are the networking Aces that you imagine floating through the event with ease, knowing everyone, or breezily introducing themselves to anyone new. Things aren't always what they seem, and these folks can make plenty of networking mistakes (such as dominating the conversation, forgetting to share contact details or having too much to drink). But this is not your goal.

You don't need to 'ace' networking events. You just need to calm your inner butterflies and get them to fly in formation. And, yes, it is possible to transform yourself from a Wallflower to a Mingler.

Networking Skills Self-Assessment

Take a few minutes to reflect on your networking skills.

1. You are going to an event with networking opportunities. Do you:

a) Turn up and see what happens?

b) Have a goal or two in mind?

c) Develop a networking strategy?

2 . As you hang up your jacket, there are 3-4 others doing the same. Do you:

a) Keep to yourself

b) Start an informal conversation about the weather

c) Introduce yourself

3. A waiter comes by with a tray of champagne glasses. Do you:

a) Accept one, hoping you won't get tipsy on an empty stomach

b) Accept one, grateful for the snack you had at home

c) Accept one and take another 'for a friend'

4. You and one other person are at the dessert table. Do you:

a) Continue to quietly study the desserts

b) Start a conversation

c) Suggest the two of you conduct a taste test

6. You are standing alone at an event. Do you:

a) Wait for someone to approach you?

b) Join a conversation nearby?

c) Wouldn't happen, why would I be standing alone?

7. You see someone standing alone at an event. Do you:

a) Commiserate but stay put?

b) Go over and introduce yourself?

c) Nothing. You are too busy to notice someone standing on the sidelines.

8. There is a group of people chatting and laughing. Do you:

a) Stay away?

b) Wander over and gently join in?

c) Happily join in, adding to the joke or just say, "You all sound like fun!"

9. The event is over, and you are on your way home. What's in your pocket?

a) A napkin and a couple toothpicks

b) A few of business cards

c) A big bunch of business cards

10. It is the day after the networking event. What do you do?

a) Nothing, other than feel grateful that you survived it.

b) Pull out the business cards, making notes and a follow-up plan.

c) Add the names to your contacts and set up a lunch date.

If you mostly answered the first option (a), then you are probably a Wallflower. Don't worry, there's lots of opportunities to transition to a Mingler.

If you mostly answered the second option (b), then you are probably a Mingler. If you answered some a's, then keep working at it. Otherwise, you are in a great spot. When you're feeling brave, you can take things to the next level.

If you mostly answered the third option (c), then you are probably an Ace. That can be a good thing, mostly, but make sure you aren't going overboard. You still need a strategy. And remember it's more important to build your network than to be the life of the party.

Networking for Introverts

Networking is much touted, but there is a bias towards extroversion in this context.

With that in mind, here are a few networking tips, specific to introverts:

- Remember that networking books and tips are geared towards extroverts.
- Reframe networking so it works for you.
- Find someone you can connect with.
- As you look around the room, ask yourself, "Where's one person I can have a great conversation with?"
- Look for kindred spirits.
- Once you've met that one person, it's ok if you want to stop there.
- Take the pressure off yourself to perform or network like the extroverts.

Keep these tips in mind as you read the rest of this chapter.

Most importantly, remember that you have permission to reframe networking so it works for you. There is no one right way to do this!

Mastering Small Talk

Does anyone ever really master small talk? Maybe. Maybe not. But here are a few hints, nonetheless.

- Remember that the banter that we call small talk is really just filler until you can land on something interesting to talk about.
- If someone asks you a closed question, pretend they asked you an open question and answer that instead. For example, if you are asked, "Did you like this morning's speaker?" respond by sharing a comment about something the speaker said that you particularly liked.
- Answer a more interesting question than the one you were asked. For example, if you are asked what you are planning to do next weekend, answer by sharing a story about the amazing vacation you have planned for next month. Or, if

you are asked if you think the wind will pick up, answer instead by telling them about what happened to your house during last week's windstorm.

• When you are telling a story, pause to create spots where others can jump in. Or create an opening by saying, "Has anyone else ever had this happen to them?!?"

• Have a mini-poll in your mind and ask everyone you meet for their opinion. Just say, "Oh, I'm asking everyone what their favorite coffee spot is. Can you tell me yours? And why?"

• Don't forget about nodding your head. As introduced earlier, a 'triple nod' when someone stops speaking acts as a signal that you are waiting for them to continue.

• Don't sweat it–have your Magic Conversation Starters ready to go and you may never get stuck in small talk again!

The Transformation from Wallflower to Mingler

Here are a few guidelines to help you transform yourself from a Wallflower to a Mingler:

- Plan to arrive early to get the lay of the land.
- Set a goal of how many people you want to meet.
- Initiate conversations versus waiting to be approached.
- Say your name with confidence.
- Have your elevator pitch ready (who you are and what you do, in 15 seconds).
- Have your conversation starter picked out.
- Share contact information.
- Leave a hand free for shaking (don't get burdened by wine, a plate of nibbles and a napkin).
- Have a snack before you go.
- Limit yourself to one drink–or stick to soda.

As you build your skills, here are 5 extra tips for 'the brave':

- Introduce yourself to someone you see standing alone.
- Leave the perimeter of the room.
- Join a cluster of people already talking (it's ok, try it; if you can't break in, just move on).
- Introduce yourself to someone you've always wanted to meet (guest speaker, industry leader).
- If you see someone you've met before, but can't remember their name, approach them and re-introduce yourself.

Here are a few bonus tips:

- Stick to events where there is a focus, such as a speaker, and avoid events that are strictly networking (unless you have a small business and are seeking leads, you're unlikely to have deep conversations at these).
- If you're comfortable, wear something that invariably brings compliments or starts conversations. This makes it easy for someone to approach you.
- Think about how you can help others make connections. For example, if you meet someone who is embarking on self-publishing their first book, and you know someone who has just done this, offer to connect them. This *is* networking!

Although they will take practice, hopefully you can now envision some of the things you can do to begin networking with increasing ease.

To get the most out of networking, however, you need a broader strategy.

3-Part Networking Strategy

No matter what type of event you will be attending, employ this three-part networking strategy to get the most out of each opportunity.

1. Have a goal

Having a question you want to be answered or something you want to learn can make the difference between randomly killing time and a satisfying outcome.

2. Take a leap

Plan to start at least one conversation or have a great conversation starter question ready if someone approaches you first.

3. Act with intention

You will be at the networking event to meet people, but unless you act with intention, you could find that you haven't really met anyone at all.

Use all you have learned to create your own 3-Part Networking Strategy for the events you attend. Review it again afterward and tweak it for the next time around.

Who knows, maybe people will be referring to you as an excellent networker in the future!

As we wrap up this chapter, here are a few helpful caveats to keep in mind:

- There is no one right way to network.
- Reinvent networking to make it work for you.
- Avoid events that are strictly for networking–look for events with an activity or speaker that are part of the agenda.
- Don't try to be an extrovert.

What do you think? Do you envision feeling more comfortable at networking events by applying these skills? Are you tempted to try? Perhaps you have been to a networking event since beginning this chapter: how did it go, what did you do differently, how did other people respond? What are your goals for your next networking event?

Case Studies

- Now that Rebecca was more comfortable sharing her ideas at work, she had a little more interest and less anxiety when it came to networking events. By honoring her need for time alone to re-energize, she found that even if she arrived late, she was in better form than if she rushed to events right after work.
- Larry had a huge boost in confidence with regards to his networking skills. Equipped with his 'story in a nutshell', a reliable set of open questions to use when meeting new people, and a few clever questions to get people he knew thinking and talking, he soon found himself networking with enthusiasm.
- Chris now felt she could survive a networking session by not clamming up if someone introduced themselves to her or asked about her life. She was thrilled to learn the 'arrive-early' approach to feel less awkward.
- Kelly already had pretty good networking skills but tried out many of the tips as he wanted to take things to the next level. He found that having a plan and acting with intention brought pretty remarkable results.

The Introvert's Survival Guide to Small Talk

While you may never love small talk, you can survive it and even enjoy it.

Here are a few do's and don'ts to keep in mind:

Do's

DO allow yourself to be interrupted.

DO create opportunities for others to jump in.

DO give interesting answers to boring questions.

DO have a mini-poll that you can use.

Don'ts

DON'T answer a boring question with a boring answer.

DON'T just stand there.

DON'T sneak a look at your phone.

DON'T fall asleep.

3 Keys to Remember

KEY 1: Pretend you were asked an interesting question and answer it.

KEY 2: Have your Magic Conversation Starter questions ready.

KEY 3: The banter is just occupying you until you land on a more interesting topic.

The Introvert's Guide to 7 Different Types of Networking Opportunities

As there are many different types of networking opportunities and call for different strategies, the following are Introvert Guides to seven common types:

- Networking Events
- Lecture-Style Presentations
- Workshops and Classes
- Luncheons
- Dinners
- Conferences
- Trade Shows

The Introvert's Guide to Networking–at Networking Events

Did you know that some events are designed solely as networking events? If you haven't encountered one yet, you may in the future. The downside is that there isn't necessarily a speaker or an activity, but the upside is that everyone has the same goal as you do--to meet as many people as possible. As others are also interested in building up their personal networks, your attempts to practice your networking skills will be celebrated.

Here are a few do's and don'ts to keep in mind:

Do's

DO take lots of business cards.

DO have your 3o-second elevator pitch ready.

DO dress comfortably.

DO wear clothes that make you feel confident.

Don'ts

DON'T just hang out at the dessert table.

DON'T just chat with people you know.

DON'T forget to ask for others' business cards.

3 Keys to Remember

KEY 1: Exude confidence.

KEY 2: Exchange contact information.

KEY 3: Follow-up with at least one person afterward.

Remember to employ the 3-Part Networking Strategy: 1. Have a goal, 2. Take a leap and 3. Act with intention.

The Introvert's Guide to Networking–at Lecture-Style Presentations

Lecture-style presentations typically have what is referred to as theatre seating, with rows of chairs, all facing forward, perhaps with an aisle or two. This format is common at conferences.

Here are a few do's and don'ts to keep in mind:

Do's

DO arrive early enough that you can get your preferred seating, especially if you need to sit in a certain spot to see or hear.

DO pick an aisle seat if you are prone to needing to get out or want an exit strategy.

DO leave your jacket or a book on your chair, then wander the room to network.

DO say hello to a couple of people and start a conversation.

DO introduce yourself to the people who end up sitting next to you.

DO think of a question you want to be answered.

Don'ts

DON'T just grab a seat and sit there reading the flyer.

DON'T just wait by looking at your Smartphone.

DON'T try to balance a coffee cup, a piece of cake, your iPad and a notepad on your lap unless you want to start a conversation with the person you spill coffee on.

DON'T be afraid to ask a question.

3 Keys to Remember

KEY 1: Arrive early.

KEY 2: Introduce yourself to your seatmates.

KEY 3: Think of a question you want to be answered.

Remember to employ the 3-Part Networking Strategy: 1. Have a goal, 2. Take a leap and 3. Act with intention.

The Introvert's Guide to Networking–at Workshops and Classes

Chances are that you have taken plenty of courses in your life, and chances are that you will take many more. Whether as stand-alone events or as part of conferences, workshops and classes are a great networking opportunity.

The two most common seating arrangements are round tables or rows of tables with chairs. Regardless of format, you want to be seated both for ideal learning and for networking.

Here are a few do's and don'ts to keep in mind:

Do's

DO arrive early.

DO introduce yourself to the instructor or workshop leader (even if you feel a bit awkward doing so, you are likely to find that you will be more relaxed once you have made this personal connection).

DO get a seat that you will be physically comfortable at.

DO be the one to pipe up and introduce yourself to the other early arrivals.

DO have a question or two in mind for the day.

Don'ts

DON'T sit with your colleagues if you aren't attending alone.

DON'T find excuses to not participate in the activities.

DON'T hide behind your phone.

3 Keys to Remember

KEY 1: Have learning goals.

KEY 2: Be open-minded to different perspectives.

KEY 3: Participate actively.

Remember to employ the 3-Part Networking Strategy: 1. Have a goal, 2. Take a leap and 3. Act with intention.

The Introvert's Guide to Networking–at Luncheons

Do you find yourself attending luncheon meetings, listening to speaker sessions held over lunch, or participating in social luncheons? With just a few strategies you can find yourself enjoying successful conversations at luncheons without giving into anxieties.

Here are a few do's and don'ts to keep in mind:

Do's

DO get a seat early so that you can see the speaker without needing to turn your chair or strain your neck.

DO ask if you can join a table with just a couple of people at it.

DO invite people to join your table.

DO have a spare pen and paper you can share.

DO have a question in mind that you want to be answered.

Don'ts

DON'T be afraid to start a new table if there is open seating and many tables.

DON'T be satisfied if the person next to you isn't talkative; turn to the person on your other side or even across the table and start a conversation.

DON'T just sit at the table looking at your Smartphone.

DON'T eat soup unless you are particularly adept at not spilling.

3 Keys to Remember

KEY 1: Get seated comfortably.

KEY 2: Plan to meet your tablemates.

KEY 3: Have a question you want to be answered.

Remember to employ the 3-Part Networking Strategy: 1. Have a goal, 2. Take a leap and 3. Act with intention.

The Introvert's Guide to Networking–at Dinners

While there are similarities between lunches and dinners, in terms of networking there are some important differences. Dinners, banquets and other sit-down affairs tend to be more elaborate affairs. Lasting longer and more formal in nature, you will spend more time with those you are seated with.

Here are a few do's and don'ts to keep in mind:

Do's

DO get a seat early.

DO start a new table at a sit-down function with many tables.

DO think of a question you want to be answered, a person you want to meet, or a personal goal for the evening.

DO carry business cards and share them.

DO look for friendly faces and ask if you can join their table.

Don'ts

DON'T wear clothes with droopy sleeves.

DON'T try to join a table with just one or two seats left, as you could very well hear that the spot is being saved.

DON'T eat food for the first time unless you have a varied palate and like most everything.

DON'T complain about the food; if something is not to your liking, just leave it aside.

DON'T reach; ask for the cream/butter/salt and pepper to be passed.

DON'T drink too much.

3 Keys to Remember

KEY 1: Get a great seat.

KEY 2: Be flexible.

KEY 3: Go easy with the wine.

Remember to employ the 3-Part Networking Strategy: 1. Have a goal, 2. Take a leap and 3. Act with intention.

The Introvert's Guide to Networking–at Conferences

Conferences offer tremendous networking opportunities. In addition to lectures, workshops, luncheons, and dinners, you will find yourself meeting other delegates during registration, between events, at mixers and other activities. It is important to set yourself up for success to get the most out of your conference time.

In addition to learning goals (the sessions you will attend) and self-care goals (healthy snacks and walks), set networking goals for yourself. A networking plan will help you leverage the best networking opportunities, avoid time- wasters that could cause you to have less time for conversation, and escape from moments of anxiety.

Note: see the next Introvert's Guide for tips specific to trade shows.

Here are a few do's and don'ts to keep in mind:

Do's

DO set goals for the conference.

DO have a question planned that you can ask of others you meet.

DO get a big picture of the conference, planning out what you want to attend, and who you want to meet.

DO have an anti-anxiety plan.

DO splurge a little and get a hotel room on-site or across the street (handy for a bit of a break; it's also handy for skipping washroom lineups).

Don'ts

DON'T attend all the same sessions if you go with a colleague.

DON'T be afraid to get up and leave a session if it is not of interest (duck into another session or take an introvert's me-break and come back restored).

DON'T spend your time between sessions engaged with your Smartphone.

3 Keys to Remember

KEY 1: Have a plan.

KEY 2: Be open and open-minded.

KEY 3: Take care of your creature comforts.

Remember to employ the 3-Part Networking Strategy: 1. Have a goal, 2. Take a leap and 3. Act with intention.

The Introvert's Guide to Networking–at Trade Shows

Trade shows, which feature vendors with booths that participants visit, are a common feature of conferences or may be stand-alone events. Trade shows are informative, however larger trade shows can be daunting, with hundreds of booths, hours of walking on concrete floors and much collecting swag and entering contests. One can leave a trade show exhausted and barely remembering who you met. For this reason, it's a good idea to have a plan.

Here are a few do's and don'ts to keep in mind:

Do's

DO carry lots of business cards.

DO study the trade show map and pick out a few booths you really want to visit.

DO start a conversation at the booths of greatest interest to you.

DO engage in conversation with other attendees.

DO set a goal, such as plan one person to follow up with afterward.

Don'ts

DON'T try to see everything.

DON'T just wander aimlessly.

DON'T get caught up in the gimmicks of collecting a trinket, stamp or contest entry at every booth.

DON'T expect yourself to go for hours without a little break for yourself.

3 Keys to Remember

KEY 1: Wear comfortable shoes.

KEY 2: Have a 3-point plan.

KEY 3: Do it your way.

Remember to employ the 3-Part Networking Strategy: 1. Have a goal, 2. Take a leap and 3. Act with intention.

Chapter 13: Special Situations

You may encounter one or more of these special one-off situations:

- Interviews
- Business Meetings
- Office Communications
- Office Parties
- Volunteering

If you do, you will find an Introvert's Guide for each at the end of this chapter.

What do you think? Do you have any special situations that aren't included in this list? If so, think about the principles in this book, brainstorm a few ideas and create your own Introvert's Guide for these situations.

Case Studies

- Rebecca had never felt comfortable at office parties, but armed with the new tips, she actually found herself recently enjoying a work-related social gathering.
- The tips helped Larry in both his business meetings and surprisingly with his family.
- Chris found herself more effective with the volunteer

groups she was involved in.

• Kelly gained great perspectives in terms of office parties, where he'd never really thought about how much to drink, or how his actions impacted his reputation.

The Introvert's Guide to 5 Special Situations

As each type of special situation calls for different strategies, the following are Introvert Guides to these five special situations:

- Interviews
- Business Meetings
- Office Communications
- Office Parties
- Volunteering

The Introvert's Survival Guide to Interviews

Interviews are a unique situation. When you are applying for a job or contract, your priority is on putting your best foot forward–and proceeding to the next step in the hiring process.

Here are a few do's and don'ts to keep in mind:

Do's

DO be on time.

DO dress professionally in clothes that make you feel confident.

DO bring a spare copy of your resume.

DO use your active listening skills.

DO ask open questions.

DO have a clean notepad and pen ready.

DO use the interviewer's name.

DO smile.

Don'ts

DON'T be late.

DON'T treat the receptionist disrespectfully.

DON'T speak despairingly about your former employers.

DON'T interrupt the interviewer.

DON'T doubt yourself.

3 Keys to Remember

KEY 1: Be confident.

KEY 2: Be prepared.

KEY 3: Be professional.

The Introvert's Survival Guide to Business Meetings

Business meetings aren't all that different from some of the networking events covered in the previous chapter, except that the focus is on the business, rather than networking. That said, there are still opportunities to network.

Here are a few do's and don'ts to keep in mind:

Do's

DO be on time.

DO carry business cards.

DO introduce yourself to everyone at the meeting who you haven't met before.

DO introduce others who may not have met each other.

DO use your active listening skills.

DO ask open questions.

DO create opportunities for introverts to contribute to the discussion.

Don'ts

DON'T be invisible.

DON'T goof off.

DON'T speak despairingly about your company or the competition.

DON'T confuse the business meeting with a personal setting; stay professional.

DON'T ask closed or leading questions.

3 Keys to Remember

KEY 1: Be professional.

KEY 2: Use open questions.

KEY 3: Meet someone new.

The Introvert's Survival Guide to the Office Communications

If you work in an office, then communications with your co-workers are part of your everyday life. Whether you mostly work alone, or interact extensively with others all day long, there are common communication situations you will face.

Here are a few do's and don'ts to keep in mind:

Do's

DO be present.

DO contribute your ideas.

DO participate.

DO use your active listening skills.

DO ask great open questions.

DO pay attention to your body language.

Don'ts

DON'T badmouth your employer.

DON'T forget to leave time to recharge your batteries.

DON'T ask leading or closed questions.

3 Keys to Remember

>KEY 1: Find ways to contribute your ideas.

KEY 2: Consider your needs as an introvert.

KEY 3: Stretch yourself, if and when you are ready.

The Introvert's Survival Guide to Office Parties

Office party? Sure, go. But don't let it ruin your career.

Here are a few do's and don'ts to keep in mind:

Do's

DO plan who you want to meet.

DO think about the best time to arrive.

DO dress comfortably and confidently.

DO pick a few conversation starters.

DO be a gracious guest.

Don'ts

DON'T drink a lot.

DON'T behave inappropriately.

DON'T put yourself in a situation where you will feel uncomfortable.

DON'T stay if you aren't having a good time.

3 Keys to Remember

KEY 1: Limit the booze.

KEY 2: Fly under the radar.

KEY 3: Find someone interesting to talk to.

The Introvert's Survival Guide to Volunteering

Volunteering is a great way to practice and enhance your communication skills. Plus you'll meet some great people while making a difference in your community.

Here are a few do's and don'ts to keep in mind:

Do's

DO have goals.

DO volunteer for short events if you want to meet lots of people.

DO volunteer for a committee if you want to build relationships.

DO respect what you need as an introvert.

DO practice your communication skills.

Don'ts

DON'T take on more than you can handle.

3 Keys to Remember

KEY 1: Be open to meeting new people.

KEY 2: Pick your projects with intention.

KEY 3: Keep track of the people you meet.

Chapter 14: Emergencies

Charles was never so glad to get back in his car. He'd scooted out of the association luncheon just as quickly as he could. He didn't know what happened. He was never great at these things, but he'd overcome his old anxiety long ago. Until today. He'd walked up to two people who were chatting, said hello and then just stood there. One never even noticed he was there. The other glanced at him once in surprise, looked confused, and returned to the previous conversation. He then realized they were engaged in a very serious personal conversation but somehow he had missed the cues. He just stood there, feeling humiliated. He extracted himself by pretending something caught his eye and wandered off. After studying a table of flyers for what felt like forever, he glanced at his watchless wrist, feigned surprise at the time and dashed off. Now, sitting in his car, he felt sick. He'd missed the lunch, and on top of his sleepless night, recent bad news and pressing deadlines at work, it was all too much. He felt all his hard work on his networking skills had been for nothing.

Angie's head was spinning. She was sitting at her desk, trying to absorb the conversation she'd just had with her boss. She'd been bugging him forever to let her make a presentation on her project to the executive, then today, bang, just like that, there was an empty slot on tomorrow morning's agenda at the quarterly management conference, and would she like to take the 15 minutes to do her thing? As she sat there sputtering, her boss had said, "I'll take that as a yes. Off you go! It's what you wanted, so now you'd better be ready!" She'd blissfully imagined she'd get a week or so's notice before having to present, if it ever happened, and here it was. Of course, she'd had the presentation ready for weeks, but mentally? It was suddenly here, and she couldn't picture being ready in the morning. She felt a sense of panic and closed her eyes. And all she could see were 200 eyes staring back at her.

What is an introvert's conversation skills emergency?

Good question.

And it's one that you get to answer for yourself.

Broadly speaking, it's anything that might throw you off your game.

Moments like what Charles and Angie were having definitely qualify.

Let's use these predicaments as a lens towards what to do if you have an 'emergency'.

The Networking Blunder - Exercise

Why do you think Charles was so upset?

What caused Charles to make his blunder?

Why do you think Charles was thrown so far off his game when he had been doing so well networking?

What advice would you offer Charles now?

What advice would you offer Charles a week from now, when he has had a bit more time to reflect?

The Looming Presentation - Exercise

Why do you think Angie is so panicked?

What questions would you ask Angie if you had the opportunity?

What advice would you offer Angie now?

What advice would you offer Angie a week from now, after she has made her presentation and has had time to reflect?

Handling Emergencies – The 5 R's

There is no formula for how to handle what feels like an emergency to you.

In the big scheme of things, no one died, and you will survive, but beyond that, how do you get yourself through these moments?

Here are a few strategies to guide you:

Retreat

If you haven't done so already, and you feel the need to, it's ok to retreat, to get a bit of distance from the situation and from other people. Take a break, take a few breaths, drink a glass of water, scribble some notes–do whatever you need to do to calm down.

Reach Out

Reach out to a friend, co-worker or networking buddy for a little advice. Alternatively, get out your journal and write out what happened and see if you can get perspective.

Reflect

Reflect on what happened, or is still happening, from a broader perspective. What have you learned? What could you have done differently? What opportunities for learning and growth do you have?

Rest

In most cases, stepping away from the situation and getting a good night's sleep can do wonders.

Rebound

Once you have calmed yourself down, and have a clear idea of what's going on, brainstorm a plan to get you back on your game. This might include self-care, such as getting some exercise, or rolling up your sleeves to rewrite your proposal.

Remember the 5R's for Emergencies: Retreat ➔ Reach Out ➔ Reflect ➔ Rest ➔ Rebound

Now, let's return to Charles and Angie.

The Networking Blunder - Possibilities

Why do you think Charles was so upset?

> • Charles is in crisis. He was depleted, made a blunder, wasn't able to respond as deftly as usual and was left speechless. He felt humiliated, even though the situation may not have been as bad as he imagined. Now, with his ego was bruised and still feeling embarrassed, his self-confidence has escaped him.

What caused Charles to make his blunder?

> • Charles had gone to an event when he was not at his best (lack of sleep, bad news, work stresses), so he was already vulnerable. This caused him to miss non-verbal cues when he blundered into a private conversation.

Why do you think Charles was thrown so far off his game when he had been doing so well networking?

> • Under different circumstances, Charles would have apologized, shaken it off and moved on. But, because he wasn't grounded, he allowed the miss to throw him completely off his game.

What advice would you offer Charles now?

> • Take a break, don't worry about it, get some rest and deal

with your personal matters.

What advice would you offer Charles a week from now, when he has had a bit more time to reflect?

> • Ask what he has learned, then reassure him that this was a blip, and he has not lost his networking abilities. To the contrary, he has survived a blunder and is now on the other side of it. Suggest he plan to get out to another event soon, but make it a particularly safe one, and be well rested when he arrives.

The Looming Presentation - Possibilities

Why do you think Angie is so panicked?

> • Angie let herself imagine that she would have lots of notice to make her presentation and was surprised. She is experiencing a combination of excitement and nervousness to the degree that it has--momentarily– stopped her dead in her tracks.

What questions would ask Angie if you had the opportunity?

> • Is your presentation ready? (Yes). What's the worst that can happen? (She might trip over a few words). Is this a friendly audience? (Yes, she knows them well).

What advice would you offer Angie now?

> • Breathe. Get up and move to change the energy. Express your nervousness if need be, then get down to business. You've got this. Pour some tea and walk through your presentation while picturing this particular audience. Tomorrow, get your butterflies to fly in formation. Remember to find a few smiling faces and talk directly to them.

What advice would you offer Angie a week from now, after she has made her presentation and has had time to reflect?

- Ask her what she learned from the experience, and what she would do differently next time. She probably doesn't need advice, as her answers are within.

As we wrap up this chapter, here are a few helpful caveats to keep in mind:

- If you find yourself in crisis, do whatever you need to do to take care of yourself in the moment.
- Breathe.
- Remember, this is a moment in time. You will get through it.
- Jot some notes to yourself that you can tuck away in your wallet to bring out and read if you get panicked (yes, we're talking about hiding in a bathroom stall, if needed).
- Refer back to Chapter 3: Social Anxiety for additional tips.
- Pay special attention to Chapter 16: Self-Care for Introverts.

What do you think? Have you ever experienced an 'emergency' like the ones described in this chapter? Do you now have things you know you could do to help you cope?

Case Studies

- Although Rebecca was growing by leaps and bounds in terms of sharing her ideas, there were a couple of points where she got totally overwhelmed with not being heard. She could no longer sit quietly on the sidelines! Each time, she learned to take some quiet time out to herself.
- Larry made a rather unfortunate blunder at a networking meeting, just when his confidence had been growing, but he didn't let it throw him off. Although embarrassed, he took stock and figured out what he needed to do to set things right. A phone call and an apology did the trick.
- Chris' biggest success came from her new ability to quell panic attacks before they started.

- Kelly's emergency came in the form of being asked to make a conference presentation on very short notice. To ensure his message landed, he thought about the different types of people in the audience and structured his words and handouts so that he would have something for everyone.

The Introvert's Survival Guide to Triumphing over Social Emergencies

We all have challenges in life, and blips along the road of wherever we are headed. When things go wrong, simply STOP, take time out and take care of yourself before you carry on.

Here are few do's and don'ts to keep in mind:

Do's

DO trust that you will survive.

DO listen to your gut.

DO tell yourself that you will be ok.

DO appreciate how far you have come.

Don'ts

DON'T beat yourself up.

DON'T panic any more than you are already.

DON'T expect more of yourself at the moment.

DON'T give up.

3 Keys to Remember

KEY 1: Retreat → Reach Out → Reflect → Rest → Rebound

KEY 2: Breathe.

KEY 3: Celebrate your victories.

Chapter 15: Written Communications

"Many introverts naturally see the world in terms of story and symbol. And when we use writing as a tool, we're able to connect the dots and lay out the patterns we see for others."

Lauren Sapala

As an introvert, writing is probably quite natural for you. By intentionally honing your writing skills and applying them to situations where you connect the dots for others, you will contribute even more to the world around you.

While our focus in this book has been on conversation skills, written communications are an important part of interacting with others.

Depending on your work, studies and interests, you may have a lot of written communications in your life or perhaps you just need to manage your email.

Either way, a few written communication fundamentals are worth your attention.

Write to Contribute

Here are just a few ways you can use your written communications to your advantage:

- Offer to summarize what was discussed in meetings.
- Offer to prepare the agenda for meetings you attend.
- Offer to draft reports and presentations for your team.

Write to Contribute - Exercise

The above suggestions have the potential to benefit you, other introverts in our organization, your team members and the company. Can you see how?

As we wrap up this chapter, here are a few helpful caveats to keep in mind:

- If you'd like to improve your written communication skills, there are many resources available to help you. Chances are, though, you are pretty good already.

What do you think? How are your written communication skills? Do they leave a lot to be desired, or do they just need a bit of attention? This is a good one to ask others about, so you can get some feedback.

Case Studies

- Written communications had always been a strength for Rebecca. She found that by applying the written communication tips to what she now understood about adapting to type, she got greater results from her emails.
- Larry began thinking more about his audience, and that most people weren't as analytical as he was, which allowed him to write emails and reports that were less dense.
- Always articulate,
- Chris learned to write as confidently as she now spoke.
- Kelly had the written communications nailed pretty much

already.

The Introvert's Survival Guide to E-Mail

You have the upper hand when it comes to email as you probably are a pretty good writer.

Here are a few do's and don'ts to keep in mind:

Do's

DO use bullet points.

DO model good written communication skills.

DO offer to summarize the meeting by email.

DO offer to send out the next meeting's agenda.

Don'ts

DON'T email when you are angry.

DON'T hide behind email.

3 Keys to Remember

KEY 1: Drafting team emails means they get your stamp.

KEY 2: Keep it brief.

KEY 3: Use bullet points.

Chapter 16: Self-Care for Introverts

"Solitude is for me a fount of healing which makes my life worth living."

C. G. Jung

Self-Care – 4 Essentials

In a nutshell, as an introvert, you need FOUR THINGS to survive and thrive:

1. Time alone daily.

2. Privacy.

3. Quiet zones.

4. Time to reflect.

It's a pretty short list.

These are the core.

Remove any one of these from your life and you will find your energy drained. You won't shrivel up and die, but you might feel like it.

How you make these happen is up to you, of course.

Other Possibilities

You may find there are other things you can do as part of your self-care plan.

Here are a few ideas:

- Learn to say NO.
- Go for a walk at work.
- Bow out from the lunch crowd.
- Put headphones on–even if you have nothing playing.
- Sitting alone in your car may be boring, but you are still alone. It counts.
- Find a quiet area in your workplace where you can get away to think. Borrow an empty office, book a meeting room, sit in the lunchroom when it's empty. Get creative.
- Look for places in your community where you can be 'alone'. Going out for a coffee isn't really time alone, and it won't be quiet, but if you can get yourself in the right headspace, it can be a pretty good alternative.
- Hang out at the library, even if you aren't there to pick up books.

Your Personal Self-Care Plan – Exercise

Pour yourself a cup of tea (or your beverage of choice) and start a fresh page in your notebook.

Jot your ideas in response to the following questions:

- Do I get enough time alone?
- What are some ways in which I can create more time alone in my life?
- Whose support do I need to accomplish this goal?
- What are some ways I can get short bits of time alone during my day, especially if I find an urgent need for it?

- What else do I need to incorporate into my Self-Care Plan (think about quiet time, time to reflect, privacy)?
- Feel free to follow wherever your mind and heart want to go. It's YOUR plan--make it work for you!

As we wrap up this chapter, here are a few helpful caveats to keep in mind:

- Learn to value what makes you tick as an introvert and carve out time to do what you need to do to take care of yourself. If that means you need half an hour of silence to restore your energy while your extrovert co-workers are at the bar, that's fine.
- Do an internet search for "Self-Care for Introverts" – you'll find some great resources.
- Follow a few Twitter, Instagram and Facebook accounts with a focus on introverts.
- Review Chapter 4: Social Anxiety and remind yourself about getting your butterflies to fly in formation.

What do you think? Do you have well-honed instincts for taking care of yourself? Do you honor what your introvert self needs? Are any of the ideas in this chapter new to you? If so, try them out. Keep the ones that make the biggest difference.

Case Studies

- Rebecca took solace in, and gathered energy from, her daily routine of time alone to recharge her batteries.
- Larry used his newly found skills to drum up a broader personal support network for himself.
- Chris was relieved to learn that the things she did naturally to take care of herself were normal and perfectly acceptable.
- Kelly learned how to give his introverted friends time to think and recharge their batteries.
-

The Introvert's Survival Guide to Self-Care

Self-care that nurtures you as an introvert is essential to your life. It is not a luxury.

Here are a few do's and don'ts to keep in mind:

Do's

DO make time alone a priority.

DO learn to say NO.

DO create quiet zones is your day and life.

DO guard your privacy.

DO speak up if you need time to reflect on a question.

DO adapt your work environment to work for you.

Don'ts

DON'T put time alone on the back burner.

DON'T take care of an extrovert's need for company over time for yourself.

DON'T beat yourself up if you don't want to be with other people.

DON'T just put up with a workplace that is not introvert friendly.

3 Keys to Remember

KEY 1: Take time to be alone.

KEY 2: Make time to collect your thoughts.

KEY 3: Keep your Personal Self-Care Plan handy!

Conclusion

Thanks for making it through to the end of *Conversation Skills: Secrets for Introverts on How to Analyze People, Handle Small Talk with Confidence, Overcome Social Anxiety and Other Highly Effective Communication Tips when Networking with People*. I hope you have found it to be both informative and practical.

Let's conclude by checking in with our four case study subjects:

- Rebecca is feeling heard and is more confident sharing ideas at work. She also feels less anxious about meeting strangers and is enjoying conversations with new people. Rebecca's secret edge is the time she plans alone each day to restore her energy.
- Larry has made great strides in his goal of improving his networking skills. The results are already showing up in his job performance, and he is more relaxed. Larry's secret edge is the genuine curiosity he has developed about the people he meets.
- Chris has achieved her goal of being less stressed at work. She is actively sharing her ideas, has a better relationship with her boss, and is no longer paralyzed if she attends a business event. Chris's secret edge is picking the person she wants to talk to, rather than waiting to be approached.
- Kelly has definitely met his goal of understanding what makes introverts tick. He has also become a better listener.

Kelly's secret edge is now having a goal for every interaction.

I hope that learning alongside Rebecca, Larry, Chris and Kelly helped you with applying the skills in this book to your own life and building your confidence.

Your next step is to put the skills into action by thinking about your communications, trying out new approaches when meeting people or sharing your ideas, and learning from both your stumbles and successes. Good luck!

Finally, if you found this book valuable, a review on Amazon is always appreciated!

Part 2: Social Skills

How to Analyze People and Body Language Instantly, Handle Small Talk and Conversation as an Introvert, Improve Emotional Intelligence, and Learn Highly Effective Communication Tips

Introduction

There are many misconceptions about introverts, such as how they are seen to be antisocial, unfriendly, shy, reserved, lonely – the list could go on and on. However, what does not get mentioned nearly enough is that being an introvert or having introvert tendencies can be a real *asset*.

The following chapters will discuss the process of developing good social skills if you identify as an introvert and draw from relevant modern examples. Topics such as dealing with social anxiety, developing introvert traits into more sociable traits, body language, and learning how to interact with different types of people will also be explored.

As a whole, the book provides pertinent advice based on modern research and an overview of some reputable people and how they socialize. The process of communication is important, and this book will enable you to understand the basic concepts of effective communication. This way, it becomes possible to understand the different characteristics of different individuals, including how to identify a liar – and this will help you, the reader, be much more effective at social interactions.

It will also cover the most effective ways of handling oneself in a social gathering, as portraying a good image among several people is an important aspect of socialization.

After reading this informative book, if you identify as an introvert or harbor introvert tendencies, then you'll be able to overcome your fears and anxieties, and generally change the way you present yourself both in professional and social settings.

An important note to remember as you read along is that you are *not* alone and there is *nothing* wrong with you. The world is full of people who have the same communication 'hiccups', and just because you will go on to master some talking techniques does not mean that the essence of who you are will entirely change. You will still be *you* – just with more confidence!

Introverts are people who get their energy from spending time alone (which is more often than not a good thing!). Like a battery, you take the time to recharge before unplugging again and stepping back out to face and interact with a beautiful but also chaotic world.

Chapter 1: How to Deal with Social Anxiety

Social skills are, unfortunately, a necessity in everyday life, whether it is in a professional or social setting. Fear and anxiety are among the major factors that determine a person's social skills, and understanding the impact they have on each person is vital. Most people are unable to stand in front of a large crowd and address them because of stage fright, and this fear always has an impact on how a message is delivered. Similarly, when interacting among people either at a social gathering or professional setup, fear and anxiety have a major impact on how a person will interact with others. It is important for you to understand, though, that fear is all 'in the mind' – rest assured as it *is* possible to alleviate it permanently with the right practice.

For most people who are just like you, either identify as an introvert or have introvert tendencies, standing in front of a crowd is as daunting as facing a bear all alone in the middle of the wilderness. This fear is developed as a result of constantly avoiding the importance of developing interactive social skills, and anxiety is inflated as a result of the realization that social interactions can be difficult. However, *it is possible* to get past this through experiences such as repeatedly talking in front of large crowds, which eventually eliminates the fear associated with social interactions. The same goes for interactions that involve one-on-one discussions where understanding different aspects of social skills can make a tremendous difference.

In order to apply the concepts mentioned in this book, it is necessary for you, the reader, to set up a foundation that will enable you to understand the best ways of improving your social skills:

Understand that fear and anxiety are all in your head (yes – it's easier said than done!): The most important part of developing good social skills is having supreme confidence in yourself. Developing good social skills means that the people surrounding you must be able to understand and interact with you in a normal way. This can only be achieved if you're confident about what you say because this lends legitimacy to you. Confidence can be developed by perfecting the elements of the message being communicated such that when you are in front of people, you can speak uninterrupted and thus inspire confidence in others.

Have an open mind: It is extremely important to keep an open mind as this will enable you to be open to different ideas. Fear and anxiety are caused by different reasons for every person, and thus it is important to remain receptive to advice and be willing to try out new things. One reason why fear and anxiety manifest for so long is that we often fail to recognize other ways that we may combat these problems. Thus, the process of improving social skills will be dependent on you being receptive to new ideas that can be implemented to a positive effect. The ideas suggested in this book are generalized and cover a wide scope of character traits, and it is important to remain receptive to the different ways of handling your improvement of social skills.

What role do fear and anxiety play in the development of your social skills and interactions?

Limits constructive thinking: Your social skills become inhibited when you focus on the fear and anxiety consuming you. This means that there is not enough time to do constructive thinking and relay a decent conversation or speech. Stage fright is an excellent example of the manifestation of fear and anxiety, and it limits the way you think and present ideas. Therefore, fear and anxiety can negatively impact social interactions because you are unable to express yourself fully, which results in ineffective communication.

Prevents effective communication: Fear and anxiety result in quietness, meekness and even confusion when you are interacting with other people. Therefore, being overcome with fear will only result in no communication at all, and this impacts the ability of others to understand you. Good social skills cannot be enhanced when you only focus on the fear because that is simply all you're thinking about. You overcrowd your head with thoughts of what your colleagues must be thinking of you, your appearance and even the sound of your voice. Thus, it becomes practically impossible to achieve effective communication in such a situation.

Distracts the listeners: Fear and anxiety not only hampers your social skills and interactions but also distracts your listener(s) from what is important. Whether it is in a social gathering or a one-on-one situation, you are more likely to get attention for your ineffective communication and open display of fear than for the message you're trying to communicate. This is ineffective when an important message has to be passed along because the person(s) will be focused on the fear you are displaying. This is a major disadvantage as it prevents the development of social skills.

Limits how to make friends: Ineffective social skills of interaction are developed because you cannot communicate out of fear and anxiety. You will spend a large amount of time thinking about your weaknesses when interacting socially with others, thereby limiting your chances of making friends. You probably find it particularly difficult meeting new people and assessing their characters, meaning that you find it incredibly difficult to make friends. This is a big disadvantage of the fear and anxiety that characterizes you because you consequently are unable to interact properly. Making friends is a critical part of interacting socially, and the inability to do this is a major disadvantage because friendship can further be a rewarding gift for people. With friends also comes the opportunity to flourish and allow yourself actually to *be* yourself, as we often befriend those who have similar qualities, opinions, and outlooks as us. Thus, the result is a positive relationship.

Communication might not be taken seriously: As already mentioned, when fear overcomes you, it sometimes shows, and this can limit the communication process as it can easily make a message dismissible. The elements of effective communication involve eloquence and appropriate body language, particularly when something important must be communicated.

Inability to effect a presentation: In a professional setting or a social situation, the ability to properly effect a presentation is affected by fear and anxiety. Proper communication requires that you reach out to everyone regardless of their characters. However, fear limits this ability because you are more focused on yourself rather than on communication. It is necessary to consider the importance of confidence when conducting a presentation as it is the only effective way of interacting with others when communicating something important.

Limits communication opportunities in the future: Your ability to communicate and relay messages in the future gradually disappears because of your inability to interact with other people socially. Fear limits different opportunities that would otherwise be available because you cannot concentrate on anything else other than your pitfalls when you are communicating with others. Romantically, it is possible to lose a mate as a result of ineffective communication because some people do not like those who are anxious or fearful. It is important to get around the problem of fear to ensure communication opportunities still exist in the future as fear makes other people have a lower opinion of you. The fact remains that social anxiety is something that can be controlled and, eventually, eliminated by understanding the basic role that fear plays in the interaction process. When you discover the influence of anxiety and fear over your life, trust us – you will be in a better position to make good decisions regarding how you interact with other people.

The secret to developing good natural charisma and getting over anxiety is, alas, through experience – and practice! Although it might sound harsh, it's a "tough love" approach: you *must* set your mind to the possibility of getting over your introvert tendencies so that you can develop more interactive ones.

But don't worry – we're here to help remember!

Chapter 2: The Importance of Social Skills

Social skills describe the basic approach to communication within society. The definition encompasses both non-verbal and verbal forms of communication because both are an essential element of good social skills. People interact with one another and even work together as a result of exercising social skills, bringing people with common goals and backgrounds together. Social skills allow for broader interactions among people from various backgrounds, thereby enabling mutually beneficial relationships to be established in society.

Everybody in society, not just you, will benefit from mastering social skills because it results in a progressive benefit for everybody concerned. First, mastering social skills allows you to improve existing relationships and allows people to feel closer to each other. Good social skills emphasize the virtues of honesty and togetherness, and this encourages closeness among different people. It is easier for somebody to like a charismatic person more than they would like an ordinary person because the former can express greater social skills. The same goes for romantic relationships because it is possible to improve such relations as a result of excellent social skills that encourage open communication. It is easier for people to forge strong relationships with each other because of social skills as it allows for easier communication and encourages action.

As touched on, excellent communication skills coupled with a good way of expressing yourself is a sure-fire way of attracting new friends. It is easier to catch the eye of somebody you would otherwise never speak to if they happen to experience your improved social skills. Everybody likes an eloquent, outspoken individual, and this is critical in the process of communicating and interacting with others. Getting a message across can be the difference between success and failure, and thus if you understand and have mastered social skills, you will rarely be misquoted. This also applies for presentations and public speaking as you will no longer struggle to make your point in front of a crowd. You will communicate with several people as though they were your personal friends.

Most professionals have achieved success in advancing their careers as a result of the mastery of social skills. Understanding how to relate to the people around you is critical for success within a professional setup. This is because it is necessary not only to be a good team player but also a manager and judge of character that positions the company for success. Social skills enable you to conduct yourself appropriately and win over several friends who end up being a big help in advancing your career. Good social skills also allow for closer interactions with customers, and they are responsible for building up a business and allowing those involved to enjoy success.

You can also enjoy a better reputation as a result of having good social skills. This is because you endear yourself to people far better than somebody who does not have good social skills. For instance, presidents and other leaders who display excellent social skills both in public and in private can command the respect of several people. As a result, they can automatically have a good reputation among different communities as compared to a person who is unable to express themselves appropriately.

It is possible to be much happier with yourself as a result of mastering social skills as compared to the depression caused by being alone. Most introverts, naturally but unfortunately, ignore the possibility of increasing their social skills because they do not see the benefit of doing it – or rather, their fear, yet again, holds them back. They would rather keep to themselves and be as private as possible as compared to getting out there to interact with other people. This concern is usually brought about by the need to live a private life and keep away from other people; however, the fact remains that society can only progress when everybody works together. Thus, the common belief by introverts is that they do not need to interact with the rest of society; however, this has the damaging consequence of bringing depression and general unhappiness. Good social skills allow you to walk around feeling free and open, never obligated into specific action but with the freedom to make choices. Interacting with other people is an essential part of ensuring happiness among a community of people, and thus personal happiness should be a critical reason for anyone to master social skills.

Should you desire a wider audience for your business or any social reason, mastering social skills can make a tremendous difference. Even internet communication, such as posting tweets, is dependent on good social skills as it will determine the nature of communication between you and your audience. Good social skills will allow you to have a much larger audience because your communication is effective and desirable to a large number of people. This way, it is possible to communicate an important message as well as advertise for your business successfully.

Another critical benefit of good social skills is that they allow you to be accepted in different social groups and among various peers. The ability to communicate effectively without fear or anxiety endears you to many different people and grants you access to different opportunities. People who explore the world and get to see many different things can do so because they are not introverts (*lucky them, huh? – but hey, it can be you too!*). Their mastery of social skills allows them to penetrate different social groups and see as much as possible. Acceptance of different peers can be possible by anybody with a mastery of social skills.

It is quite difficult to "make it" in society alone because we rely on each other one way or another. So, here are some vital points on how to help you with your introvert tendencies:

Match conversations with friends and diversify: Speak to a close friend or family member to improve your social skills. It is critical to get a trusted person's help because they will be honest and guide you through the process reasonably. There is also the need to be respectful of their opinions as there is a reason you have selected them to help you. Practicing forthcoming conversations, whether it is in front of a gala dinner or trying to get a date, will help as it will allow you to anticipate what is coming. Diversifying is also an important aspect of improving social skills because it is necessary to interact with people outside of your normal scope of friends or even culture. Learning the perspectives of life from somebody new is important in helping you to master social skills because it gives you a different perspective. People from different cultures interact in a manner that you might not be used to and the experience itself will bring new importance for you. Having a full mastery of social skills will open up your mind to new ideas and diverse ways of thinking.

Practice in front of the mirror: This is a necessary action because you have to instill confidence in yourself. Look at your face in the mirror, how you are dressed, and picture what other people will think about you. It is necessary to have confidence and use both facial expressions and other modes of body language as you communicate. The purpose of looking at yourself in the mirror is to understand that *there is nothing wrong with* you in your presentation and that you should have more confidence in yourself when you are in front of people.

Read more about social skills: There is a lot of content online that can inspire you to understand more about social skills and how to master them. This book offers a similar guide in these steps as practicing them enables you to build confidence in yourself progressively. Reading appropriate content online will provide you with the knowledge base you need to make better decisions and conduct yourself with more confidence with other people. Adding this knowledge is a necessity as it will allow you to be better placed to avoid your anxieties and develop greater confidence when facing a group of people. This also applies in a romantic situation.

Remember, practice makes perfect: It is important to keep up with practicing your social skills. After all, the experience of interacting with more and more people will be responsible for eliminating the fear and anxiety that holds you back. Continuously understanding that interacting with people gets easier day by day will help you develop strong social skills, and you *will* end up feeling confident in your interactions with others. Eventually, social interactions will stop being a problem because the constant practice has made you get used to being around different company. You will understand how to conduct yourself in different situations.

Get Inspiration from well-known figures: Reading up on people who are excellent at social skills is another way of preparing yourself to improve your social skills. Emulating a leader or celebrity figure will inspire more confidence and prompt you toward developing better social skills. You can emulate them because you feel comfortable with them and how they present themselves. This will be possible by copying some of the trends that you like, and it will allow you to understand that all the fear that's holding you back, causing you continuously (and annoyingly) to falter, is just in your head. An inspiring figure can be a useful guide on how best to conduct yourself in a social gathering to ensure that the people you are communicating with understand you well and even like you. Take, for example, a handsome actor; it is possible to emulate some of his or her actions and even statements when on a date. It can make such an encounter so romantic that it guarantees success within a short period.

Chapter 3: Introvert Traits

Are you actually an introvert?

This is an extremely important question to answer as it will determine the extent of your mastery of social skills. An introvert is a person who prefers to be alone in a surrounding that is calm. For the most part, they exert a lot of energy in the socialization process, but this is not to say that all introverts do not have social skills. A good example is a person who prefers to sit by his or herself on a balcony as a way of relaxing as compared to an extrovert who is more likely to go to a party in a similar situation.

There is nothing wrong with being an introvert; in fact, studies suggest that up to half the population in the United States are introverts. So, how do you know if you are an introvert?

Socialization: Attending parties constantly, engaging in frequent casual chats and seeking attention are activities most introverts would consider to be a chore. For them, socialization is done in a meaningful manner where the party attended will not be too loud and there will be less casual chats and more meaningful conversations. Being an extrovert seems a lot of work because you have to constantly deal with several people, leaving little time for deeper connections.

Networking is difficult: Most introverts do not find this effort appealing, and for them, networking is only done on an as-needed basis. The effort put into getting so many friends that you might only have one chat with them is undesirable for introverts. Thus, if you find that networking is a more difficult task than sitting down in a math class, then you could be an introvert. Social media is a particularly excellent platform for understanding the nature of extroverts. Most of them will post several personal pictures, spend lots of time engaging in conversation and having very large followings. In order to acquire this status, it is necessary to do a lot of networking to engage with as many people as possible to boost your popularity.

You have your own world: Do you constantly find yourself slipping into some fantasy world, maybe one you thought about or frequently dream about? Do you enjoy spending a lot of time in this fantasy world, and when you get out, do you usually feel recharged? Then you probably are an introvert. The fact that you have your own little world that you can slip into whenever you want to is a telling character trait that shows you are creative and spend a lot of time to yourself.

Spend a lot of time pursuing interests: Introverts are usually organized and systematic people to the extent that they always have goals they are pursuing. An introvert will set a target for themselves, and the task can range significantly in difficulty, but it is still a challenge. As time passes, the targeted task will eventually be completed, and this is probably going to take up a bulk of the time. These contrast the traits of an extrovert who is more institutionalized and the tasks they are likely to be pursuing will be professionally related. It is rare for an extrovert to spend much time with themselves as they are being swamped by friends constantly or online on social media.

You enjoy spending time alone: This is a commonly discussed trait about introverts that sometimes confuse others to think that they are anti-social. The simple fact remains that introverts prefer meaningful company, and when it is not there, they would rather be by themselves.

An extrovert society is alien: Most introverts find it very difficult to socialize and keep up with the world of an extrovert. The fact that there is almost no time to spend to themselves is worrying enough to see the world of an extrovert as very alien. An introvert needs lots of time to themselves as well as to conduct only a few meaningful conversations at a time. This is not possible for an extrovert, and it does make their world seem very different from that of an introvert. Generally, the latter would prefer to keep to themselves and not dwell among circles of people where they feel uncomfortable.

You work best alone: The pleasure of getting to do something by yourself is climaxed by the eventual success. An introvert would prefer not to blame somebody else but take on the challenge by themselves. Help can be solicited for a complicated, technical project, but the introvert will oversee the entire process with a precision that will end up impressing everyone around them. An extrovert would prefer to solicit as much help as possible and probably excel more working in a team. An introvert will do all the work and be very satisfied at the end of the day, a contrast to how extroverts work.

You spend much of time in your head: If you find that you daydream so much that sometimes it can distract you, you probably are an introvert. Spending a lot of time to yourself and enjoying it more than interacting with others shows a deeper nature of your intuition.

You have a close circle: Most introverts prefer having only a close clique of friends that they can trust and actually engage in conversation. Extroverts are outgoing people capable of having a conversation with people of multiple character traits at once and enjoy it. This is very different from most introverts who prefer spending quiet time with close friends that allows them to have philosophical discussions or talk about shared interests. This is perhaps a reason why introverts are termed as anti-social because they will not make friends with people they cannot have a discussion with, but will have very close bonds with people they share character traits with.

You are in constant search of knowledge: An introvert is never satisfied with what they know; they are constantly exploring to learn as much as possible. Most introverts like holidays that allow them to explore and interact with nature because it allows them to see the world and discover new things. In the same sense, they will spend lots of time buried in books trying to discover something new.

You stay out of the spotlight: Introverts prefer less attention; it is very difficult to find them at the core of disturbance. They would rather be away from prying eyes and let somebody else gain the reputation and recognition because the actual process of socializing is too tiring for them.

You are better at writing than speaking your thoughts: If you find yourself preferring the art of writing than speaking or performance, then you probably are an introvert. This is a discussion that several introverts usually have, particularly when comparing a movie to a book it is based on; most introverts usually prefer reading the book than watching the movie because it leaves greater room for imagination and enjoyment of the story. This is a different case as far as extroverts are concerned because some of them probably appreciate movies more than the books because a movie offers an opportunity to interact with others and getting to watch it in numbers.

You do not always have all the answers: Just because introverts are different from extroverts does not always make them smarter or more knowledgeable about things. They are just normal people but behave differently from the extroverts, and this has more to do with the brain than actual choices. There is a difference in the release of dopamine in the brain between introverts and extroverts, and this offers a solid account for the differences in character. Therefore, extroverts should not blame introverts and put them under pressure that they should know everything because they have an equal opportunity to get answers to the questions they have. This book will help you because it will show you that you should not be confused about whether you are an introvert.

Introverts do not hate people: It is commonly believed that just because an introvert does not like to socialize much, it means that they hate people. Introverts simply seek a meaningful connection each time they interact with others and end up establishing very close bonds with others. Therefore, introverts can easily be the best of friends.

Introverts do not necessarily want to be extroverts: Introverts are proud of themselves and how they conduct themselves. This is why they rely on their intuition to determine their behavior rather than on what the majority is doing. Thus, introverts do not necessarily want to be like everybody else and are pretty satisfied with themselves.

Introverts are not socially awkward: Introverts are surprisingly sociable people – only they keep a few friends and refrain from constantly chatting with people they do not know. This positive personality does not necessarily translate to introverts being socially awkward; they are the opposite of that.

Introverts are not rude: One might get the impression that an introvert is rude because they do not want to engage in conversation or even be at the same event. The simple fact remains that introverts are interesting people and are always looking to spend their time constructively; this does not mean that they are rude.

Introverts do not need to change: Introverts are very proud of themselves and sometimes might be forced to think about changing in order to fit into a social gathering. The simple fact remains that introverts are more likely to be accepted and liked by others if they maintain a specific character about them that comes to be associated with them.

Chapter 4: Goals

To improve your social skills, it is important first to set goals that are attainable. Consequently, you have to follow through with the set actions to achieve success in interacting better with others. This is necessary because failing to plan is planning to fail, and so it is necessary first to highlight areas of weakness that need immediate improvement and setting the right goals to achieve this.

Some might find this step a little too tiring because it will require a lot of preplanning and even reading, but it is necessary to understand its importance in improving social skills. Towards the end of this chapter, there will be a practical example set on how to set goals and successfully achieve them.

The following lists six reasons why setting goals are important in the process of improving your social skills:

Allows you to identify challenges beforehand: The importance of setting goals is so that you can understand the hurdles that face you before you have to interact with others. This is essential if you are going to get past your socialization problems, and it does not mean that you have to change your personality. The beauty about setting goals is that you can acknowledge the difficulties that face you before delving into them. This will allow you adequate time to be mentally prepared and is the first step towards understanding social skills.

Enables you to earn experience: The planning stage is important in any part of a strategy. Therefore, it is the perfect way for you to gain experience in some of the advantages and disadvantages of mastering social skills. It is rare that a plan goes exactly how you envisioned it, and this experience is useful for anybody learning social skills. This is because it is necessary to realize that there is no point in beating yourself down after one interaction because there are always several of them. Preparing for the next hurdle is more important, and each interaction should be treated as a learning experience.

Allows you to get a better understanding of your weaknesses: It becomes much easier to handle the specific weaknesses that inhibit you from interacting with others by first identifying those weaknesses. Everybody has different types of weaknesses, from hating long conversations, talking about certain topics and interacting with specific types of personalities. Identifying these weaknesses will enable a lot of time to be spent trying to understand how to tackle the problem and to practice. For instance, an introvert who does not like long conversations can find a smooth way of excusing themselves and slipping away.

Helps you practice: It is important to be able to recite your actions and prepare yourself on how to interact with others. This is the importance of setting goals as it enables you to have that critical mental preparation that will make all the difference. It is important to see yourself as a normal person and build up confidence, and this will readily be achieved by practicing beforehand. For example, it is possible to write out a short script and play it over to yourself or in your head. The importance of this is to give you a scope on the level of interactions you will have to engage in so that you can be prepared.

Helps you gain confidence: The process of setting goals will allow you to come to the task with the challenges that lay ahead and be able to implement a workable strategy. This is important because it will give you more confidence, an important trait you will need to have when mastering social skills. Nothing is intimidating about standing in front of a group of people and speaking to them, even if it is a romantic situation and you are trying to speak to the opposite sex. The fact remains that everybody likes somebody who can display confidence, and if you can, the chances are high that you will be liked. Setting goals beforehand, therefore, is critical to you attaining confidence and enabling you to understand the social skills you need.

Allows you to solicit the help of a friend: Setting goals will give you an opportunity to ask a close friend to help you master social skills. This is because there will be time for you to consult and practice together with your friend, allowing you to put into practice what you have already learned. This is a pretty effective technique as your friend can tell you how you are coming off and give you some tips on improvement. Setting goals enables you to foresee challenges that you would possibly encounter while interacting with others, and the help of a friend should make the entire process much easier for you.

Toby is an introvert, and he only has a few friends. However, he is still outgoing when you get the chance to interact with him, and he has recently been promoted to be the manager of his entire branch. He rarely attends parties, but not only will he have to attend the one celebrating his elevation to the position, but he will have to give a speech and interact endlessly with others. He only has a week to prepare, and his biggest concern is that he does not want to attend the party because he is not good at socializing. Therefore, he set himself the following goals and implemented them before the week was over:

Attend the neighborhood meeting: Being an introvert, it was the first time Toby was attending a neighborhood meeting. He did so to overcome his problem of having to engage in long conversations that were not particularly beneficial to him. However, by the end of the night, he was surprised by how invigorated he felt because he was able to speak to some of his neighbors whom he did not know but had some shared interests. He was able to overcome the problem of constantly fearing drawn-out conversations as they take up so much time and end up being very tiring. But in Toby's experience, the meeting was a success because it was preparing him for what was about to come.

Spending time in front of a mirror: Toby enhanced his understanding of facial expressions and body language by performing in front of a mirror. He recited a provisional speech and observed himself, gaining confidence and even deciding the best way of dressing. This was a good action because it was evident that the process was not too difficult to implement when trying to understand social skills. Spending time to himself to practice was important as it gave him a rough idea of how to conduct himself and even what to say.

Reading up about giving speeches: Toby found this topic to be surprisingly exciting because several good examples are presented online. Giving a speech is quite exciting, particularly when you have prepared for it, and Toby found that it was going to be easy for him to prepare the right words to say for the occasion. However, his main concern was stage fright because he was not used to speaking in front of several people at once. Even in the office, he was more of a man-manager because he liked working closely with each of his subordinates and carefully prepared them for their tasks. However, he found subtle advice by reading up on speeches about the best ways of overcoming stage fright, including focusing on the main elements of the communication but maintaining casual eye contact with the audience. The information turned out to be useful and reading up on it certainly gave him more confidence to prepare himself for the upcoming banquet.

Watched old Churchill tapes: Toby ended up spending an entire night watching old Winston Churchill tapes and spending time, in particular, watching how he gave speeches. He found the experience to be so intriguing that he was unable to sleep that night, but he did enjoy how Churchill delivered his message in the past. He watched everything about the great leader, coming to appreciate the importance of mastering language in communication, as well as the role that confidence played. His confidence was boosted tremendously after watching the tapes, and he started to think differently about how to overcome his socialization problems.

Practiced with his wife: Practicing with his wife turned out to be equally useful because he was able to get good advice on how to change some of his actions. His wife played the perfect role of an extrovert, putting Toby under pressure at different instances in order to help him get used to the day he was about to experience. Toby was able to identify further weaknesses in himself as his wife played the role of an extrovert, and this was crucial in helping him prepare how to conduct himself.

Setting these goals in advance turned out to be an excellent idea for Toby. The day turned out to be a good one for him because the practice that he was able to do throughout the week enabled him to socialize very well. He ended up having a lot of fun and endeared himself to his subordinates. After that day, he was already looking forward to his new role and interacting more with the employees at the organization. Understanding social skills requires goals to be set so that the process can be streamlined for success.

The example above is not to say that introverts can master social skills within a week. For most people, it will take varying amounts of time to understand basic social skills that allow them to spend extended amounts of time with extroverts. The fact remains that introverts will always be interested in and look forward to spending time with themselves, but it is also important to find a perfect balance that allows them to spend time with the people around them. Mastering the social skills necessary to be considered as "one of us" among a group of extroverts will take time and will require much practice. The importance of setting goals can make a significant difference in the mastery of social skills.

Chapter 5: Analyzing People

Analyzing people is a very important part of mastering social skills. The process of analyzing people gives you a better perspective on their character, behavior, and preferences. This is important to understand both in a professional setting and a social one because it enables you to tailor your interactions to each person. Everybody likes to feel special, so treating them in their own unique way is an excellent way of getting them to like you while you enhance your social skills. There are many reasons to analyze people:

To avoid surprises: Analyzing people will enable you to avoid compromising situations because you will be in a position to understand their preferences. You will not make mistakes ordinarily attributed to somebody who does not know how to deal with certain character traits. For example, it will be possible to avoid a scenario where you make a joke about a specific profession when it turns out the same people you are joking with happen to be in that profession! Analyzing people will give you tell-tale signs of who they are, and you will be in a better position to interact with them.

To judge character better: If you are going to interact with people successfully, it is important to judge their character to understand the type of conversation you will have with them. This is the reason for conducting analysis on people because it sheds a little light into who they really are and their motivations. This allows you to be more efficient with your decision making when interacting with such characters, and it becomes possible to know what to avoid when interacting with them. Judging character is a good way of better understanding a person and being in a position to interact well with them.

To prepare for interaction and avoid mistakes: Analyzing people gives you an opportunity to mentally prepare yourself on how to interact and what to say to them. It provides an opportunity to mull over appropriate subjects of conversation that will keep both parties interested, and it also highlights the best way of presenting yourself. This way it becomes possible to avoid common mistakes involved with social etiquette, and it limits the number of embarrassing moments for you. Analyzing people beforehand gives you the chance to ensure your interaction is a total success.

To better understand the context of interaction: The process of analyzing people within a certain context provides a better understanding of the interaction and how to conduct yourself. This is because it will provide information on the type of people in the social gathering. There will be a better understanding of the general crowd and the reasons for meeting up, thereby allowing you to behave in a specific way and get a better understanding of social skills.

There are a number of ways in which to analyze people. Below is a general guide on how you can achieve this:

Pay attention to posture: One of the subtlest ways of analyzing people is noticing how they position themselves. Different body postures are indicative of different moods that the person is experiencing, and this will be useful in understanding how to approach the person and what topics of conversation are most suitable. If a person's body posture is slumping, it is indicative of sadness and thus will be inappropriate to approach them and discuss an upcoming funeral.

Notice their appearance: The immediate appearance of a person speaks volumes about who they are and what they like. A good, positive appearance featuring good dressing and a generally happy posture means that the person is in a good mood and probably would be up for a conversation. The appearance of a person is one of the most direct forms of communication, and when generally looking at a crowd, it can dictate the type of people as well as their motives. A poor appearance discourages much interaction, and such people might not be the best to hang around with. It is possible to make important social decisions based on how the person is dressed.

Body Language: This describes the general body movements of a person and can play an important role in determining how you interact with them. For example, crossed arms and legs when sitting down can indicate the person is in a serious mood and does not have the time for jokes. Lip biting can suggest somebody who is nervous or agitated while the way somebody is leaning can be indicative of the people they like and those they would rather stay away from. Hiding the hands is another subtle form of body language that is indicative of someone's secretive nature.

Facial Expressions: Facial expressions are also an important way of analyzing other people in a social setting. A clenched jaw or teeth is indicative of somebody who is not at ease, and thus interacting with them should be done carefully. A crow's feet smile is indicative of somebody who is happy, and thus engaging in a merry conversation would not be off. A person with pursed lips is indicative of bitterness or even anger, and a person with deep frown lines is equally not happy or stressed. Thus, understanding these facial expressions is instrumental in analyzing people and forms an excellent basis for mastering social skills.

The tone of somebody's voice or even laughter: A low-pitched voice or laughter is indicative of somebody who is more relaxed and at ease. It will be best to introduce simple topics and chat belatedly with such a person in a social setting. A high-pitched voice or laughter, however, can be indicative of more than a single emotion;

an agitated, angry person is likely to speak in a high-pitched voice, but somebody laughing equally loudly would be indicative that they are in a very good mood.

Pay more attention to a handshake: A simple handshake can be the basis for analyzing somebody because it can speak volumes about their state of mind and their mood. From a handshake, it is possible to tell whether you will be engaging with somebody further in conversation. Aggressive handshakes might be indicative of a loud and brash personality, a typical characteristic of extroverts. It might be simple enough to have a few words with such a person and move on because interacting with them might prove tiresome. However, a gentler handshake might speak of the personality of the person, and it might be easier to have a conversation with such a person in a social setting.

Watch their Eyes: It is possible to learn a lot about somebody simply by watching their eyes and monitoring how they observe everybody else. Somebody whose eyes are constantly darting all over the place might be indicative of a nervous person. It is likely that the person is also an introvert and is uncomfortable with being in such a setting. A person with a fixed facial expression with eyes trained on one place even if they are alone can be indicative of sadness or calmness.

Follow your intuition: You should analyze a situation for yourself by looking at everybody and remembering the aspects of social skills you have already mastered. You should always follow your gut feeling when making a decision because it is surprising how important a role intuition plays in the decision-making process. Having confidence in yourself will enable you to analyze people without much effort, and this will be a big plus when interacting with them. It enables you to develop a special mastery of judging character and understanding the behaviors of others even before you fully interact with them.

There are many factors for you to consider when you successfully analyze people in order to improve your social skills:

Improves communication: One critical benefit of understanding how to analyze people is that it makes the communication process more efficient. It becomes easier for you to make decisions based on your knowledge of the character and behavior of the people. Communication becomes simple enough because you can identify a single way of spreading a message to other people in the most appropriate manner possible. Analyzing people has the advantage of being able to speak to them comfortably.

Reduces chances of offending others: Understanding how people behave and interact with one another eliminates the chances of offending them when interacting with them. For instance, if you are speaking to a group of health professionals, it might be inappropriate to suddenly start talking about how healthcare has worsened over the years as they believe themselves to be dedicated professionals. Analyzing people beforehand has the benefit of helping you avoid the small offenses and being in a position to make appropriate decisions based on what you already know. This way, interacting with them becomes much easier.

Offers an opportunity to make friends: It is possible to understand the characters of different people as a result of analyzing them, and it makes it better to know whom to make friends with. Analyzing people will reveal basic facts about them, and this puts you in a better position to make judgments about their traits and whether you can spend time with them. You will be able to get information about them prior to actually interacting with them, and this can show you whether you would be interested in befriending them and furthering your friendship with them.

Allows efficient interaction with others: Analyzing other people will reduce the chances of you making mistakes when interacting with people because you have a better understanding of their preferences. It becomes much easier to be in a social setting where you will interact with different character traits, and it allows you to display your social skills to some of the people. Mastery of social skills will be dependent on your ability to understand the people around you because they make up the society in which you live in. As a result, the socialization process becomes much easier, and being nervous around other people slowly becomes a rarity.

Chapter 6: Body Language

Body language as a term describes the communication that somebody makes by using a part of their body to indicate their emotional state, to point out something, or to dismiss something. This is one of the oldest forms of communication and remains an important part of developing social skills because it helps to analyze people. Body language is a subtle way of communicating because it is difficult to misinterpret what is being communicated to another party. The clarity of body language makes it an assured way of understanding other people because how they behave with their bodies communicates volumes about them.

It is important to read body language in the process of mastering social skills because it will form the basis for your interactions with other people. The communication that you will get from their bodies will provide you with ample data to make decisions on their characters and behaviors. Understanding each person around us to the maximum is probably impossible because it would take up a significant amount of time. However, understanding the basic aspects of a person's character will make it easier for you to interact with them because you will know what to talk about and avoid what offends them.

The other advantage of understanding body language is that it enables one to be efficient in their interactions because they have a basic understanding of other people. Body language is an important form of non-verbal communication that, if understood, makes interacting with other people very simple. There is no need to bother interacting with a person who is letting off a negative vibe the whole evening; it is better to interact with the person on the dance floor the whole night because he or she is energetic and likely to be available for a good conversation.

There are many important forms of body language that you need to understand in order to know how to apply them in basic social situations. The following body language techniques are the basic forms of expression that people utilize whether consciously or unconsciously. They form the basis of understanding the character and state of mind of a person in that instance, and this makes it easier to interact with them. Every form of body language is a communication attempt by a person, and it is important in understanding social skills:

Head held in the hands: When you come across somebody in this posture, their body language easily suggests one option: sadness. Somebody who is literally hiding their face in their hands shows a great level of sorrow, and it would probably be best to console the person or let them be. This is an obvious body language communication, and it does not leave much to the imagination because the sadness of the person is obvious. It would probably be best not to crack jokes with them but try to come to terms with their somber mood.

Nose rubbing: Somebody who is constantly rubbing their nose probably knows something you do not or is very excited. For example, if you happen to be having a conversation with somebody who is constantly displaying this body language, he or she is probably excited about knowing something you do not know. It might be useful to engage them further in conversation to understand what they know, and it is also important to keep it respectful.

Monitoring such body language expressions helps to understand the intentions of a person, particularly in a social context, and is a significant step towards mastering social skills.

Fidgeting: If someone is constantly fidgeting, it is highly likely that they are nervous about something and would not be willing to discuss it further. It is important to take note of such expressions as it helps in understanding what somebody is thinking and thus sets the grounds for interaction. A fidgety person will be at ease and will also speak with a lot of nervousness, making it difficult to understand them. Therefore, the best approach is to let them be or, if you have to speak to them, keep in mind that they are nervous.

Leaning at a distance: This is another important form of body language that indicates the likes and dislikes of somebody. If you come across somebody who is leaning close to somebody else or a group of people, this is indicative of his or her likeness for them. They are likely to be close friends, and people always lean close to the people they trust the most. However, leaning away from people would be indicative of a sense of mistrust, and if you walk into such a situation, you could be walking into a tense scenario. Therefore, how somebody positions themselves in a social gathering speaks volumes about their character.

Locked Ankles: When somebody has their ankles locked, it is indicative that they would rather not be disturbed or they have information they are not willing to share. Just like the gesture, locked ankles signify the withdrawal of the person because he or she is not that interested in interacting. It would be better to limit your interaction with such a person because they are not openly receptive. If you have to interact with them, however, keep it short because the person would only be interested in speaking if the matter was of absolute importance.

Restlessness: General restlessness speaks for itself because it is an indicator as to how comfortable a person is. Somebody who is constantly pacing up and down, unable to remain in one place at a time, is indicative of a nervous or agitated person. Such a person is likely to have their emotions running high, and so interaction should be minimized because it would not be possible to determine how successful one would be in interacting. Reading such signs will enable you to know exactly the sort of people to speak to, keeping in mind that restlessness shows that somebody is highly emotionally charged.

Active: An active body language indicates the eagerness of somebody to engage in an activity and might be an appropriate person to interact with. An active person will dance around, speak to several people and generally try to be outgoing in a social gathering. Such a person is likely to be in good spirits and should be easy to approach as they are in an openly interactive mood. It would be interesting to test your social skills with somebody resembling these character traits because they are openly receptive to interacting with almost anyone.

Arms crossed over chest: This is indicative of somebody who is in a serious mood and would prefer to minimize jokes and engage in constructive conversation. This body posture is a signature appearance for any child who ever made their parents cross and had to answer to them. Generally, interacting with such a person will involve a serious conversation where your social skills will be put to the test. It is important to remain calm and patient when interacting with such a person or else you will draw their retribution. Understanding the best approach to speaking to such a person will be a tremendous help in your quest to master social skills.

Drumming Fingers: Somebody who is displaying this body language is probably nervous and would like to minimize interactions. The drumming of the fingers means that the person has a lot on their mind, and unless you are a close confidant, they would not be willing to divulge this information. If you are on a date and they are constantly drumming their fingers, you might want to get into it a little more. Dates can be nerve-wracking sometimes, and talking about it with the opposite sex might create the light mood necessary for the interaction.

Nail biting: Another sign of nervousness is when somebody constantly has his or her fingers in their mouth. Most people bite their nails in an apparent distraction to their thoughts, but in reality, they think about it more when they are biting their nails. This is a classic type of body language, and it might be wise to approach such a person carefully – unless you know what is making them nervous. Interacting with such a person will involve a hushed, gentle conversation but it is unlikely to last very long unless they are willing to share the cause of their troubles.

Rubbing the hands: This is a body language expression that shows anticipation and excitement over something to come. Somebody who is constantly rubbing their hands probably has something interesting to say because they are openly showing their anticipation. Interacting with such a person would be interesting because they would be concealing the main aspects of their message while at the same time talking excitedly. Interacting with such a person would be a good experience for mastering social skills because it will involve you analyzing the person and determining whether he or she is being honest or not. This forms a basis for most decisions when making new friends.

Head tilted: This is indicative of somebody who is bored or sad, and thus will warrant a different approach when interacting with them. Somebody who is bored is very likely to tilt their head and stare nonchalantly into the distance probably deep in thought. They will not speak much, and approaching them might not change the situation much because they will not be looking to have a conversation. A sad person also tilts their head, and they will also not have much to say because some sorrow will be consuming them at that moment.

Placing the tips of the fingers together: Some people usually focus on touching just the index fingers, others choose to do this with all the fingers. Either way, it is an expression of power an intelligence over the audience of the person involved. Touching fingers together shows some level of superiority, and it might be useful first to know the person before interacting with them. Somebody who displays this body language is more likely to have something to say and so listening and talking less might be the best interaction in this case. A person with this personality will have a lot to teach you in terms of social interactions, and it will enable you to master the basics of social skills.

The process of analyzing people to the best possible result is not always possible because some people are not entirely sincere about their body language. However, even seasoned psychologists can tell when somebody is telling a lie, and thus it is possible for anybody else if they make an effort. The simple fact remains that understanding how to analyze different people is an instrumental part of mastering social skills and forms the basis of better interactions. Body language cues are the most common ways of "reading" people as it allows you to use your intuition.

Chapter 7: Face Reading

Face reading is an intriguing method of analyzing other people because it focuses entirely on the expressions appearing on the face. In several instances by psychologists, they have attained success in determining character traits just from face reading, and some have been able to come up with diagnoses for behavioral problems. The concept of face reading is not new, however, and it forms an essential part in understanding the basic social skills. Learning to interpret the facial expressions of others is a crucial part of how you interact with them.

Face reading can be very complicated, and maybe this is a reason why it is not very common. Psychologists will insist that only 'professionals' can successfully conduct face reading exercises because they are trained to do so. They would probably be right because there are five main pitfalls associated with face reading that might be necessary to know when attempting to do so. Understanding these pitfalls will help improve your judgment of other people just from their facial expressions and enable you to master crucial social skills:

An expression may mean two different things: It is completely possible to misread a facial expression because it might mean two different things at once. A wink might be a gesture from a prospective lover who wants to have a conversation at that moment; the same facial expression can also be a gesture for you to leave with the person, and it is probably going to be accompanied by shaking of the head. Therefore, this confusion has made many people mistake a facial expression for a specific meaning, and it can often get awkward.

Complete misinterpretation: A person might opt to assume a facial expression is the total opposite of what it actually is, even though the facial expression has more than one meaning. One might take shaking of the head to mean that a person is happy when the opposite is true. Such mistakes are common and can be a hindrance to socializing because they create tense moments. It is necessary to be more patient and observe somebody before settling for their facial expressions because a misinterpretation will be the difference between a successful interaction and a failed one.

Extreme temperatures: Some people are too quick to judge character simply by looking once at the person and immediately making a conclusion. Funnily enough, extreme temperatures do affect the facial expression on somebody's face, and if you are quick to make a judgment, you will miss what they are actually feeling. When it is too hot or too cold, somebody can easily interpret the facial expression on your face to denote displeasure, and this can create an awkward scenario. Sometimes the opposite is true, and it is possible to assume that the person is happy; either way, it is necessary to observe this pitfall before concluding an analysis on a person on this basis.

Faking a facial expression to throw off another person: This is also a common practice among people who have something to hide. Some people will fake their facial expressions to avoid having discussions about either their disappointment or joy. Some people will behave like they are happy, but after speaking to them, you come to realize that they are actually sad and even sarcastic about it. Others are likely to have a sad expression on their faces, but in reality, they are very happy and just do not want to talk about it.

Unfamiliarity with certain facial expressions: Some people simply do not understand some facial expressions. This can be a serious disadvantage because it will be impossible to understand them – the chances of offending somebody because of failing to understand their facial expressions can be disastrous in an interaction. It usually helps when the facial expression made is understandable, but it is very possible to get lost during social interactions if you do not understand a facial expression. As a consequence, people are likely to talk about you right in front of you without you even knowing it.

The following is a list of facial expressions that are useful to know as they help in improving mastery of social skills:

Stroking the chin: This is an obvious facial expression that shows the person is deep in thought, and it might be best if they were not interrupted. When in a social setting, it will be advisable to be courteous to such a person. Approaching them slowly and politely will be the most appropriate way of interacting with them, and be mindful about keeping the chitchat to a minimum.

Pursed lips: This is a common facial expression for anybody experiencing bitter emotions and even anger. It would be best to approach such a person carefully because their emotions might implode at any moment. For instance, a person seated by themselves in a social gathering with pursed lips may best be left alone if you have no idea what to say to them. However, if you are in the mood to console them, you might find a way of interacting with them, and it will be up to you to improve their mood and make them smile.

Nodding: You are probably speaking to somebody who is in a good mood or in agreement with you if they are constantly nodding. This is a sign that the message being relayed is acceptable, and that they also approve of your company because they are openly expressing themselves. A nod is likely to be accompanied by a smile and other forms of body language that indicates agreement. It is easy to interact with such a person because they are openly receptive and likely to engage in conversation more easily.

Crow's feet: This is a big smile on the face that can sometimes almost stay permanent if a person is in a good mood. It is called crow's feet because it forms running lines across the face that look like the infamous bird's legs. A person with this facial expression is more likely to be open and in a good mood, and it should be simple enough for you to interact with them. A happy facial expression opens the door to conversation and happy interactions, and this is always a good character trait that introverts look for in prospective friends at social gatherings.

Smacking the lips: This is usually indicative of appreciation or general delight at what is currently happening. Smacking the lips shows obvious acknowledgment to something nice, and the person is usually in a good mood. If delicious food is laid on the table at an interactive party, several people are likely to smack their lips as they eagerly anticipate the delicious meal. The same applies when somebody sees a beautiful person – they might smack their lips in appreciation of the person's beauty, and this is a positive facial expression. When you observe somebody in this state, it becomes quite simple to interact with them.

Deep frown lines: This facial expression suggests that somebody is unhappy or deep in thought. The deep frown lines appear clearly on the face and influence a negative look. Interacting with such a person must be done quickly because they probably do not want to engage in conversation for a long time. It is necessary to be observant of this facial expression as it will help reduce the chances of approaching the person and offending them. If you see somebody sporting this facial expression, do not expect the happiest of conversations with them.

Clenched jaw/teeth: Somebody who clenches their teeth are probably nervous, angry and/or agitated. For the most part, this can be a sign of frustration, and clenching the teeth or jaw is just one way for the person to cope with the problem. They might not want to talk much judging from their facial expression, and so it might be necessary to keep interactions to a minimum.

Winking: Somebody who is winking at you might be trying to communicate that they like you and might be interested in talking to you. However, winking is a diverse facial expression, and it is possible to wink to denote direction or just simply grabbing your attention. When the opposite sex winks at you, it is fairly obvious what their intentions are; however, when a close friend of yours winks at you, they might be trying to get your attention or just simply motioning to you. Either way, it is an important facial expression which everybody understands and makes it easier for people to interact with one another.

Shaking of the head: This is a tell-tale sign that somebody is not happy or they do not approve of something. If you happen to be at a social gathering and see somebody shaking their head rigorously and continuously, they probably do not accept something they are being told. The shaking of the head is a surefire indication of disagreement, and it can easily prevent further interactions among people. It is also possible that somebody is mourning a loss, and this can be done by shaking the head. Interacting with this person must be done in a considerate manner because they are not in the best of moods.

Chapter 8: The Four Personality Types

The four personality traits that have commonly been used to distinguish among the temperaments of different people are choleric, sanguine, phlegmatic and melancholic. Hippocrates was among the earliest to describe these four personality types as personality traits and behaviors affected by four bodily fluids. The early Greeks had managed to coin these personality types as temperaments, and they used them to distinguish among people from their character and traits. In the modern world, the four personality types have been used to categorize people accordingly.

Galen was another important philosopher who was responsible for coming up with the personality types by linking them to physical conditions in the world. According to him, the four personality types could be linked to dry/wet and hot/cold situations. These earthly substances were linked to the temperament of a person and used as a basis for coming up with the personality types. Bodily humor played a significant role in determining the four personality types and quickly became associated with everybody. Medical science has progressed since and the personality traits are used by psychologists today to great effect to understand each person and provide an apt diagnosis.

Different aspects of personality are responsible for determining each of the four temperaments. However, it is not unusual for a person to display more than one type of personality trait depending on their mood and what type of activity they are engaged in. There is no standard combination for any of the personality traits as it is impossible to pinpoint to a person's temperaments. Linking each of the personality traits to an element in the world makes it easier to understand the inspiration behind it and the actual personality trait of the person:

Choleric

A choleric personality is one which describes a decisive and independent person who is driven to achieve specific objectives. Such people are usually extroverts and enjoy interacting with others as this is an important aspect of how they socialize. Such people tend to be leaders because they are constantly setting goals for themselves, and they also tend to be outgoing but not shy. This personality trait can be linked to brash leaders who are always at the forefront of attention and looking to provide guidance to everybody else.

One of the major characteristics of this personality type is that the person is usually outgoing and ambitious in their nature. Such people are always looking to discover and lead by example, and it is very difficult not to notice them in society because they make an effort to be seen. This personality type is linked to fire as a comparison to one of the elements in the world, and this signifies the ability of the person to rule over others. People who have this personality trait also like having a fact-based opinion of the world. They are also very straightforward in their views.

A good example of a choleric personality type is a leader such as Donald Trump who enjoys being at the head of any social and professional group he is involved in. He is very goal-oriented and will pursue his interests with intense vigor while at the same time emphasizing his leadership skills and the need for everybody to support him. Trump is a typical choleric leader because he also looks at the world from a fact-based approach and it is not easy to convince him otherwise. His personality trait also characterizes decisiveness as well as ambition as he has come to be known throughout the country.

Sanguine

A sanguine personality is described as one that is very active, social, and enthusiastic. A person with this personality type is easy to talk to because they enjoy it, and they are never satisfied with doing nothing. It is quite difficult to find such a person seated by themselves without anything to do because they are always all over the place. The noisemaker of the classroom tends to be sanguine because they are rarely calm and 'to themselves'. They enjoy interacting with others greatly, and they can be 'the life of the party' because their liveliness can be infectious.

The talkative nature of such people is an important characteristic that marks out a sanguine personality. They enjoy being part of a crowd, and they are very social people who are easy to approach and interact with. Sanguine personalities tend to be charismatic, and this can explain why several people like this specific personality type. Similarly, this personality type describes an extrovert who is more likely to be at a social gathering than at home alone. The earth element linked to this personality type is air, and it signifies the social usefulness of the person.

An example of a character that can be linked to this personality trait would be a celebrity like Justin Bieber. A person such as this would enjoy the company of others and even be a daredevil when in the company of friends. Such a person enjoys risky activity and will probably engage in a risky activity faster than they will have time to think about it. Such a person would enjoy performing at parties and generally hanging out with everybody and getting to know every single individual at the event.

Phlegmatic

This personality type differs significantly from the first two as it describes a person who is relaxed, peaceful and quiet. Such people are more composed and would prefer their own company rather than hanging out at a noisy place with lots of people. A phlegmatic individual tends to be easygoing, and it would probably be interesting to interact with such a person because it would be a very calm and relaxed interaction. Such people would prefer to stay away from trouble, and they are known for generalizing their thoughts and opinions on most matters.

Some of the major characteristics of individuals who possess phlegmatic personality traits are that they tend to hide their emotions and keep to themselves. It is difficult to know what is going on in the head of a phlegmatic individual because they do not speak much and would rather conceal their feelings. However, they are sympathetic individuals who display typical characteristics of introverts and are well known for making compromises. Such people tend to be very caring and openly receptive to other people. The element linked to this personality trait is water, and it describes a person who usually focuses on getting what they want in a reserved manner.

A good example of a person displaying this trait would be a primary school teacher. Most of these individuals tend to be sympathetic and understanding, particularly of young ones, and they spend a lot of time helping out their students to be better people. Classroom teachers sometimes do not speak much and only do so when the situation is absolutely necessary. The classroom teacher will be open to engaging with their students but only as much as they can assist them appropriately. They will not be overly outgoing, but they will be receptive enough, particularly to the students and open for interaction.

Melancholic

People who feel very deeply, and think in the same manner, display melancholic personalities. They are even quieter and reserved than phlegmatic people, and they tend to spend a lot of time by themselves lost in their own little worlds. They have very active brains, and they are known to be very creative because they spend a lot of time thinking. Individuals who possess this personality type are very analytical and take everything with the seriousness it deserves; they like details and would likely understand absolutely everything about the things that surround them.

Some of the major characteristics of this personality type include self-reliance and reservation that makes them unique from the rest of the population. It is not usually easy to spot a melancholic individual because they tend to avoid being singled out in a crowd, even if it means awkwardly mingling with those around them. As a classic introvert personality type, melancholic people tend to strive for perfection, and this usually results in them being very organized. The element that represents this trait is earth, and it signifies somebody who avoids too much interaction with the rest of the group.

A good example of individuals who display this character trait would be book authors such as Stephen King. They tend to be thinkers who spend a lot of time to themselves and are constantly organizing their thoughts to come up with different deals. Stephen King is a person very much reserved to himself and enjoys the time he spends alone as it offers him an opportunity to think of new book ideas. Stephen King is less likely to attend a party and more likely to be very tidy and detailed because his profession demands this of him.

Understanding the different personality types is instrumental in ensuring that you master the social skills necessary for interacting with everybody else. Comprehending the different personality types makes it even easier to analyze people from their body language and facial expressions. It becomes possible to make accurate judgments about somebody's character and preferences, thereby minimizing the chances of making mistakes when interacting with the individual. A key part of developing your social skills is learning to differentiate between the different personality types as it allows you to understand the manner of interaction to engage with each person.

Chapter 9: How to Detect a Liar

In the process of social interaction, it is possible to come across liars who will try to derail your understanding. Such people are not uncommon in a social gathering, and there are also liars in a professional setting. The important thing for you is to understand when a liar is in action so that you are not misguided as it can cause some embarrassment when interacting with other people. The truth is always important, particularly when a decision must be made, and so understanding how to spot liars is extremely important.

Most people in society who have already mastered social skills are good at spotting liars from tell-tale signs. Liars behave in a specific way, and it is possible to tell from their body language and facial expressions. Factors such as the tone of their voice and interactions with other people are also indicative of a liar, and it is advantageous to spot one to avoid being misled. Psychologists have developed several methods of spotting liars in a social situation, and the following methods are useful in ensuring you keep away from such individuals:

Staring but not blinking: if you want to attain a mastery of social skills, it is important to distinguish between a truthful person and a liar. Most liars usually do not blink when staring at you because they want to be as convincing as possible. They will give you a cold, hard stare in an attempt to make you believe that what they are saying is honest. In reality, however, the cold, hard look has been forced on in order for you to believe that they are quite serious with what they are saying. They will likely maintain this stance for as long as possible provided you appear to be following their story.

Hands stay out of sight: This is a common trait among liars where they tend to keep their hands directly away from your sight as they try to tell you something. Psychologists attribute this behavior to the basis that one is trying to hide something, and they are likely to indicate it through some form of body language. The fact is, a liar will be hiding something away from you as they tell you one thing when, in fact, it is the opposite. Detecting this type of liar will require you to have some understanding of the basic body language expressions.

Repetition: This is another interesting trait of a liar because sometimes they might do it consciously or unconsciously. A liar will constantly repeat the lie because it is likely to sound true if it is said over and over again. They rely on familiarizing you with the lie as frequently as possible so that it becomes 'normal' to you. They can also repeatedly lie unconsciously when telling a long, complicated lie and this usually exposes them in a social situation. Constant repetition will indicate the person is nervous and doing a difficult job trying to twist a narrative so that it sounds as real as possible.

Pausing for a long time: If you find that having a conversation with somebody is difficult because they are constantly pausing, it is highly likely that they are spending much of the time lying to you. Liars usually pause for long periods in order to prepare what they are going to say. Every statement they make in such an instance is tailor-made for the occasion, and they do so to conceal the truth and convince you of something different. Long pauses are quite concerning, and they leave the listener in doubt because it is almost impossible to have a single conversation continuously. The occasional interruptions because the person must think or pretends to have zoned out is indicative of a deceptive character. It is necessary to be observant around such a person because it is highly likely that most of the things they are going to say will be far from the truth. A truthful person will be able to keep up with a conversation without frequent pauses because there is not much to think about but speak with an open mind.

Talking too much: Somebody who is also speaking too rapidly to give you time to contribute to the conversation is probably lying. Giving away too much information when having a simple discussion can be indicative of a lying personality. It is necessary to be careful with such a person because they will focus on bombarding you with too much information for you to think of anything else. This is dangerous because they can transform simple statements into believable words when they are, in fact, the opposite of what they actually mean. Be wary of somebody who speaks too much because the value of what they are saying might not be worthwhile.

Rubbing the chin and mouth: A nervous person who is trying to get away with something is usually twitchy and very much on edge. Having a conversation with somebody who is constantly rubbing their chin and covering their mouth might show that they are hiding something. Consequently, the conversation you will have with them might not be a frank one because of the person's need to hide the actual facts. Covering the mouth usually symbolizes the need to be quiet and keep the actual facts away from a statement.

Strange body language: It is likely that somebody is telling you they are fine and well when they are nervously twitching and jerking. Body language is an important expression that can help anybody looking to master social skills spot a liar. A person can say one thing, but it is very possible that their body will communicate something entirely different, signifying that they are lying. When somebody speaks to you, pay attention to the way they are positioned and any strange movements they make. This might be the difference between you knowing whether they are being honest with you or not.

High-pitched voice/laughter: A person speaking with a very high-pitched voice and laughing very loudly is probably nervous because they are trying to hide something. This is particularly suspicious if there is no call for being loud in any way. The high-pitched voice is probably trying to drown out the conflict in the liar's head because they know that whatever they are saying is not truthful. The high-pitched laughter also covers for the fact that they are faking their laughter in an attempt to fit in and lure you away from the truth.

Sudden movements with the head: A person who is lying will make sudden movements with the head, particularly when they are making a false statement or opposing something with you. They might jerk their heads because they are trying to hide the fact that they are being dishonest with what they are saying. These sudden movements are suspicious, particularly when having a normal conversation, and they should show you that somebody is trying to hide some truth. If you make an accusation against them, they are also likely to jerk their heads because they are trying to fight with the truth and they know it.

Clearing the throat a lot: If it is almost impossible to have a conversation with somebody because they are constantly clearing their throat, it is indicative of them hiding something. Clearing the throat is a signature way of secretly communicating to somebody else that you are telling a blatant lie. Be wary of somebody who is constantly clearing their throat in conversation even if they are healthy because it is likely that what they are talking about is not truthful. In such an instance, you are better walking away from such a conversation than bearing the continuous throat-clearing exercise.

Shuffling of the feet: Somebody who is telling a lie and is nervous about it will constantly be shuffling the feet in a bid to make themselves as comfortable as possible. They will be scared as what they are saying is dishonest, and they will move about and be fidgety. Their nervousness will be obvious to see because they will not be comfortable being around you or engaging in conversation. Instead, they are probably going to be more of a flight risk because they will not want to hang around long after telling their lies.

Avoiding/ignoring some questions: Liars will often avoid questions or statements of fact by changing the subject or simply remaining quiet. If you find that you are speaking to somebody but they are constantly changing the topic and you find yourselves speaking about something else, they are probably concealing a lie. This is an important aspect of understanding social skills because it is necessary to spot those who behave very nervously under pressure. When somebody ignores your question, you might as well end your interaction because you cannot be sure anything else they say will be honest.

Aggression: Some liars get overly aggressive particularly when they are called on what they are saying. Instant aggression is a good sign that you are talking to a liar because it shows that they are willing to go to great extents to cover up information. Aggressive behaviors compensate for the lack of ideas because the individual has no choice but to forcefully back whatever they are saying even though it has already been debunked. A truthful person will always maintain their cool even when they are being discredited because they have nothing to hide.

Failing to deny: If somebody goes as far as refusing to be honest, even though new information has been revealed to show that they were not accurate, then this is indicative of a liar. Total rejection of somebody else's opinion and sticking to a path that everybody else is opposing shows that the person you are dealing with is not honest. A truthful person never conceals information when asked because they have no reason to twist the reality; whereas a liar will have something to hide. Therefore, they will fail to deny, in some instances, repetitively, and this will show their true nature.

The most important thing associated with understanding the nature of a liar is that it enables you to boost your mastery of social skills, and it becomes difficult for other people to tell you otherwise. The objective of detecting a liar is to prevent being lied to, but it also offers an excellent opportunity for you to understand people better. This chapter links with Chapter 5, which provided information on analyzing people, because true mastery of social skills depends on the understanding of these basic facts. Use the information provided in this chapter to your advantage to determine whether it is worthwhile to interact with some individuals based on their ability to be honest.

Chapter 10: Make Body Language your Superpower

Getting your body language right can be very useful in the process of mastering good social skills. This is because it is possible to communicate very effectively with other people by way of body language, particularly when what you say aligns with the motions of your body. A good mastery of body language can make you an instant hit because people will always associate their interactions with you by associating specific types of body language. For example, it is a fun way to interact with an umpire or referee in the real world by pointing at them for fun the same way they do when officiating a game.

Therefore, the following are practical tips on how body language can be used to advance your social skills:

Positivity is infectious: Many people might not be aware that by simply remaining positive, it has a corresponding effect on the people around them. Remaining positive can involve distinctive forms of body language such as moving about lightly, singing gently or interacting in a very friendly manner with everybody around you.

Either way, it is an excellent way of improving social skills as it endears you to everybody around you.

A good example of this is taking a morning run where you say hello to everybody and wave at them happily. This sense of joy is likely to infect everybody, from the postman to the ordinary people going about their duties. Taking a run through town in this kind of attitude is an excellent way to show the importance of having positive body language constantly. This is because it makes everybody else feel the need to emulate you, particularly when responding to you.

Dressing colorfully and flashily: How people dress and present themselves is crucial to determining their social interactions. It is quite rare to find somebody interacting with the garbage collector hard at work because the conditions around them might be deplorable. In the same respect, it is very possible to interact easily with a flashily dressed attendant at a restaurant because they have caught your eye and left you with several questions. Dressing well and matching it with positive body movements, such as gracefully walking, ends up being an important determiner in your mastery of social skills.

A good example of this can be seen when somebody is going to work and is dressed appropriately and exuding positivity. A pilot, for instance, walking through a crowd in the airport not only draws respect because of his or her profession but also their attire as well. With a smile on their face and a spring in their step, he or she is likely to spread that positivity easily, and everybody in the vicinity would not mind interacting with them. Outward presentation is an essential part of body language that can make you likable among several people, thereby helping you tremendously to boost your social skills.

Constantly smiling and offering a firm handshake: Another way that body language can improve social skills immediately is by smiling and happily shaking hands with other people. Smiling is an integral element of body language and a basic facial expression that can guide people towards liking you. Extroverts who are constantly socializing understand the secret to smiling, and they do it to keep the attention of several people at once. A firm handshake is equally important because several people take pride in this and use it immediately to judge somebody.

A good example of this is a customer representative who has to meet with several clients in a day. The business the representative is conducting will be successful if they can handle as many clients as possible, satisfying them successfully and ensuring that backlog is kept to a minimum. A customer representative can achieve this simple, standard goal by smiling with their customers whenever they walk up to them and offering a firm handshake. A weak handshake sometimes denotes disinterest from the person, and so it is important that the customer service representative makes the client feel as welcome as possible.

Hand gestures: This type of body language is particularly useful when trying to explain something technical to a single person or group of people. Hand gestures help to show emphasis at different points of conversation, and this highlights what is important and noteworthy. It is simple for another person to follow what you are telling them because you are providing descriptive guides by using your hands and motioning in different ways. Hand gestures are a basic form of body language and a crucial way of discussing technical matters that require demonstration to make them easier to comprehend.

A good example of this is when you are introducing a new product before your company's board members and trying to get them to sell it. You are likely to make a PowerPoint presentation where you highlight different merits of the products, its price, and the associated business expenses. When having this technical conversation, you will use hand gestures at different points of the presentation, for instance pointing at the profits to emphasize the likely benefit that the company will enjoy in the near future. Hand gestures are instrumental in helping to show what is important by matching them with speech, and this helps in improving social skills immensely.

Rubbing the hands together: This is another type of body language that can help you improve your social skills. When communicating with somebody, you can rub your hands to indicate anticipation of something good, particularly when you match it with speech. Rubbing your hands together will ensure the listener remains calm and on your side because they can also feel the positivity you are exuding. It shows that you have confidence in what you are pursuing and that you can give a fairly accurate forecast of what is about to happen.

A good example of this is when delivering news to an expectant father. If he is waiting outside a maternity room and the doctor appears, he can rub his hands as he approaches the father with a smile on his face. The father might not even have to ask because, from the body language of the physician, it is likely that he has good news for him. Rubbing the hands in such a manner shows that there is positive anticipation to account for and that the father should have every reason to be a happy man.

Leaning in one direction: This is another telling type of body language because it involves positioning your body towards something you like, with the opposite being true. If you like somebody and you are on a romantic date, you might find yourself leaning closer towards them. An interesting person will have something nice to say, and they will constantly keep your attention, hence explaining the positioning of your body. If somebody is uncomfortable or not speaking the truth, they might lean away from you as a form of protection and also in the hope that you will not realize what they are concealing.

A good example of this is a romantic date where the positioning of your body can tell whether the evening is going well or not. If you find that the opposite sex is spending a lot of time trying to get closer to you, this could mean that they really like you and would like to hang onto everything you say. Their body positioning can easily tell you everything you need to know about your social skills because they will show their displeasure or pleasure with their body movements.

Speaking while exposing your palms: This is another important form of body language that expresses innocence to emphasize that what you are speaking is the truth. This is a gesture that is used on several occasions, and it always shows that the speaker is willing to be called on what they are saying. It is a sign of sincerity, but liars can also use this body language gesture to justify anything they are saying. Typically, this gesture can even be used to indicate surrender, whether it is an actual conflict or simply in conversation. Understanding this basic hand gesture is important towards boosting your social skills.

A good example of when this gesture is put into practice is when somebody is trying to justify a basic truth. For instance, if you are trying to tell a friend that Alaska is part of the United States, you are likely to expose your palms with a slight shrug of the shoulders to indicate that you are telling the truth. Similarly, worshipers usually raise their hands and expose their palms to the sky symbolic of the fact that they surrender to God's will and will worship His name. This hand gesture shows innocence and a willingness to accept what is before us.

Nodding and shaking the head: An excellent way of keeping a conversation going without interrupting it is by nodding and shaking the head. These are important body language expressions that are very standard and basic to understand. Nodding is indicative of agreement where a conversation can keep going as long as the listeners are nodding. This silently acknowledges the fact that they are listening while at the same time agreeing with the points being presented. When the listeners shake their heads, it can be either that the speaker was not audible enough or they oppose a point that has been raised.

A good example of this can be seen when a group of people is strategizing and trying to put different parts of a plan together. When the speaker explains the basic parts of the plan, everybody will nod and keep up with the conversation. However, when something is said, and the majority of the people do not agree, they will shake their heads, and disgruntlement is likely to follow. These simple body movements can help improve social skills because they ensure efficiency even in the simplest of conversation.

Chapter 11: Handling Small Talk as an Introvert

An introvert is a person who prefers to keep their own company in a peaceful surrounding. This is a stark contrast to an extrovert who prefers the tumultuous company of several friends in a lively environment. This shows that introverts are poor at handling small talk because they rarely engage in it and only do so in the company of very close friends. Most introverts are deep, meaningful people and are always looking to be talking about something interesting. Some of the topics that introverts talk about range from changing the world, bringing peace everywhere, and conspiracy theories. Introverts are always unique minded people that have no interest in the system and the current order of things. They always think big, and as a result, some of the actions they take can attract more attention than they believed so. Introverts do not find the process of socializing and even engaging in small talk as fun – in any way. An introvert would rather discuss an upcoming business plan than spend an hour engaging in small talk that will bring no significant benefit at the end of the day.

Why is small talk difficult and desirable for introverts?

It is a waste of time: Introverts do not take much pride in wasting time talking over matters that have already been said. Instead of seeing the appeal of simply discussing something casually with friends, an introvert would rather spend that time more constructively to gain something at the end of the day. For example, an introvert would rather discuss a plot for the next book they want to publish as opposed to chitchatting about the latest celebrity on the news.

Socializing is tiring: Introverts find it difficult to sit around and have long conversations that are not particularly beneficial because it is tiring. As mentioned, they prefer to have deeper, meaningful conversations and keep the small talk to a minimum. They also find it difficult trying to fit into crowds they already know are a poor fit.

Introverts have a smaller circle of friends that they are comfortable with for small talk: Introverts usually have a tightly-knight friendship with a few people, and it is probable to find them engaging in small talk with their friends. However, when it comes to engaging with other people, it is difficult because there is a lack of understanding between the two sets of people. Introverts want to talk about specific things and will be interested in new ideas and information. Small talk, though, is not desirable because it is not as interesting as it is speaking with their friends, making it undesirable for them.

There is little desire among introverts to master social skills: Introverts are barely interested in keeping up with the basic social skills that would otherwise make it easier to engage in small talk. Introverts would rather interact with close friends and enjoy a stimulating environment because they find it tiring and a waste of time engaging in small talk. Their little desire to improve their social skills contributes to the difficulty they experience just sitting down for a few minutes and having a light conversation. A mastery of social skills can make all the difference in tolerating and even enjoying small talk.

Preference for their own little worlds: Small talk is a daunting task for introverts because they are constantly locked in their own little worlds and would prefer to stay there. Small talk has no place for their little worlds because the latter usually is the most comfortable place for an introvert. An extrovert, however, would not mind engaging in small talk to relax because they can manifest their personality. Therefore, the fact that introverts are usually lost within themselves makes it difficult for them even to concentrate when others are engaging in small talk.

The following are practical tips on how an introvert can tackle the problems associated with small talk:

Nodding to keep attention: There is nothing wrong with nodding along when somebody else is speaking because it means that you are attentive and agree with them. The essence of small talk is to engage in a manner that does not create conflict, and thus nodding along, regardless of what is being said, is one way an introvert can keep up. It is better to nod along than be rude and openly show your disinterest in the subject because patience is an essential element of mastering social skills.

Trying to change the subject subtly: It is also all right to try and introduce a new subject of conversation in order for you to genuinely participate in the conversation. As an introvert, you will be driven to discuss something that is of meaning, and there is nothing wrong with getting the rest of the people involved. However, it is important to change the subject slowly and respectfully because you do not want to imply that what everybody is engaging in is a waste of time. Instead, be subtle about introducing a new topic that will make you feel participative.

Asking questions to try to keep up interest: Another good tactic is asking questions at different points during the small talk to spike your interest. This is likely to show your host that you are not knowledgeable on the subject, and they will end up sharing intricate details and spike your interest. Asking questions will also reveal little things that you did not know, and this will end up drawing you in to socialize with the rest of the people. Appreciating the essence of small talk can begin by asking friendly questions that help to enlighten you.

Soliciting a friend's help to keep up: It is possible to ask a friend to give you information when engaged among a group in small talk. A close friend can help you keep up and even appreciate the conversation by pointing out different things and answering your questions. Having a friend along makes the situation a bit easier because you can have some practical guidance on how to interact with the rest of the people. With time, small talk stops becoming difficult and undesirable because you have gotten used to it and have been guided appropriately.

Venture into common small talk topics: It might be that you are familiar with common small talk topics that you can engage in, maybe political gossip or sports. Sometimes it helps when you steer the conversation in this direction as it will provide you with a topic that you can mutually discuss with other people. This is an effective way of getting around the boredom created by small talk because you can try and talk about something you are more familiar with. This way, the monotony associated with small talk will reduce, and it will be possible to see it as a positive way of interacting.

Crack a joke: Another equally effective way of getting around the problem of the boredom created by small talk is cracking a joke. This is a common way of breaking the ice in several social interaction instances, and it will do the trick if you're trying to fit in among a group engaged in small talk. It will draw the approval of everybody else, particularly if you tell a good joke, and it will enable you to be a part of the group on the basis of your contribution.

Tell an interesting fact: It is possible to completely change the dynamics of small talk by talking about something real and interesting. This will draw the attention of everybody and become the new subject of conversation. Telling an interesting fact is just as important as changing the subject because it gives you control over the conversation and you can decide what everybody else will talk about. Give an interesting fact such as the largest aircraft in the world; such topics will solicit the interest of everybody else and will give you the chance to engage in much more interesting small talk, thereby getting around the problem.

Speak about an interesting travel experience: This is another way of getting around the problems presented by engaging in small talk. Instead of having to talk about a topic that you find boring and unhelpful, it might be better to talk about different parts of the world. This is an excellent social approach to improving your social skills because you can connect with different people who have shared interests. It is very rare to be in a group of people who have no interest in travel because people are constantly talking about other parts of the world. It is possible to avoid the difficulty and undesirability associated with small talk by introducing interesting travel topics about exotic places in the world.

Do not remain silent, no matter what: Somebody who does not contribute to the conversation will quickly be seen as boring because they are doing nothing. This is the wrong way of approaching the issues associated with small talk because as much as it can be tedious, it is better to say something than remain quiet. Silence can be a direct implication that everybody around you is boring, and this will be the wrong way of approaching the challenges of small talk.

Kindly excuse yourself: It is not rude to kindly excuse yourself and walk away when people start small talk. However, what is important is to excuse yourself decently, so you don't spark anybody's attention or seem offensive. There are many ways in which one can excuse themselves, but it is always best to apologize as you stand up to leave. A respectful exit from the place will earn you a future place among the friends whenever you are ready to hang out with them.

Chapter 12: Introvert Problems and Relationships

Introverts face many challenges as a result of lacking social skills that enable them to make more friends. This is also true in the dating field where they struggle to woo mates as compared to their extrovert friends who can woo as many mates as possible. The opposite sex has always been a subject of conversation for introverts because they are constantly seeking the best way of approaching them and confessing their love. However, whenever they do get an opportunity to do this, it comes off badly, and they end up embarrassing themselves.

When setting up a date, it is important to consider the following factors:

Choose a scenic location that both of you approve: It is important to go out on a first date to a scenic location that has meaning for both of you. This can be a restaurant or a national park; either way, it is important that the place has meaning because it will help establish a connection between the two of you. A good first date is essential in determining whether a relationship will be successful, and so extra attention must be paid into that first impression.

Talk about shared interests: The most efficient way that you can keep up with a conversation while out on a date is by talking about shared interests. Get to know your date a little more, and you will find that he or she is open to discussing subjects that are of interest to you. If they are a historian, talking about the history of the country and tackling old-age dilemmas might be an excellent way for you to connect. You will find yourself speaking freely, and you will derive happiness as a result of spending your time constructively.

Do not bring up sex so soon: This is a common mistake among guys who are too quick to bring up sex and quickly discourages the opposite sex. When it comes to a meaningful date, it is important to take your mate slowly and allow him or her to get to know you more. You will be surprised that after only a short wait, he or she will suggest it. Do not make the mistake of rashly bringing up sex or setting any conditions because that is likely to ruin the relationship that has already been established.

Avoid long pauses: Remember that when it is a date, it is just the two of you. Do not bore your mate by remaining quiet and handling the conversation because it is important that you equally contribute. A date will be more successful if you both contribute to the conversation and try to interest each other. Do not be too focused on trying to make the date as memorable as possible because this is likely to distract you from your mate. If you are going to pause, stare deeply into their eyes and let them know that your full attention is on them.

Use respectful language: Before you know somebody well, it is always important to use respectful language and minimize the slang while on a date. Formality is important, and this will endear the opposite sex to you more than if you insist on using disrespectful language. How you present yourself to a date is important in determining whether you have a future because no one wants to hang around someone who is not properly cultured. Compose yourself throughout the evening and make sure that when you speak, you sound right.

Always be on time: This is another common mistake that sometimes people make whenever they have a date. It is okay to run late once, maybe twice, but never make it a habit. It is extremely irritating and does nothing for your mastery of social skills because the opposite sex is likely to become fed up with waiting for you. Always keep time dates and do not make rash promises that will result in your date having to wait for you for extended periods. Value their time because wasting it while on a date is also ill-advised; pay full attention to them while you are together because if there is something to do, it can always be done some other time.

To have a successful conversation with the opposite sex, there are a number of factors to consider in order to instigate a personal conversation successfully:

Be gentle and respectful: It is of the utmost importance that you treat your date with careful regard and always consider their wishes highly as it will determine the bonds of your friendship. Most people think that acting brashly and noisily will impress your date, but nothing could be further from the truth. The opposite sex usually likes somebody who is calm because it makes it easier to approach them and talk privately. Be gentle and mindful of the people around you so that you don't offend your date because a private conversation should remain as such. Humble yourself and be close to your date so that you can talk softly and gently. This will be an excellent way of improving your social skills and securing a good friend.

Have constant communication: It is important to speak continuously to the opposite sex whenever you are not together, but be careful and do it respectfully. Know their routines so that you can have specific chat times during the day and in the evenings. Send each other messages to find out how the other is doing, and limit the conversations to casual talk and not technical talk. Being in constant communication means that you are thinking about one another and it will enable you to master the basic aspects of social skills.

Listen to their problems: You must always have an ear to listen to the problems being experienced by the opposite sex. It is a good way of opening up a personal conversation, but it is important that you are meaningful and understanding of the problems that they are experiencing. This is important because it shows that you truly care for them and enables you to master important social skills. Your empathy in such a situation will allow you to establish a much closer relationship with the person, and they will, in turn, be open to talking to you.

One-on-one conversations are just as important as over the phone: You should place a lot of value on communicating with your partner because it builds upon your trust for each other. One-on-one conversations are just as important as when you speak on the phone, so you have to keep it respectful. This also applies to messages, and it is necessary not to bombard the opposite sex with too much technical talk. Focus on speaking about them, their day, how they are feeling, and what you can do to make them feel better.

Minimize friends when having personal conversations: Sometimes you might always want your close friend beside you, even when you are on a date. While this is okay probably for one occasion, it should be something that is never attempted. You should take pride in the alone time that you spend with the opposite sex, and they will appreciate you more when you have enough time for them. Constantly having your friend when you are spending time with the opposite sex is an indication that you do not enjoy their time so much. This could easily spell the end of the relationship because you must always set aside time for being with the opposite sex away from your close friends.

Reciprocating in a romantic relationship is just as important as being respectful. There are a number of ways that you can achieve this:

Giving gifts: You should focus some of your time shopping to find some of the finest gifts that you can share with the opposite sex. Gift giving is a respectful action as it shows you value the other individual, and it is an excellent way of reciprocating their love to you. When you give gifts, you have to be mindful of their value and significance, so you don't offend the opposite sex.

Do not forget anniversaries and birthdays: Reciprocating somebody's love also involves being mindful of significant days in their lives and celebrating it with them. Anniversaries are important because they show the scope of a relationship, and it enables mutual respect to be established between the two of you. Birthdays are also an excellent way of showing love towards each other and making it a special occasion certainly boosts the love between the two. Basic practices such as these improve your social skills and enable you to be a sensitive and reasonable person to your mate.

Be there for them during hard times: Times of sorrow are typically the most challenging for any person, and thus having a friend who can be by your side is extremely important. If you show your mate support at a time when they are saddest, say someone has died in their family, it establishes strong bonds of friendship that are very difficult to break. It is a great social skill to be considerate and have empathy.

Do not cheat: It is also important not to make the mistake of being dishonest because this can destroy years of friendship. Unfaithfulness is one of the worst things that can happen to a relationship, and it can destroy years of hard work mastering social skills. Always be honest with your mate whenever you have a conversation and confide in them. This will allow you to build your trust and respect for one another with time, and pretty soon, you will never be uncomfortable around them. Developing good social skills is dependent on honesty, and the lack of it only guarantees the destruction of a relationship.

Respect family and friends: It is imperative to have absolute respect for the family and friends of your mate. This is paramount to achieving success in the relationship because it will make them like you even better. A relationship will become prosperous if each of you can approve the friends around your mate as this will be a sign of you joining that circle as well. Respect for the family will also make you be a part of it, and your mate will respect you even more as a result.

Chapter 13: Introvert Problems in an Open Workplace

Introverts behave uniquely in an open workplace because they are forced to interact with others while at the same time remaining reserved. One of the most important characteristics of an introvert is their pride in their alone time and an opportunity to disappear into their thoughts. An open workplace is perhaps one of the worst places an introvert would want to be because everybody has access to them. There is no time to think independently because they always have to work. Should they get a little free time to think for themselves, they are likely to be interrupted by the numerous people working in the office. It becomes a necessity for them to understand a few basic social skills in order to work with their colleagues and be a part of the larger business team. The process of learning social skills has always been a problem for introverts because they see it as a waste of time. Their behavior has always been unique as much as they have been accused of being vastly different from the rest of the population. However, it is important to discuss the specific way in which introverts behave in the open workplace as it will shed light on the social skills that need to be mastered.

Introverts keep to themselves: Even in an open workplace, introverts will try to reserve the tiny bit of independence they can. They have a well laid out workspace of which is like their own little world where they get their work done. They keep interactions to a minimum because they spend much of their time focused on their work, and they rarely engage in other activities. It is difficult to interact with them unless you approach them. Otherwise, they remain incredibly focused on their work.

They rarely engage in small talk: As previously mentioned, it is hard to find an introvert busy contributing to small talk, and this also applies in an open workplace. In fact, despite small talk being a standard way of interacting with other work colleagues, introverts prefer to keep to themselves and only speak when they have to. This is not to say they never engage in small talk, but it is a rarity compared to the rest of their extrovert work colleagues, and it easily singles them out in the workplace. Introverts are not chatty people, and the chances are high that they will be the quietest people in an office block.

They work best outside teams: Introverts prefer to do things by themselves, and this means that they never work well in teams. They would rather accomplish a project by controlling the main aspects of it and only solicit outside help for technical responsibilities. Introverts like taking full charge of a project and they rarely adopt a hands-on approach unless it is absolutely necessary. When working in teams, they might not contribute much in terms of speech, but they always get their share of the work done efficiently. Introverts are the lone wolves of the office who sometimes can be relied on as a last resort when handling difficult tasks.

They are tidy and precise: Introverts are surprisingly straightforward when interacting with their employees, and they are well organized as well. Since they keep personal discussions at a minimum, interactions with other employees are on the basis of their responsibilities. They can easily be singled out in the office for their tidiness and organization as compared to their extrovert colleagues who would rather spend free time with friends than organizing their desk compartments. Introverts also appreciate timeliness and are always the first to work every morning, maintaining that precision frequently.

They mainly engage in technical talk: When introverts do decide to engage in conversation, it will be business jargon and technical talk more than small talk. Introverts will always try to find usefulness in the way they spend their time, and this means passing it by talking about constructive subjects. They will probably try and solicit the assistance of their fellow employees in a project they are doing in the workplace, and they can also talk about different types of business opportunities. The conversations that are conducted by the introverts of the office tend to be different from the typical small talk that most are used to.

Quiet and reserved: This is the classic trait of the introvert in the workplace because they do not interact much with the people around them. Instead, they prefer to spend their time working on their projects and less time interacting with others. They are rarely involved in the affairs of other people and prefer to keep to themselves as much as possible. They can barely be heard even in group meetings because they rarely see the need to address a large crowd of people. If they do have a problem in the office, they will seek to resolve the issue with their supervisor or manager.

Excited by company projects: The introvert is always looking to further projects within the company and attain as much success as possible. This is a crucial passion for them and expresses a reason for their involvement in the workplace. An introvert takes their work very seriously and also takes pride in when their ideas prosper along with the company. This is another possible conversation item for introverts within the workplace because they will always be talking about new projects and promoting ideas that might change the dynamic of their surroundings.

Rarely attends parties and retreats: The classic introvert does not frequent office gatherings unless it is necessary. It is possible to fail to spot them at a party or a retreat because they would rather be spending their time more constructively. This would be the kind of opportunity that at extrovert embraces with all their might, but an introvert would rather be in a much calmer environment that they have control of. This behavior might seem anti-social, but it is just a classic characteristic of the introvert; understanding the important aspects of social skills will be crucial for change.

It is possible for the introvert to take action to excel in their social skills while at work. The following are practical tips that can help you while in the workplace:

Work in teams: One possible way that you can excel at social skills in your place of work is by being comfortable working in a team. This will give you the opportunity to interact with several people and have a chance to create bonds. Working in a team is special because you will get a chance to appreciate the contributions of each person and learn a thing or two about social interactions.

Forge stronger bonds with workmates: It is possible for you to forge stronger bonds with fellow workmates by identifying hobbies that you can both engage in. This can be anything, from playing chess to sharing funny stories. It is necessary to have a work colleague as a close friend but not necessarily in your closer circle of friends. Having a good friend at work can make all the difference in trying to master social skills that will make it much easier for you to interact with the rest of the office.

Spend time at retreats and parties: Another good way of ensuring that you spend as much time as possible with work colleagues is attending parties and work retreats. If you hear somebody is having a birthday party in the office, attend it and try to practice some of the small talk as mentioned earlier. It is an excellent way of broadening your social skills, and attending the corporate retreats, too, will be an excellent idea and a chance for improvement.

Active participation in staff meetings: It is important for your voice to be heard in the office, and one effective way of doing this is participating actively in staff meetings. This will give an opportunity not only to your work colleagues to notice you but management as well. Practicing formal ways of addressing others in the workplace should be looked up to provide a better picture of the expectations. Participation in the staff meetings will get you noticed and give an opportunity for others to approach you. This will be a good way of breaking the ice and furthering your social skills in a professional setting.

Read up some more about socializing in a work environment: The internet is awash with several articles that will provide information about active ways of participating in the office. This will broaden your understanding and enable you to find definitions to terms you were not aware of. Reading up on the subject will give you theoretical knowledge from which you can practice by being more active in the workplace. Diversify your sources of information as this will prove important in finding the right advice about social skills. Reading will enable you to identify the challenges you experience and offer you an opportunity to research the solution.

Organizing get-togethers: It is also all right to take the initiative and organize an event that brings work colleagues together. This would prove to be a success because work colleagues will never forget a display of kindness and will constantly talk about it in the office. This will be an excellent way for you to boost your reputation and interact with people you normally would not. It will also help in establishing a good reputation in the office, and such an experience can easily increase your mastery of social skills in a professional setting.

Having a positive outlook: It is important to exude positivity while in the office because it will rub off on others to ensure a good working atmosphere. Talking with a smile on your face and being courteous to everybody else are important traits in ensuring that relations are excellent. In the work environment, you can greatly improve your social skills simply by being polite and helpful. Other work colleagues appreciate kindness and positivity and will often reciprocate goodwill to the benefit of everybody working there.

Chapter 14: Introvert Problems at Social Gatherings, Events, and Parties

Social gatherings, events, and parties can be one of the worst destinations for introverts. This is because they are forced to interact with other people and be in an environment where they feel out of place. Yet these events are important for work colleagues to pass on important information and to give them a chance to interact on a friendly basis. There are a number of measures an introvert can take to improve their social skills to fit in among crowds. However, it is important first to understand the challenges that introverts face in such situations:

Stage fright: This is a serious problem that faces any introvert because they are not used to taking to the stage and addressing a large number of people. Stage fright is a serious problem that hampers the delivery of any message that an introvert has because most people will be paying attention to their follies. This problem sometimes overcomes the speech ability of the individual, and they end up standing on stage for minutes on end either saying nothing or just stammering incomprehensible words. This happens as a result of having to face too many people at once, something that most introverts are not used to.

Discomfort engaging in small talk: The main type of conversation at a party or event will be characterized by small talk. Thus, introverts will be very uncomfortable in such a setting because they are not familiar with small talk and neither do they have an interest in it. They are uncomfortable needlessly contributing to a conversation they are not interested in, and they are likely to spend their time wandering about looking for something interesting.

Too many unfamiliar faces: Introverts are very uncomfortable around people they do not know, and the fact that their social skills are not the best does not help the situation. Too many unfamiliar faces usually make most introverts coil up in silence because they have nothing to speak about to a stranger. This is a contrast to an extrovert who will relish the opportunity to meet somebody new and talk to them. The fact that there are too many faces that the introvert is not familiar with makes it a problem for them to be at the party.

Opposite of a relaxed environment: Parties, events and social gatherings are the opposite of what an introvert might consider comfortable. This is because they prefer relaxed, serene environments where they can have a chance to disappear into their thoughts and own little world. This is not possible at a party because of all the distractions, and this makes it a serious problem for such character types.

Too much noise: Events are always noisy occasions, and introverts do not like such environments. If you are an introvert, you will try to complete your business at such gatherings as fast as possible so that you can return to the peace of your home. Noisy places make it is almost impossible to think clearly or make rational decisions in all the mayhem. It is far much more preferable being in a silent place with minimal interruption than to be in a flashy party with all the noise and activity around you.

Drifting off/boredom: It is easy for an introvert to get bored at an event, particularly if they do not know too many people or have an interest in what is being spoken about. Since they will be keeping interactions to a minimum, it is highly possible that they will want to leave as soon as possible because they'll be wasting their time. Such events can be time-consuming, and if they feel that they are not getting any value from them, they are likely to drift off easily. This is another serious problem that introverts have to deal with constantly as a result of having to attend social gatherings.

Spending too much time practicing: There is nothing wrong with planning, but spending too much time doing it can be catastrophic. As much as mastering social skills is important, it is necessary that it is done in moderation to avoid any nervousness. The process of learning social skills should be fun because it will be based on an introvert's experiences. Having a friend to help is always a good idea because they will act as a useful guide as the introvert sharpens their skills of interaction. They should take note of the time they spend in front of a mirror to prevent making themselves nervous and spoiling hours of good work.

Exhausting: Socializing can be very tiring for an introvert, particularly if they are not used to it. Events involve walking around, greeting several strangers and forcing conversations with them. They might also have to talk in front of a large group of people, and maintaining their interest in the event might prove to be a significant challenge as time goes on. Dealing with other people and having to bear the enormity of the interactions can be energy-sapping, and this presents a critical problem for introverts.

There are a number of solutions that you can observe in order to go about the challenges you experience at these events:

Practice giving speeches: This is good advice for anyone who has stage fright because you will be in a position to communicate to a large group of people without making any errors. More importantly, you will have overcome your nervousness as a result of the practice, and this will be instrumental in your mastery of social skills. The practice will also help you prepare to give an appropriate message so that you can overcome a critical problem you experience at social gatherings.

Avoid bringing up work-related issues at the party: There is no point bringing office affairs to the party, even though it is a corporate event. The aim of the party or gathering is to get people to interact, honor hardworking individuals, and create a sense of positivity among everybody else. It is important to keep up the spirit by having interesting conversations and ensuring everybody is as comfortable as possible. Office issues will only kill the momentum of the party.

Appreciate small talk: You must appreciate the essence of small talk as it is the most effective way for people to interact. Small talk allows individuals to bond because you can observe more about their character traits and behavior from the way they talk. These conversations are the life of the event or the party because everybody wants to be casual and speak freely. If you appreciate this as well, then you're on the way to mastering social skills, and you will be able to have many more friends as a result.

See it as an opportunity to make new friends: You must appreciate the party because you are not going to have too many chances to meet people of great diversity. A party allows you to meet many different personalities, and this can be a good opportunity to make friends and learn about new cultures. You need to develop a different perspective about parties because you can easily change your life by meeting new, interesting people. This will enable you to see more meaning from such events, and you will come to appreciate the essence of such social gatherings as they directly contribute to the improvement of your social skills.

Have a drink, try to relax: The most direct way of running away from the challenges of having to interact at a social gathering is to get into the mood. After all, if you cannot beat them, join them. You can easily find yourself having a good time if you keep to yourself but have a drink and try to enjoy some aspect of the party. It is very likely that others will join you, and this will improve the spirit of the gathering, and it will make you appreciate the people around you even more.

Enjoy the music/dance/be lively: Get on the dance floor and move about even if you do not know how to dance. Try and release yourself into the moment because it will help you understand the people around you a little better. It is not necessary for you to be a professional dancer to have a good time because the event is all about releasing that stress and trying to have a good time. Be lively and walk around because this will ensure that you do not get bored. Do not remain fixed in one place at a party because you will not enjoy the real reason for being there.

Link up with people of common interest: While walking about, it is possible to eavesdrop on loud conversations with people who have similar interests. Hang out with them because they will make the event much more fun for you. Listen to what they have to say and contribute to the conversation as this will be an excellent chance to interact. Hanging out with people of shared interests will be a significant boost to your social skills, and it will help make things livelier for you.

Leave early: If you are really not enjoying the party or event, then forcing yourself to be there is not going to help. There are no social skills that you will learn if you are desperately bored and disinterested. The best thing for you is to leave early, but try to prepare for the next gathering by familiarizing yourself with the basic concepts of social skills. At the end of the day, patience will play a big role in your mastery of social skills, and forcing yourself to be a part of larger groups of people will not help.

Chapter 15: Emotional Intelligence

Emotional intelligence refers to the ability to learn and manage personal emotions as well as those of others. It is a way of controlling the way you feel and handling your feelings for other people in society. Handling your emotions is extremely important as it takes you a significant step forward towards understanding yourself. People who have emotional control have better mental health and can interact much better with others in the community. However, it is important to distinguish between emotional quotient (EQ) and intelligence quotient (IQ).

Definition: Whereas emotional intelligence refers to the ability to manage one's own emotions as well as of others, intelligence quotient refers to the result of a standardized intelligence test that shows a person's capability for logical reasoning. There is a clear difference between the two because one handles with emotional control and the other deals with the level of intelligence of a person. Emotional control involves important decisions regarding how a person relates to themselves and the people around them. Intelligence quotient, however, is the result of an academic endeavor where a statistic is worked out to determine the logical capability of the person.

Ability: Emotional quotient helps a person to identify and express their emotions in society to ensure effective communication. Controlling emotions also means understanding those of the people around you, and this is an important aspect of mastering good social skills. This is different from the intelligence quotient that involves learning to implement knowledge that has been acquired over time. The intelligence quotient shows the ability of a person to retain knowledge over a definite period and how developed their logical and abstract thinking is.

Recognition: Emotional quotient provides recognition to almost anybody in the community with emotional challenges to understand them and learn to deal with them. This is an essential aspect of this factor because it can affect anybody in society. This is a stark difference to the intelligence quotient that identifies only those who excel in the standardized tests. This type of test helps to understand people with mental challenges as well as those with high intellect in the community. Therefore, both tests help to recognize different sets of problems and each aim at tackling the challenges they represent.

Guarantees: Learning to control our emotions by understanding the implications of the emotional quotient enables the individual to achieve success in life. This is because they can focus their emotions on productive endeavors to guarantee success in their efforts in life. This is an important aspect of emotional intelligence because it shows the individual's ability to be in control of themselves. This is a stark difference to the intelligence quotient that helps in understanding somebody's knowledge to guarantee success in school. The intelligence quotient focuses on somebody's ability to learn as opposed to their emotions, and it highlights how best they absorb and retain information over a period of time.

Measures: The emotional quotient provides a measure of how robust a person's emotions are and their ability to control the emotions of others. This means that it assesses the level of happiness and sadness, for example, of the individual and determines how much in control they are and of the people around them. This is different from the intelligence quotient that provides a measure of how intelligent the individual is. From this measurement, it is possible to determine just how smart a person is and how much they have learned and are willing to improve.

Acquisition: Emotional intelligence is something that is learned through time, and it is highly dependent on a person's social skills. Mastery of social skills allows a person to develop emotional intelligence, and this allows them to live a much healthier life in light of all the challenges that exist. As for the intelligence quotient, it is acquired at birth where everybody is born with different levels of intelligence. This is an important difference between the two because one can easily be altered by understanding the importance of social skills while the other is an inborn ability.

What is the importance of emotional intelligence, particularly for you?

It enables a person to have a better understanding of themselves: Emotional intelligence reveals to a person their weaknesses and allows them to improve on these. It is possible to understand what makes a person sad most of the time and develop a mechanism to avoid such emotional problems. Understanding yourself better is a key aspect of mastering social skills as it reveals dark inner secrets about you that you might not want to confront. Similarly, you are in a better position to interact with others as a result of understanding their emotional state.

Learning how to control emotions: Another important aspect of mastering social skills is being able to control emotions and ensuring they do not get out of control. It is possible to spot people who remain very cool, even in sad circumstances such as a funeral without breaking a sweat. Such people have control over their emotions, and it is something they have to learn over time in order to remain composed and understanding. Emotional intelligence allows you not only to control your emotions but also those of the people around you.

To understand others: When you get a better perspective of how emotions affect our lives, it becomes easier to relate to and understand other people. In this instance, emotional intelligence offers a brief moment where you can look into another person's weaknesses and better relate with them. Controlling the emotions of other people can be a tremendous help to both parties because you can help each other avoid different problems associated with emotional control. It becomes much easier and straightforward to deal with people because you develop a better understanding of their preferences and their ability to remain cool in different types of situations.

To cope with pressure and make better decisions: Having emotional intelligence also helps you get around difficult times by providing you with the mental control you require. It becomes a straightforward process handling different pressures of life, and it becomes possible to understand how to motivate yourself. Emotional intelligence, therefore, allows for better decision making because it becomes much easier to control sadness and happiness. The same applies to your friends because you are also in control of their emotions and thus able to guarantee a favorable state of mind. Coping with pressure in life is a sign that you are mastering social skills and are thus able to interact successfully with other people.

There are a number of approaches that can be relied on to improve emotional intelligence and guarantee a much happier life:

Reading up about the concepts: One of the best ways of adding to your knowledge of emotional control is reading up about it and mastering the technical terms. Several online sources will give you appropriate information for learning about emotional control and the measures you can take in your life. Finding out the information for yourself is extremely important in determining success because it provides an inner understanding of the basic concepts of emotions. Reading up online will enable you to come across several works by psychologists on the subject that will give you proper insight into the best approaches for emotional control.

Soliciting friendly help: The assistance of a friend in the process of controlling emotions is invaluable as they will offer practical advice based on what they know about you and their own knowledge. Friendly help will give you a chance to practice your emotions without things getting out of hand, and this will be an effective way of developing your emotional intelligence.

Learning more about social skills: This is an excellent opportunity for you to understand how to apply different types of social skills in different situations in your life. Emotional control enables you to get a better picture of how to apply social skills to control not only your moods but that of the people around you. The importance of social skills becomes more important as you control your emotions because they are responsible for how you present yourself in the community. Getting more information on social skills will enable you to interact successfully with everybody else.

Handling emotions: The most important aspect of mastering emotional intelligence is that it opens the doors towards handling your emotions. You understand the power of sadness and happiness at the same time and how best to apply them to improve your mood and others. Emotional intelligence is linked to mental health because it is about finding the most appropriate way of living with yourself and achieving maximum happiness. If it is possible to guarantee your happiness, then you are in a position to influence the lives of other people around you positively.

Before concluding the chapter, it is important to understand what empathy is. It is an important aspect of emotional intelligence because it refers to the ability to share and comprehend the feelings of another person. Empathy is an important aspect of mastering social skills because it shows an understanding for the people around you and your willingness to help. Taking into consideration how others are feeling can also improve your emotions because there is a positive impact on your emotional control when you make other people happy. Having empathy places you in the shoes of another individual and enables you to have a proper understanding of what they are going through.

Chapter 16: Practical Communication Tips (Additional Tips)

The following list provides helpful communication tips that can assist you in socializing with other people in different circumstances:

Conversation starters: There are many approaches to starting a conversation with a stranger, and the setting of the place is just as important. If you are trying to woo a mate, how you start a conversation will determine whether you will make friends with them. Approaching them with an interesting comment about where you are is a good way of beginning as this will provide you with the attention you need. For instance, if you are at a wedding and you see a beautiful person, you can approach them by commenting on how beautiful the wedding is and how much you like the cake. Conversation starters are also important in a professional setting because they break the ice and allow you to interact with somebody new. Approaching a person by way of small talk is an excellent way of tackling this as it will give you a chance to introduce yourself and your topic of discussion.

How to speak clearly and confidently: There are a number of approaches you can utilize to ensure that you are audible and confident when you communicate with other people. One thing that helps increase confidence as you interact with other people is expressing yourself via your body language and facial expressions. When it is possible to appropriately match your body language with what you are speaking about, you can communicate your message clearly. Many people take body language very seriously, and most of them use it as a basis for communicating and understanding other people. How you present yourself and communicate with your body will determine the clarity of your message. For instance, when presenting a new product to prospective customers, using body language to provide emphasis ensures the clarity of the message you are communicating. If you can achieve this, you end up being more confident because you are approaching the problem of communication with precision. Confidence is created by your ability to be effective at your communication, and this can be furthered by gauging the emotional state of everybody. Match what you are saying to them with the tone in the room; do not communicate excitedly among people who are somber and the opposite is true.

How to stop shyness: There are a number of approaches that can be used to help stop shyness when interacting with other people. First, speaking eloquently on a topic you are interested in helps to get rid of shyness because you can focus on something you know and provide much more information about it. Being knowledgeable about a subject allows you to speak frankly about it without feeling weird in any way or being intimidated by any of the listeners. Another way of avoiding shyness is by maintaining a good mood because it allows you to laugh and engage with other people. Being in a good mood can make you easily forget that you are among several people, and this is an effective way of relaxing and enjoying the company of other people. Shyness can also be avoided by constant practice over time, particularly with the help of a person. Shyness is an indication of inexperience in social circles, and getting to spend more time with other people makes you get used to them. This prevents shyness from becoming a serious problem because you familiarize yourself in front of other people and thus become familiar with how to conduct yourself.

Make people like you immediately: Another important aspect of socializing is getting people to like you instantly as this makes it easy to socialize and enables you to be accepted in their circles. As always, somebody with something interesting to talk about will be instantly liked because they have interesting information to share with the rest of the group. Appreciating the essence of small talk will enable you to come up with intriguing things to talk about, and all attention will be on you because you happen to know exactly what to say. People will also like you immediately if you display the basic tenets of good social skills, such as politeness and empathy. Somebody who is considerate and respectful will easily be liked because they can conduct themselves very well around other people. It is also a good idea to be inquisitive when the situation permits because other people like answering questions, particularly when it applies to them. Understand the type of people that you are around because an inquisitive nature will endear you to one of them and you can interact on that basis.

How to make friends: The most straightforward way of making friends is by being respectful and considerate of other people. In an event or even a professional setting, it is extremely important to be patient and courteous as you interact with other people because a good nature quickly attracts people of a similar nature. Be casual at the same time as interested in the people you are with because a positive attitude will make them like you within a short period, and you will be able to make friends and have fun. Always have something interesting to talk about as this is the main aspect of the interaction between two people. Your intelligence can play a big role in securing friendship because you can pursue topics of similar interest with the respective individual. Find common ground with a colleague and focus on discussing specific subjects; over time, you will be able to make friends with them because there will always be a chance of regular communication. Successful interactions are responsible for making new friends, and this becomes even more important by understanding the basics of having good social skills in society.

How to talk to anyone with confidence: Confidence is something that you can gain over time through practice, and it is important also to have a courageous spirit. Confidence cannot be acquired if you are weak at heart because it requires you to interact with others wholesomely and understand their emotions. Comprehending the art of speech giving, for example, is critical to developing confidence because the basic lessons earned in this endeavor help create confidence in a person. Somebody must be brave and willing to stand in front of other people without feeling any form of intimidation, and it is possible to achieve this by mastering social skills. Preparation is everything when you want to talk with confidence because you can organize your thoughts systematically. Planning ahead gives you a chance to find out difficult aspects of what you want to talk about, and arming yourself with this knowledge is pivotal in ensuring your confidence is there. Confidence can also be acquired by understanding the emotional state of the person you are speaking to, which will give a better perspective on their state of mind. This way, you can speak without fear of offending them, and you build your confidence more as you understand their character and traits.

How to charm anyone: One of the most important aspects of being charming is the ability to be knowledgeable in what you want to discuss as well as having good social skills to communicate. A charming person is always intelligent and can discuss almost anything without any fear. Shyness is not something you will find on a charming person because they can give themselves confidence when they interact with other people. Being knowledgeable on a specific subject and maintaining it as the topic of conversation will guarantee that you are charming because you are talking about something interesting. Maintain the concentration of the other person by sticking to a subject you are good at, and this will make them like you immediately. Being charming is also about being respectful to the person you are communicating with and making them feel as comfortable as possible with you. Everybody likes another person who treats them with careful regard and understanding of their likes.

Communication skills (general): Communication skills can be learned over time, and the key to success is to improve on your ability to communicate. The first step is understanding the basics, such as body language and facial expressions as they form an important basis for successful communication. Learning to communicate with ordinary bodily cues greatly improves communication skills because it is possible to reach out to a large number of people. Communication skills can always be improved through practice, and asking a friend to help in this situation can be a good idea. Try out different communication techniques, learning to understand their differences depending on the different situations that they are applicable. Achieving success in social skills means that the mastery of good communication skills is inevitable. This will allow you to speak to people of different personalities and enable you to diversify your friends. Communication skills can also be learned by observing the way other people communicate, particularly extroverts as they have a natural appeal interacting with others. Emulating the way extrovert people interact and communicate with other people will give you an insight into how to develop your communication skills.

Chapter 17: Inspiring Individuals

Introverts have much to learn from leaders of the world and celebrity figures on the most effective ways of acquiring social skills. Emulating the example set by well-known characters can be of significant help in understanding how to interact with others. A good majority of the people who make the headlines are usually extroverts, and the example they set can be a useful guide on developing social skills in society. Several extrovert people get their inspiration from such figures, and the same can be applied for introverts looking to boost their social skills. The following is a list of well-known individuals that can offer you an example on how to interact in society:

Donald Trump: The character of the President of the United States offers an example of how leaders speak and exercise their social skills. The president is open and brash when addressing the public, and he manages to maintain the concentration of the people by being outgoing and fearless. This is an important trait for you to learn because it shows a standard way of gaining the attention of everybody else and maintaining it. However, it is necessary to learn the importance of being humble by watching any fiery Trump speech.

Keanu Reeves: The famous actor is the opposite of Trump and displays a very reserved personality both on the screen and in real life. The actor shows that it is not a must for you to be excessively loud and brash if you want to communicate effectively. Being confident in yourself is just as important a trait like any other, and it is responsible for keeping the attention of your listeners. One can focus on speaking more sense than being very loud, and this will be instrumental in successfully interacting with other people.

Barack Obama: This is a character that is very much loved by everybody else, and this is because of the intelligence he displays while speaking. One thing we can learn from Obama is that preparing yourself before addressing other people is extremely important. It makes all the difference in what you are going to say and how you will deliver this message. Approaching interactions with other people by relying on intelligent appeal keeps up their concentration and enables them to like you even more. The main take from Obama is that you can also be humble and respectful, but be mindful of what you say to other people.

Theresa May: The British Prime Minister is also a quiet talker but very effective in getting her points across. This is because she speaks firmly and with confidence whenever she is presenting her points, and her stone-faced approach to handling issues should be an inspiration for an introvert. Observe how she handles the media because she demands respect subtly by presenting herself appropriately. Be firm and unwavering in the way you present your information, and you will find it easy to interact with like-minded people.

Pope Francis: The Pope is a humble and even shy individual and speaks quietly even when addressing a multitude of people. This is an important trait to observe in the head of the Catholic Church because it shows there is no need to be loud and brash. Approaching a conversation with good grace and humility endears the people around you, and they will offer you an opportunity to speak as a result. The lesson that can be learned from the Pope is that silence is not a bad thing when interacting because it is better to be composed than to expose your ignorance by being too loud.

Oprah Winfrey: This is an open person who likes to talk freely and fearlessly with her audience. Her communication technique is reliant on providing lots of information, body language and consideration for the language that she speaks. Oprah is a good example of the importance of confidence when communicating, and her social skills have been developed based on this trait. The importance of being open-minded is evident when listening to Oprah and it is possible to learn a great deal about social skills by looking at how she interacts with her audience.

Vladimir Putin: The President of the Russian Federation is a firm talker, and he provides inspiration on how to interact with others. Putin shows a unique way of communicating because he rarely incorporates body language and facial gestures but still manages to come across clearly. The clarity of the message being communicated is important as is confidence and firmness. Putin always prepares for his press conferences, and even when he responds to questions, there is a sense of preparation with the meticulousness he gives to every response. He shows that it is possible to minimize other forms of bodily communication yet be very effective when reaching out to other people.

Beyoncé: This is a well-known celebrity who has built her reputation on producing good music. Her communication style is based on several things, from her dressing to the calmness of her voice. She always insists on addressing each person individually, and she has a general demeanor for when she performs on stage. The lesson we can learn from this celebrity is that presentation plays an essential role in how we communicate. Your social skills are likely to be enhanced if you can present yourself before others ostentatiously to keep their attention.

Melania Trump: This is another silent speaker, and she displays the signs of an extrovert by how she remains withdrawn. She speaks very gently and shows the necessity of having information beforehand whenever addressing other people. There is no need to be excessively brash because it is still possible to get a message across even by remaining calm and composed. It is better to draw the respect of others by maintaining your cool rather than attempting something big and ending up not communicating effectively.

Conclusion

Thank you for making it through to the end of *Social Skills: How to Analyze People and Body Language Instantly, Handle Small Talk and Conversation as an Introvert, Improve Emotional Intelligence, and Learn Highly Effective Communication Tips*. It should have been informative and provided you with all of the tools you need to achieve your goals.

The information provided in this book offered guidance on the best ways that an introvert can socialize with other people in society and fit in comfortably. This is because introverts tend to be withdrawn, and many people assume that they lack the social skills to enable them to display extrovert behaviors. The first sections of this book provided information about introvert traits and how to deal with social anxiety. Practical advice was given on how to set objectives in order to improve social skills and allow introverts to be in a position to interact with others successfully.

The book emphasized the importance of maintaining good social skills as this is the key to successfully fitting into society. The book also provided information on the best ways of analyzing people, and there was much information about body language and facial expressions. There was also a discussion of the different personality traits as well as the best approaches for introverts to interact with other people. The focus was on the challenges that introverts face, and there was even a discussion on small talk and how to conduct it successfully. The book further described how to interact at social events and gave practical advice on social skills in such situations, as well as a discussion about emotional intelligence – an important factor to consider when understanding how to deal with other people.

The book rounded off by providing practical communication tips and listing some popular figures to provide inspiration for learning social skills.

The next step is to go forth and start utilizing the tips, tricks, tools, and techniques provided in this book to begin realizing your social skills potential and become confident and empowered as your journey into the world of social skills improvement progresses.

Don't judge yourself if your progress is slow at first – just stick with it, and you'll see how much you can achieve. Moreover, there are likely to be techniques that come more naturally to you than others, so don't worry – it evens out, and you will become more confident with your social skills the more you practice.

Part 3: Small Talk

A Shy Introverts Guide to Being More Likeable and Building Better Relationships, Even If You Have Social Anxiety, Including Conversation Starters and Tips for Improving Your Social Skills

Introduction

The following chapters will discuss what you need to know as an introvert, or someone who is shy, about starting small talk. As an introvert, you probably would rather spend your time at home, reading a book, watching a show, or doing another hobby that might not be considered "social". This is how you recharge your batteries and get a break from all the socialization that you get at work or at school.

But there are just some situations where you need to talk to other people, and the small talk that ensues can be difficult, and often brings you to a screeching halt with nothing to say.

This guidebook is going to help you deal with social conversations, and can make you an expert at small talk, no matter what your experience level was before. If you are a shy introvert, being able to hold a conversation and turn that simple small talk about unimportant topics into a deeper conversation later on is so important, and will help you to make the lasting friendships that you need and desire.

In this guidebook, we will look at a few different topics, especially about how introverts and shy people are two different personality traits (you can be shy without being an introvert, and not all introverts are shy), and how they view the world differently.

From there, we are going to explore valuable tips that will empower you to become great at small talk. We will look at how to become an active listener, rather than just thinking about what you will say next, how to be more likeable, and more.

There are so many instances in our lives when small talk can be important. And for a shy introvert, these times can prove to be a challenge. Most introverts would rather just stay home and not do too much socially. But they may still need to show up to events for family and friends, for work, or to make some new friendships. This guidebook will provide the tools needed to really get some great results with small talk, while still celebrating all the things that make an introvert unique!

Chapter 1: What is Small Talk?

Before we explore some tips that will help you improve your small talk skills, we first need to understand what small talk is. Small talk is a type of socially acceptable conversation that is essentially meaningless when it comes to its content, but it can serve an important function in certain situations and contexts.

For example, in many English-speaking countries, it is seen as unfriendly or rude for people not to participate in small talk. When you are looking for the right subjects to talk about with this kind of polite conversation, it is expected that you will stick with non-personal comments over non-controversial subjects.

Small talk is a way to be pleasant, for a few friends to catch up quickly, or just to pass the time when you are waiting for an event or in line, it is not the time to get into all of your political views or try to get a debate going. Keeping the conversation as light and breezy as possible is the key to ensuring that the small talk goes well.

A good example of small talk is discussing the weather. In fact, this is one topic that many of us already use on a daily basis when we run into people that we see only occasionally, or when we meet someone new. For example, you may find that as you chat with the cashier when getting your groceries that you talk about the weather, or a bit about your plans for the weekend.

Making conversation like this can sometimes be related to the situation at hand, such as waiting in a line. How many times have you been waiting in line at the store or at the post office and then started talking to someone nearby about how slowly the line is moving that day? You may use small talk and other forms of communication with those you see each day, but who you don't know very well. Another good example is a person that you run into in the halls of your apartment, but never really talk to for more than a few minutes.

Small talk can also be common at parties, such as when the guests all know the host, but they don't really know each other that well. During this time, it would be considered rude, and a little bit awkward, if no one mingled or talked to each other. So, each person will start getting together and talking about inconsequential subjects to help break the ice.

One way that this can be done—especially at a party—is with a compliment, such as one woman complimenting another on her dress. While compliments are acceptable, they also shouldn't make the other person uncomfortable, by referring to the person's body or sounding like a pick-up line. Guests who are at the buffet table could talk about the food that is offered, as they decide what to put on their plates to eat.

The point here is that small talk is not supposed to be very in depth. Since most small talk occurs between you and someone you don't know at all, or at least someone you don't know very well, you really don't want it to get much deeper than how long the line is taking or the weather recently. Keeping things light and airy is the point of small talk. The more general you can keep the topic, the better it is for everyone involved.

There are some people who love to use small talk. They may like to communicate in a verbal way with other people, or they may find the silence uncomfortable in some instances. There are others who like to meet new people and find that they really enjoy talking and learning more about them. Some people don't like this small talk at all, and often dread going out or going to a party because of it.

Every person deals with small talk differently. Some people find that they can meet up with anyone and form a connection with each person they come across. And then there are those who really struggle with small talk and maybe carry around a list of topics with them so that they can think of things when the conversation tends to lag a bit.

For many introverts, engaging in small talk is a challenge. They may already have a hard time talking to other people, especially those they don't know well. Perhaps they are already struggling with the venue or the situation they are in if it happens to be loud, new, or something that they don't particularly enjoy doing.

There are also some social constraints that happen with small talk, which can make it difficult to know what to say, putting further pressure on introverts who struggle with being out and around other people. Add to this that many introverts are shy, and small talk can be a pain. Just because someone is an introvert and needs quiet time alone, without being around people all the time, doesn't mean that they don't like people at all. They just need to take a different approach.

This guidebook will help with this. With some practice, and some time, even the shyest introvert will get better and they will see success. Anyone can learn how to use small talk to their advantage, they simply need to be ready to take some time to learn how to do it!

Based on the majority of the research that has been done on the topic, most people are happier, and experience a greater sense of well-being, when they are around other people. Being alone and in isolation for more than short amounts of time, even if you tend to prefer this, can be hard on the health. People who engage in conversations that are more meaningful, rather than just small talk, have a greater sense of wellbeing as well. But how do we build up to those deeper conversations? We need to start with small talk.

You usually don't end up in a deep and meaningful conversation with someone you just met. Instead, you start out with some basic small talk, and then, over time, you build up to the deeper conversations, the ones that are so good for your health.

If you are an introvert, or shy, or emotionally sensitive, small talk can be difficult, as this kind of conversation seems pointless and empty of meaning. However, it is unlikely that you can meet someone new, or even start a conversation with a friend, by just diving right in to any big issues that you have.

Always remember that for the most part, small talk is just the beginning of your connection with other people. It is going to be hard, and there will be times when you aren't going to want to do it. Maybe it feels the same as having to go out and get groceries and clean the house before you can have company over that you enjoy spending time with. The preparation is going to take work, and it is not going to be much fun. But once you have the company over and enjoy yourself, all that work seems worthwhile.

This is also true for meeting people and engaging in small talk. It is hard to do, and sometimes it doesn't always go the way that you would like. But after you have made a new friendship or a new connection with another person, you will find that the small talk was all worth it. You will feel good that you went out to a social event and made an effort.

When you work to build up your social skills with small talk, you will find that it becomes much easier to reach the deeper conversations and relationships that you desire.

Almost everyone runs into some trouble when they are working with small talk, and only a few people are naturally good at it. But if we want to be able to form deeper connections, friendships, and relationships that are so important to our wellbeing, we need to start somewhere, and that somewhere is with small talk. This guidebook is going to provide you with a lot of tips and tricks that you can use to get better at small talk, and to help you see the best results possible in no time.

Chapter 2: Understanding the Introvert and How They Interact with the World

Introversion and extroversion occur on a spectrum. What this means is that there are different stages or degrees of introversion, and no one person is completely an introvert or extrovert.

There are some innate qualities that many introverts share, including a love of introspection, a need for solitude, and a slower, more focused style of communication.

It is common for many introverts to feel overstimulated and drained by social interactions, and they may put up a wall around themselves to help them cope. When this happens, it may lead others to believe that an introvert is standoffish and cold, but most introverts are not actually this way.

Our society has a lot of myths about introverts. We have come to believe that being an introvert is a bad thing. The world values extroverts and assumes that everyone should strive to be that way. And for those who fail, this can lead to them being looked down upon. But our world needs to be made up of both introverts and extroverts, and we can always learn from the opposite personality type.

Though each introvert is different, there are some common challenges and some common traits that they all share.

Introverts love to work with introspection

For an introvert, the idea of introspection comes naturally. Introverts love to explore their imagination, and all the colorful landscapes that exist there. Often, this inclination to daydream is criticized, and they may have been told at one point or another that they should stop and get their heads out of the clouds. The problem here is that there are some good reasons for introverts to be this way.

An introvert may feel like the outside world is an assaulting force—at every turn, once they leave their home, there are "energy vampires" that threaten to suck them dry. The introvert may turn inward as much as they can in order to feel a level of comfort, and to help them conserve their energy. This love of introspection also brings direction and meaning to their life.

Solitude is essential

Many introverts enjoy solitude, but this is often more than just a preference. In fact, this solitude is crucial for their happiness and health. Introverts need to have time during the day to be alone and recharge their batteries.

They may often feel pressure to get out of the house, usually from either well-meaning friends or those who just don't understand how an introvert functions.

If this pressure pushes the introvert to the point of being exhausted, they can become grouchy and irritable. They will then feel guilty for acting this way to their friends, and they may start to blame themselves for not being able to be "on" all the time.

If you are an introvert, it is important that you learn how to say "no", so that you can seek out the solitude that you not only crave, but also need, to survive. This will help your life to feel lighter. You can still go out, but you will also take the time to be alone and recharge, without guilt, which makes all of those social situations a lot more bearable. Even small talk will become easier to endure if you have been able to take a break and seek out solitude ahead of time.

The quiet introvert

Introverts are known for being quiet. While the rest of the world seems to praise extroverts who like to talk—seemingly just to hear themselves speak—introverts are generally quieter and will think more carefully before they talk.

An introvert's brain often works on the idea that less is more with conversations. Even though this is just the natural way that many introverts are, they may feel judged if they are asked, "Why are you so quiet?"

Studies have shown some big differences between the brain of an extrovert, and the brain of an introvert. One of the key differences between these two types of people is the way that information travels through the introvert's brain. Information takes a longer pathway and is processed more deeply, and this could be one reason why most introverts take longer to verbalize their thoughts.

Other characteristics of an introvert

1. Introverts are sometimes also highly sensitive in nature.
2. Introverts are often better at writing compared to speaking.
3. Introverts tend to prefer deeper conversations, rather than having to deal with small talk.
4. Introverts have a tendency to overthink things.
5. Introverts generally like to have structure in their lives, and to stay with their established daily structure.
6. Introverts have a rich inner life and are more likely to explore spirituality.
7. Introverts commonly dislike spending time talking on the phone.

The dilemma of most introverts

In our culture, extroversion is considered the norm. In fact, it is often seen as the superior personality type. But introverts really don't need to be transformed, fixed, or cured, so that they can be turned into extroverts—and this isn't possible anyway.

Extroverts are not superior, and neither are introverts. Both are completely different personality types at opposite ends of a spectrum, and they have different behaviors, desires, and needs from each other. This means that it is important for some understanding between the two groups, rather than pressure for the introvert to change.

Remember that there are also many different types of introverts. Some would rather spend the majority of their time at home and only go out on occasion. Others may find that they like to go out quite a bit, but they still need a break at times, so that they can replenish their energy.

Just because they are different from what is considered "normal", this doesn't mean that they should try to make themselves any different or try to turn into extroverts.

How an introvert sees the world

Introverts see the world in a different way than other personality types. They like to be at home, reading a book in comfort. They often prefer spending time with just a few close friends and family, over meeting new people and always being out. And even though they don't mind other people, they do usually prefer to work on their own.

Some other things that are important to note when it comes to understanding an introvert and how they interact with the world around them:

   1. They are more likely to make themselves an expert in one

thing, rather than a jack of all trades; introverts excel at focusing on a single skill or exercise until they master it. This allows them to shine at hobbies, such as playing a new instrument, painting, or performing magic tricks. It is far rarer to come across an introvert who has a more generic skill set. They like to focus on just one thing and master it, rather than trying to do a lot of different things.

2. They like to write to express themselves. An introvert is perfectly able to speak on a given subject, but they would rather use writing to put down all of their thoughts instead. You may find them with some paper and a pen, and they generally prefer to contact others with the use of emails and texts.

3. They really don't like to speak on the phone; the thought of a phone call that is planned can send some introverts into a meltdown. They can't stand this form of communication, and actively avoid it as much as possible. They try not to answer phone calls, unless they know that it is urgent, and will put off making calls until it is down to the last minute.

4. They think very carefully before writing or saying anything. No matter what kind of communication the introvert uses, they will be cautious and think through the points carefully before making them. This can mean that conversations will not be as fluid in their execution.

5. They like deeper conversations, but they do not like small talk. Discussions that are all about superficial matters can be hard and taxing emotionally for an introverted person. Instead, they will often choose to engage in conversations that have a deeper meaning and purpose. This is one of the reasons that some introverts aren't the best at meeting new people.

6. They like to look at the big picture, rather than jumping to conclusions. An introvert is someone who tries to look at both sides of the story, before they make any of their decisions. They don't want to be too rash, and they want to

make sure that they understand what is going on, and then make the right decision on the matter.

7. They will hold back when they are in a crowd. Introverts are more likely to find a small group of those they already know at a party, and then stick with them. But if they can't find anyone they know, an introvert will often speak to new people, though they may try to withdraw a bit and not communicate in the crowd.

8. They can succeed as a performer if they like, but they are not that fond of the limelight. Some introverts are good at performing, whether that is with acting, putting on a show, or just giving a presentation at work, but even if they do perform, they don't want the focus to be on them personally.

9. They often do their best work on their own. This may not be because they don't like other people, but because they prefer to just get the work done quickly, or in a certain way. Even when they are working alone, rather than as part of a team, they will get a lot of amazing work done, and usually they can get it done faster than others.

10. They are rarely bored, but they can get easily distracted. If you give an introvert a day at home alone, they will still be able to find many interesting ways to keep themselves busy and have fun. They might get lost in a book for hours, or find a room to clean or a game to play. Sometimes they have a hard time staying on track, but they will rarely ever be bored.

11. They are thorough and pay close attention to detail. This makes introverts valuable help in any situation where it is important that even tiny details are exact.

12. They are more drawn to being alone, and might pick out a somewhat solitary career path. Since introverts do so well working on their own, they will be drawn to a job where they can at least spend some of the time working individually on projects.

13. They will react differently to their surrounding environments. They may spend more time in their heads, and

this means that things like sporting events, concerts, parties, and other social events won't give them the same rush that others experience.

14. When their energy is all gone, they are going to shut down. When an introvert has used up their energy reserves, they will close off and stop doing anything. They won't try to push through this exhaustion, and often they won't be able to find a second wind. Introverts don't seek out company to recharge their batteries, they just need to have some quiet time alone, without all the stimulation. It is better for them to recharge at home, where it is quiet and they don't have a lot of expectations put on them.

Just because someone is an introvert doesn't mean that they can't learn how to use small talk and get the benefits from it at the same time. An introvert may have to put some effort in to get better at small talk, and they may have to step out of their comfort zone a little bit to make it work. But if they can step out of that zone, they will be on their way to communicating better and making more friends in the process.

Chapter 3: Are There Any Advantages to Being Shy?

There are many people in our world who are considered shy, which means that they are nervous and timid around other people. Some people are incorrectly deemed as being shy because they are an introvert and they want to be left alone to recharge on occasion, rather than going out all the time. But others may be so shy that they share some of the same symptoms as those who are dealing with SAD or social anxiety disorder, but to a lesser degree. However, most people who are shy can learn to adapt to their surroundings and function in a world that is dominated more by the extroverts and outgoing personality types.

Many times, in our society, a shy person will be seen as abnormal or looked down on. Society has learned how to value extroverts who are outgoing and ready to be sociable all the time. While there is nothing wrong with being an extrovert, and our world needs them to function, there is also nothing wrong with being shy or being an introvert.

At the same time, someone who is shy may find that it is easy to get down on themselves because of this. It may seem like everyone around them is doing better socially, and they are going to be left behind.

At times like these, it is sometimes a good thing to consider the great advantages or benefits that come with being shy:

1. The modesty can be attractive.

You will find that most people who are shy are also modest. They are the last ones to announce their own accomplishments, and they might not even consider letting the world know what is amazing about them. They may even take this so far as shrinking away from any compliments or downplaying any of their own positive attributes.

Of course, you may find that having too much of this modesty eats away at your self-esteem, but a healthy dose can be a trait that is attractive to many. At the same time, as someone who is shy, you must be careful not to cross the line from modesty to self-deprecation. Some of the tips that you can use in order to make modesty work for you, and not let it go too far, include:

- Accept any compliments that others give you in a gracious manner.
- Recognize when you have achieved something important. Try to stay away from the idea of downplaying your successes and saying that they are just due to luck.
- Learn how to stand up for yourself if you ever feel that someone is taking advantage of you.
- Offer as much praise to others as you can. This can help you to understand what is of value and to accept praise yourself.
- Try to be as realistic as possible, rather than thinking that all things are bad, or all things are good.

2. Shy people will think before they act on something.

If you are already socially anxious, or at least just shy, then you are probably going to find ways to look before you leap into anything.

This is a helpful trait to have when it is time to think critically about many important life decisions. Thinking carefully, and then planning things out before acting on them can be important when you are setting up goals for the long term; avoiding any unnecessary risks; or even when it comes to planning for the unexpected.

To support this theory, there was a study done in 2011 that compared the behavior of apes and human children. This study showed that human children would show more behavior in line with shyness compared to apes, and these children were less likely to approach something that was new. This could be used to suggest that humans may have developed the ability to look before they leap, so to speak, through this leaning towards being shy.

On the other hand, this tendency to think through things before taking any action needs to be moderated a bit. Thinking through where to work or what school to attend is a good thing. But thinking too long and hard about something that is meaningless, such as your lunch, can cause problems. If fear of taking a chance seems to be what is holding you back from some of your goals, then this means that you also need to learn to take a leap and just trust that things will work out well for you.

3. Shy people can seem more approachable.

Other people like to be around those who are shy because they don't act superior and this can often make it easier to talk with them. As long as it isn't too extreme, shyness, along with the self-effacing and modest nature that goes with it, is seen as non-threatening to others and can mean that they feel as comfortable as possible around you.

You need to be careful though because sometimes too much shyness can be misinterpreted and can make a person seem standoffish or aloof. If this is something that you are struggling with, you could start out slow. Start by saying something like: "Hello" and trying to smile at people so that you can show that you aren't really stuck up, you are just someone who is shy.

4. Shy people have a calming effect.

Sometimes shy people provide a calming influence to those around them, especially those individuals who are more highly strung. While shy people can deal with inner turmoil, their outward appearance is often calm, and they can seem like they are on an even keel emotionally. This calmness could end up having a positive effect on those who are around you.

However, if you feel that you are dealing with some inner turmoil, it is important to realize that it is fine for you to reach out to others for help. If your shyness means that you need to wear a mask all the time, see if you can start by opening up to one person about how you are feeling and see how much of a difference it makes for you.

5. Shyness can develop empathy.

Having a shy personality means that you are more likely to be an empathetic listener, which makes it much easier for others to open up and be honest with you. Having empathy for others makes you a compassionate friend, and it also suits certain careers. One of these positions could include a human services role, or any job where you need to help someone and there is one-on-one interaction.

6. Shy people tend to be more trustworthy.

We are always looking for those around us who are trustworthy. We want to find someone who will show up on time when they say they will. We want to find those who will help out or bring something if they promised they would. And we would like to be able to find someone who we can talk to, who wouldn't go and tell someone else and share our secrets.

Since a shy person isn't going to go around and toot their own horn, they aren't going to be the first ones who tell others about their own accomplishments. This also means that others are going to believe and trust them more. In some cases, this can even make a shy person into a better leader than an extrovert.

7. The ability to overcome many different things.

It is rare for someone to be really outgoing as a child and then become shy as an adult. Usually shyness is something that a person has had to struggle with their whole life. They have had to learn how to adapt to their surroundings while being shy, and to handle the difficulties that come when others don't understand why they behave in a certain way.

Since these people have struggled with shyness for so long, they really know what it is like to battle, endure, and overcome challenges. Without the struggle that they have gone through against shyness, they wouldn't have been able to develop the ability to cope with the different difficulties that come up in life.

8. Shy people often have deeper friendships.

Many times, a shy person will outwardly look like they are an introvert. However, shy people often do want to go out and socialize, but they are afraid to. They might not feel comfortable with small talk and would rather form some deep and meaningful connections with a few close friends. As a result, shy people spend time investing in a friendship with someone who understands who they are and why they are acting in a certain way, but it does take some time to develop.

Chances are that when a shy person does develop a friendship with someone, these friendships will be deep and long lasting.

9. Shy people can be dedicated employees.

There are a lot of jobs out there that will ask employees to focus and concentrate in a solitary role, and this an environment that shy people can flourish in. Not having a lot of social ties means that they will have fewer interruptions and less need to validate what they are doing in the eyes of others.

10. Shy people experience their rewards more fully than others.

There has been some research done that shows how the brains of shy people react more strongly to both positive and negative stimuli than others. What this means is that a shy person finds social situations more threatening compared to some of their outgoing friends, but that positive situations are also more rewarding. The increased amount of sensitivity to reward means that the shy person may find more value when it comes time to work towards their goals.

Having some daily shyness that isn't going to prevent you from participating in life and achieving your goals can have a lot of advantages. However, if the shyness becomes too severe and it starts to cause issues with the way you go about your day, this is not helpful, and you will need to work on improving. If you are already dealing with social anxiety or shyness that is severe, you should talk to your doctor and maybe seek the help of a mental health professional to get things straightened out.

Chapter 4: What is the Difference Between Being Shy and Being an Introvert?

Despite what a lot of people may think, being introverted and being shy are not the same. They may have a lot of similar characteristics, and on the surface, they can look the same, but they do have some big differences. An introvert enjoys spending their time alone, and they can sometimes feel drained emotionally if they spend a lot of time out with others. But a shy person doesn't enjoy being alone, they are just afraid to interact with those around them.

Let's consider two children who are in the same classroom. One of these children is shy and the other one is an introvert. When the teacher organizes an activity for all of the children in the class, the introverted child might prefer to stay at their desk and read a book because they find that spending time with the other children in the class can be stressful. But the shy child would really like to join in with the others, but they stay at their desk because they are scared to go over and join them.

Introversion is an intrinsic part of a child's personality and you won't be able to change or force them to act against their nature. But children who are shy can be helped to overcome this shyness. There are some introverts who are also shy, but this isn't true of all the introverts you meet. In fact, some of these introverts have excellent social skills, they simply choose not to interact all of the time because this leads them to feel drained, and they need to spend some time alone so that they can recharge their own emotional batteries.

While it is possible to use different techniques and even some therapy to help a person who is shy to overcome this obstacle, trying to turn an introvert into someone who is outgoing, or into an extrovert, will cause them a lot of stress and could make their self-esteem drop. Introverts are able to learn some different coping strategies that will make it easier for them to deal with a variety of social situations, but no matter what, they will always be an introvert.

Those who are dealing with shyness have a hard time when it comes to meeting and talking to someone new, and they don't like to find themselves in a brand-new situation. They might even feel so much fear about being in these situations, that they have physical symptoms, like blushing, shaking, sweating, and heart palpitations. It can sometimes be severe enough that it can cripple the individual and impact on their mental and physical health.

Of course, everyone can be shy in different types of environments, and there are a lot of different degrees when it comes to shyness. Most people are shy without having it turn into a problem and they will be able to use techniques to get over it.

Shyness and introversion are two personality traits that are often written down as the same thing by those who don't have to deal with both, one, or the other. Outgoing extroverts find it hard to see a big difference between these two personality types, and they just assume that all people who are shy are introverts, and all introverts are shy. But this is not the case. It is possible for these two personality types to exist inside one person, but it is not a guarantee.

We have all been to one of those parties. There is that one person that is standing to the side, or maybe they are still within the group, but they look like they do not want to be there at all and are just waiting for the best chance to leave. In some cases, if you are an introvert, you are that person. Many people don't take the time to learn about these two personality types and how they differ, and they will brush it off, and this can get really grating on the individual, who feels like they are misunderstood.

One study that was done by the Salk Institute for Biological Sciences suggests that there is actually a different way that the introverted brain registers the world around them compared to others. When researchers took the time to study the activity in the brain of someone who is an introvert, it was found that the same amount of electrical activity occurred when they looked at an inanimate object and when they looked at another person.

This could really suggest another reason why a lot of introverts just don't want to look for social interaction. They not only get tired from doing it and feel a bit drained in the process, they may also find that this social interaction isn't stimulating to them at all, so they don't want to waste their time with it.

The introvert will go out on occasion. It isn't like they will never talk to others or that they avoid talking at all costs, and they do have friends as well. But they know their limits, and they know when they would rather be at home doing something else. And since introversion is more of a biological personality trait, most of those who are dealing with it are going to be completely fine heading home at the end of the day to be alone or spending their break time reading a book, instead of interacting.

While an introvert would choose to stay home on a Friday night because they don't see the interaction as stimulating, or they need to recharge their batteries after a long week, a person who is dealing with severe shyness may think that their only choice is to stay home, even though they wish that they could be out and about instead.

There are also some extreme cases where those who suffer from this kind of shyness will find that they can't function in many situations. For example, they may find that they can't ask for something as simple as directions from a stranger. Or, they may find that they aren't able to go to the front of a check-out line because then they will need to interact with another person.

Introverts are good at finding small groups of friends. When they have some people that they are close to, they can be great listeners, and they will provide thoughtful advice and be empathetic. But a person who is shy may find that it is more difficult to form the close friendships that they need. They may even feel awkward around people, including family and those that they have known all of their lives.

Introverts who are not also very shy can be fine if someone comes up to them and begins a new conversation out of the blue, even if the long conversation leaves them tired. But someone who is shy may find the thought of starting a new conversation—especially if they need to initiate it—terrifying.

The main difference between these two traits is how the person feels about the lack of social interaction and companionship. An introvert is fine with this. Even though others will assume that they aren't okay and will try to convince them to go out, the introvert is usually happy with the results that they have. But for someone who is dealing with shyness, they tend to wish that they could go out and have more friends. They are the ones that feel there is something holding them back and they just aren't able to put themselves into the situations that would make this possible.

Chapter 5: Social Anxiety is Holding You Back and How to Leave It in the Dust

Social anxiety is the fear of feeling negatively judged by those around you, which can lead you to feel inferior, depressed, humiliated, embarrassed, and inadequate. If you become irrationally anxious in social situations and think that you will be much better off alone, then you may be dealing with social anxiety.

Social Anxiety Disorder (SAD), which used to go by the name of social phobia, is a much bigger problem than researchers initially thought. It is now estimated that millions of people throughout the world are dealing with anxiety each day, whether they are experiencing one of the specific forms of the condition, or just generalized social anxiety.

In the epidemiological studies done in the United States, Social Anxiety Disorder was found to be the third largest psychological disorder in the country, and only after disorders like alcoholism and depression. In fact, it is estimated that around seven percent of the population of the United States suffers from some form of social anxiety right now, but the lifetime prevalence rate for developing this kind of disorder is somewhere between thirteen to fourteen percent.

Of course, these are just estimates and there could be many more people who suffer from social anxiety that either don't realize it, or don't seek help for the condition. These numbers are just based on those who have gotten help because they already knew that they were dealing with social anxiety in their lives. In any case, the numbers are high and show how prevalent this problem can be.

Social anxiety can manifest in many ways, and one example that affects many people, even on a small scale, is the fear of speaking in front of groups. Those with more generalized social anxiety feel uncomfortable, nervous, and extremely anxious, no matter what kind of social situation they are dealing with at the time.

When things like anticipatory anxiety about being in social situations, feelings of being inferior, embarrassment, depression, indecision, worry, and self-blame are present no matter what kind of life situation you are in, then this is generalized social anxiety at work.

The symptoms of social anxiety disorder

There are numerous symptoms that can show up when it comes to suffering from social anxiety disorder. People who are dealing with this kind of disorder often experience a significant amount of emotional distress when they are in a variety of situations, including:

    1. Any interpersonal relationships, whether they are romantic in nature, or friendships.
    2. When participating in group activities, and they know that they will need to say something.
    3. Most social encounters, but especially when going to meet up with strangers.
    4. Meeting people who are in a position of authority, or who are considered "important" people.
    5. While being observed as they complete a task.

6. If they are the center of attention, no matter what the reason is.
7. If they feel they are being criticized.
8. Being introduced to someone new.

Of course, these aren't all the symptoms that you could face. The physiological manifestations that come with Social Anxiety Disorder can also include things like muscle twitches of the neck and face, trembling, difficulty swallowing, dry throat and mouth, excessive sweating, turning red or blushing, a racing heart, and an intense fear of what is going to happen next.

Those who are dealing with Social Anxiety Disorder already know the anxiety that they feel is extreme, and that it really doesn't make any sense. Even though these individuals are facing their fears each day when they leave the house, their feelings of anxiety persist and show no signs of easing.

Treating social anxiety

It is not always easy to seek the help that is needed to treat any mental health issue, whether it is Social Anxiety Disorder or another condition. If you are already reluctant to talk to strangers, or other people in your life, then how are you supposed to ask for help? If you have let this anxiety go on for too long and you are now at the point where you are avoiding any social contact, or it has started to control your life, then it may be time to talk to a mental health professional.

It is never a good idea to let this social anxiety go on unchecked. If you become scared to deal with other people, or to get into any kind of social situation like eating in restaurants, public speaking, dating, or attending parties, then this could signify a problem. When you start to cut yourself off because of social anxiety, you may develop low self-esteem or feel depressed.

The first thing that you need to do is make an appointment with your doctor. There are a few ways that the doctor may determine if you have social anxiety, including:

1. A physical exam. This helps to assess whether there is any medical condition that you have, or if you take any medications that can trigger these symptoms of anxiety.

2. By discussing your symptoms and how often these symptoms occur and in what situations.

3. By reviewing a list of many different situations to see if these seem to make you anxious.

4. Asking you to self-report on questionnaires about the symptoms of social anxiety and see if you match up.

5. If you meet the criteria that is listed in the Diagnostic and Statistical Manual of Mental Disorders. This is something that is published by the American Psychiatric Association.

There are a few different types of treatments that your doctor may choose to prescribe. Since just facing your fear won't do much on its own, and often makes the situation worse, the doctor is likely to offer a few other options. Treatment will depend on how much this anxiety is affecting your ability to function in your daily life. Some options that you can usually investigate include talk therapy or psychotherapy, medications, or both.

First, let's explore psychotherapy. In therapy, you are going to learn how to recognize and then change the negative thoughts that you are having about yourself. You can then move on to developing skills that will make it easier to gain confidence in all social situations.

There are a few options available for this, but cognitive behavioral therapy (CBT) is considered the most effective when it comes to anxiety. This type of therapy can be successful whether it is done in a group or individually.

When dealing with exposure-based cognitive behavioral therapy, the patient is gradually exposed to situations that they fear the most. This can make it easier for individuals to improve their coping skills and can help them to deal with any situations that induce anxiety. Another way to do this is to participate in skills training or role playing to practice social skills and gain some confidence and comfort. Practicing this kind of exposure to social situations can be a good way to help challenge any worries that you have.

There are also a few different types of medication that can help deal with this kind of anxiety. One common option is selective serotonin reuptake inhibitors (SSRIs). It's thought that these have a good influence on things like mood by boosting serotonin levels in your brain. Your doctor may otherwise suggest that you need to take some medications like Zoloft or Paxil depending on how severe the anxiety is.

Of course, the need for medication needs to be weighed against any possible side effects. Since many of these medications might cause a lot of side effects, the doctor could start you out with a low dose first to see how you handle it. You will then need to follow up a few times to help adjust the medication to the dosages that you need. It could take you up to a few months of treatment with a particular medication before you notice an improvement to your symptoms.

Some of the other medications that your doctor could prescribe to you to help with social anxiety and its symptoms, include:

>1. Antidepressants. You may have to work with a few different options in order to see if they work for you. There are many different types of antidepressants, and they all have a variety of side effects. The therapist or your doctor will most likely want to try them out to see what works the best, with the fewest side effects, for you.
>2. Anti-anxiety medications. Some medications known as benzodiazepines help to reduce how much anxiety is felt in some individuals. They can work very fast, and you may notice a change in the symptoms quickly. However, these are strong and tend to be habit forming and sedating so if you are prescribed these, it is going to just be for the short term.
>3. Beta blockers. These are medications that will try to block some of the stimulating effects that come with adrenaline. These can help to reduce symptoms like shaking voice and

limbs, pounding of the heart, blood pressure, and heart rate. They can be used on an infrequent basis to help you control your physical symptoms in some situations that may bring up your anxiety.

It is important to remember that any treatment for Social Anxiety Disorder isn't always going to work quickly. You can continue to work with therapy and take medication for many months to help you out. The symptoms can fade over time, and often after you build up some confidence with the way things are going, you will be able to discontinue the medication. To help you make the most of your treatment, try to attend all of your appointments for therapy, challenge yourself by picking out goals and pursuing them, and take any medications as directed.

Chapter 6: Good Listening Skills Can Make Small Talk Easier

Small talk can be a lot of work for many people who don't like trying to think about inconsequential topics to keep the conversation going. They may be uncomfortable with getting the other person to start talking, and they want to make sure that they don't say anything that is going to offend the other person or to cause a big lull in the conversation.

One of the keys that you can work on to make sure that you can get small talk to work well, is to listen. The more that you can listen and gather from the other person, the easier it is to keep the conversation flowing.

Here are some of the key skills that you need to use in order to practice active listening, so that small talk will be more effective for you:

Don't do all the talking

It is common to get nervous when talking to others. To avoid any silence when the conversation comes to a stop, we may overcompensate and start to talk aimlessly, barely letting the other person talk at all.

If you don't pause to allow a natural back-and-forth, then you risk turning the conversation into a monologue. The good news about active listening is that you don't have to talk too much, as you encourage the other person to do most of the talking.

This doesn't mean that you should just stand there and say nothing the whole time. But if you use active listening to bring up the right questions, you may be able to keep the conversation going for quite some time, without really having to do much talking at all.

For example, you can ask more questions about the topic at hand; you can ask for clarification; and then you can ask a few more questions to bring the conversation back up again when needed. Talking is important but try to get the other person to do a lot of talking, while you listen, as much as possible.

Try to put the speaker at ease

When you start small talk with a new person, whether you have met them before or it is the first time that you have ever spoken to them, try to put them at ease as quickly as possible. It is natural for both you and for them to be a bit nervous by the situation, but if you are able to put the other person at ease, then you are going to feel more at ease as well.

Your job here is to try to help the other person feel like they are open and free to speak about anything that they want. Remember their concerns and needs, and listen to what they have to say. Make sure that you use nods or other gestures and words to encourage the other person to continue with what they are saying, and to show that you are truly interested.

Eye contact can be so important here. Do not look at the floor, look at your hands, or look at other things that are going on around you. This is going to send out the wrong message, and makes the other person feel like you are bored with them, or that there are more important things for you to focus your attention on.

Strong eye contact, without staring and seeming aggressive, is so important. You need to look the other person in the eyes, while smiling and appearing attentive, to show that what they have to say is important and you are listening, understanding, and appreciating the conversation.

Find ways to remove distractions

There are always going to be a lot of distractions that show up in the world around you. Whether it is from your phone beeping, from others walking around, and even from your email. But if you let yourself get distracted by all these things, then your attention is taken away from the conversation at hand. How are you supposed to be effective at engaging in small talk, or any kind of communication, if you are so distracted that you can't even hear what the other person is saying?

When you are working on your listening skills, make sure that all the distractions are put away. Turn off the computer, the phone, and the television, to make sure that there is no chance that they will get in the middle of the conversation. Don't look out the window, pick at your fingers, shuffle papers, or doodle. This kind of distracted behavior sends a message to the other person that you are bored or disinterested in them and what they have to say. If your roles were reversed, how would that make you feel?

If you can, it is also important to avoid any interruptions. While you may not be able to avoid these all the time—for example, if you are at a party and someone walks over and interrupts, there isn't much you can do—you can try to avoid them as much as possible.

You want to make sure that you can put your full attention on the speaker, and that you make them feel at ease and like the most important person around. You can't do that if you are constantly checking your email on your phone, looking out the window, or looking around the room.

Empathize

Empathy is one of your strongest tools in communicating and

forming meaningful connections with others. It is easy to come off as thoughtless or insensitive if your ability to experience and express empathy isn't well developed. When you are talking to someone, try to understand how they are feeling from their point of view. Even if what they are experiencing and talking about isn't something that you have gone through personally, and even if it isn't something that you understand all that well, it is still important to find some common ground and then use that to help you to empathize with the other person.

For example, if you find that you don't respond much if another person is obviously feeling very happy or sad, or if you give harsh, tone deaf responses to a friend whose dog has died—because they should have "expected" it, since dogs don't live as long as humans, then you might need to work on developing your emotional empathy.

It is also important to develop cognitive empathy, which involves trying to understand how someone is feeling from a more logical perspective. For example, if you get annoyed at someone else who is not as educated as you, simply because they don't know something that you think should be "obvious", you need to work on improving your cognitive empathy, and understanding that not everyone has had the same opportunities as you to advance their studies.

If possible, let go of any preconceived notions that you have about a person. When you start out the conversation with an open mind, it is easier to have some empathy with the speaker and to respond appropriately. Reading widely and on a wide range of topics is another great way to expose yourself to many different viewpoints and life experiences. Not everyone has the same reaction to events as you do, and it's important to recognize this and to try and learn about someone else's viewpoint, which can help to develop your empathy.

Of course, there may be times when the other person is going to talk about a topic, or say something, that you don't really agree with. This doesn't give you the right to just barge in and start talking over them or putting them down for their perspective. Instead, if you do disagree with that person, you can wait and construct an argument later that will respectfully respond to what they said.

Even if you do decide to counter what the speaker has said because you don't agree with them, this doesn't mean that you should close your mind and ignore their feelings. When it comes to any kind of communication, whether it is in the form of small talk or not, it is so important to keep an open mind to the opinions, emotions and views of others. Even if you don't end up agreeing with them completely, you may be able to learn a few things along the way.

Don't interrupt with your own solutions

We are taught as children not to interrupt other people when they are talking. But much of what we see on television and in popular culture shows that it is just fine to interrupt someone and put in your own solutions.

Interrupting is one of the worst things that you can do when trying to have a conversation, whether you are talking to someone you just met, or someone you have known for a long time. When you interrupt, it is sending the message that:

> 1. This isn't a conversation. I see it as a contest, and I plan to win it.
> 2. I don't have time to wait around for your opinion.
> 3. I don't really care what you think, but I think that you should listen to me.
> 4. What I have to say is way more relevant, accurate, or interesting compared to what you have to say.
> 5. I'm more important than you.

Each person thinks and speaks at different rates. If you are already a quick thinker, and an agile talker, then it is going to be a burden for you to relax your pace if you come across a communicator who is thoughtful and a bit slower to express themselves.

Making an effort not to interrupt the other person helps to keep the conversation at an even pace and to ensure that you actually hear what the other person is saying, rather than talking over them.

Any time that you are listening to someone talk about one of their problems or another issue affecting them, you should work hard to not just suggest solutions. Most people aren't really looking for advice because they just want to be able to talk and let off some steam. If they do want some solutions, they are going to specifically ask for it. You need to listen and help the other person find their own answers. Somewhere down the line, if you are absolutely bursting with a great solution, at least ask the other person whether they would like to hear the idea first.

Wait until the speaker pauses before asking for any clarifications

When you don't really understand what someone is saying, it is fine to ask them questions to make sure that you understand what is going on. It is much better to ask them to backtrack or to ask some questions to make sure you fully understand what is going on, rather than just continuing the conversation and being confused the whole time.

But make sure that you don't interrupt the other person when you ask for clarification. Wait until there is a natural pause from the speaker. Then, you can ask something like: "Back up a second. I didn't understand what you just said about..." This allows you a chance to get clarification, but it also shows the other person that you were listening to them and that you really want to hear what they have to say.

Ask questions but stick to the topic

During a conversation, there may be many points that come up that can lead to a conversational tangent that gets things off track. For example, at lunch, a colleague starts telling you about their recent trip overseas. In the course of this talk, they mention visiting a mutual friend. This can lead you to ask questions about that one mutual friend, and soon the topic has moved off from the original discussion about all of the amazing places that your colleague saw on holiday.

There is nothing wrong with asking questions to explore different elements of a topic—in fact, this can often help a conversation to evolve and flow well—but try to keep things relevant and on the same topic that the other person wants, at least to start with. If you notice that the question you have asked is leading the speaker astray, then you should take the responsibility to get it back on track. This can make the person you are talking to feel like they still have control over the conversation, and it helps you to practice going with the flow.

Pay attention to some of the nonverbal cues

There is a lot that the other person can say with their words, but there is even more that the other person can say that is nonverbal. It is possible to glean a lot of information from another person without them even saying a word. This can even happen over the phone, with the help of listening to the inflections in their voice.

There are a lot of different nonverbal cues that you can pay attention to, when it comes to having a face to face conversation with another person. You can see whether the other person is irritated, bored, or enthusiastic just by observing their body language, the sound of their voice, and the expression on their face. These are all clues that you shouldn't ignore.

When you are listening to someone else and trying to glean everything that they want to tell you, you must be careful of what else is being said below the surface of their words. What the other person is saying out loud will only convey a fraction of the message. The nonverbal cues are just as important.

Show some regular feedback to the speaker

When trying to connect with another person during a conversation, it is important to give regular feedback. If you just stand there passively looking like a blank slate, not responding to them in any way, it will make the other person feel as if they aren't getting through to you and they will start withdrawing from you.

It can help to mirror their posture and body language, for example. You can also show the speaker that you understand where they are coming from by saying things like: "I can see that you are confused", "What a terrible ordeal for you", or: "You must be thrilled" in response to their story. If you are talking to that person and you find their thoughts and feelings unclear, then you can simply go through and paraphrase the message, as you understand it, on an occasional basis.

From there, you can just nod and show that you understand them with the help of appropriate facial expressions. The idea here is to give the speaker proof on some level that you are listening and that you are still following along with them on their train of thought.

You need to be an active listener when you are using small talk. Too many times we get involved in our own thought processes and expectations about how a conversation should unfold, instead of letting it flow and evolve naturally. If two people meet who are doing the same thing, then the conversation will come to an awkward halt.

But when you become an active listener, you will find that you can learn so much. You can easily catch on to the topics that the other person is bringing up, you can understand and respond to the cues that they send, and ask interesting questions to propel the conversation. You can feed off that and keep the conversation going for much longer, without feeling worn out, worried, or strained to find more topics to discuss.

Chapter 7: Tips to Start a Conversation and Keep It Going

Not knowing how to keep a conversation going can really harm your social life. Awkward silences can be uncomfortable for everyone, but the good news is that there are different things that you can do to get around them.

For many people, one of the most daunting things about meeting strangers or trying to make new friends is the risk of not knowing what to say. But if you do know how to start and keep a conversation going, it can make socializing much more enjoyable, and help you to create some lasting friendships.

Why do I run out of things to say?

One habit that gets in the way of a dynamic, flowing conversation, is filtering. This is the process of holding yourself back from saying something out loud, until you have had a chance to filter it first. This supposedly allows you to make sure that the sentence you are about to say is interesting, smart, impressive, or cool, and that it won't embarrass you.

While this approach may make sense in your head, it is effectively killing your conversation ability.

Another problem that can come up is not learning how to get in the mood to start a new conversation. For example, if you just spent a whole day studying or analyzing intense subjects, you might find it quite hard to switch off from thinking about these topics, before you are ready to talk and interact with people on a social level.

How do you overcome this issue? You can overcome it in a simple way by learning some new skills to get yourself in the right mindset to associate with others socially. Here are some tips and important points to consider, so that you never run out of things to say again. Once you can do this, you will find that it is much easier to talk with people and make new friends.

How can I keep a conversation going?

There are a few different skills that you can develop to help keep a conversation flowing.

1. No filtering.

The first thing is to stop filtering yourself all the time. You are only hindering your own confidence if you keep stopping yourself from saying what is on your mind, with thoughts like: "Would I sound stupid if I say this?"

The best way for you to practice speaking more freely is to start with people that you know at least a little bit. It is sometimes fun to find out that you can say whatever comes mind during a conversation, and as long as it isn't widely inappropriate, no one is going to judge you for sharing your thoughts. People aren't really that interested in whether or not what you have said is "cool" enough. They are too focused on trying to keep the conversation going and on how they come across to you, so just talking and being yourself by bringing up any subject that comes into your head can make a big difference.

2. "Interesting, tell me more!"

This is an approach that can work a good ninety-nine percent of the time, and it is a surefire technique that beginners really like to work with. People love to know that you are truly interested in what they are telling you. If you can show them a bit of genuine interest, it is more likely that the person you are talking to is going to hang around longer. This is a great way to keep a conversation going without much effort on your part.

There are some variations of this phrase that will also encourage the speaker to keep on talking, such as asking follow-up questions in response to what has been said.

When the other person sees that you are actively listening and interested, it will help put them at ease and they are going to be more engaged and willing to share information with you.

3. Stories can come from everywhere.

A good story can get everyone involved and keep a conversation going with ease. You don't have to exclusively draw from the experiences in your own life when you are starting a conversation. It is perfectly fine to use stories that didn't happen to you personally, to help keep the conversation going. For example, you can talk about something that your friend told you; an anecdote that you heard on TV; or even what you read in the news.

This technique is a great way to make any conversation that you are having more interesting, with more of a natural ease, avoiding all the silences that can show up and make things more awkward.

Additional tips to enhance your conversations

Some other ideas that will help the conversation go smoothly when using small talk, include:

- Be interested in what they have to say. You need to find ways to be really interested in the conversations that you have with other people. If you don't seem interested, whether or not you are is irrelevant, because the other person will get

bored or frustrated and will walk away from the conversation in no time.
- Ask lots of questions. When the other person brings up a new topic, start to ask questions about it. This shows that you want to learn more, and it will do wonders to keep the conversation going. It can also work well if you don't know the topic that the other person brings up, because then you can participate and learn along the way.
- Be good at listening. If you let your mind wander too much and don't really listen and pay attention to what the other person is saying, it is hard to take in what they tell you. You have to make sure that you can take in all of the information that they provide you, instead of going around in an endless loop of questions because you weren't really giving it the attention that it needed.
- Make eye contact. Maintaining respectful eye contact is another way to let the other person in the conversation know that you are listening to them. If you are constantly moving your eyes around, then you are going to appear distracted and like you are not that interested in what the person is saying.
- Consider keeping a list of topics to hand. Sometimes it is hard to think of topics when you are meeting with someone new, and you may feel some anxiety about this. If the conversation is already moving and flowing along, you may not even need the list, but having it in the back of your mind just in case the conversation starts to lag, can take some of the pressure off.
- Find some common ground. When you find something that you and the other person have in common, you may want to try and stretch that thread into a longer conversation. You can pay attention to find some common ground during the discussion, or you might be introduced by someone who already knows what mutual interests the two of you share.
- Use conversation "threading". This is where you pick up on

multiple points of interest in a statement made by another person. You can then ask various questions to branch off the conversation, for example, if someone says: "Last week, I traveled to Alaska for work", you could ask if they like to travel in general and discuss some of your own stories about traveling. You could also ask them where they are working, or what they thought about Alaska. This opens a lot of doors, as you can naturally direct the way you would like the conversation to go.

• Practice and get out there. The more that you can practice small talk, the easier it will be. You can practice conversing with anyone around you, whether it is someone at the grocery store, a family member, or a friend. You can even try if you are online in a video chat. Over time, this will make small talk feel so much more natural and will help to build your confidence.

• Know when it is time to put an end to the conversation. This is a very important part to consider for any conversation. If things are going well, then it is hard to figure out when to end things. You don't want to interrupt the other person, but you do want to make sure you leave before the connection runs out. It is easier to end too early, and leave them wanting more, than to talk with them for too long and have either of you get bored. When you are ready to end the discussion, make sure to let the other person know that you would like a chance to talk with them later, and then share contact information so that this is possible.

Now that you know some of the tricks that you can use to ensure your conversations don't stall, the next thing that you need to do is practice using these techniques. The best way to practice is to get out there and use them the next time that you talk to someone new.

Of course, if you have been struggling with the issue of small talk for some time, it is a good idea to start by implementing just one of these ideas at a time, and find a way to add your own twist to it, so you aren't overwhelmed. From there, you will be able to slowly implement these tips and engage in some of the best conversations of your life.

Chapter 8: Can I Make Friends as an Introvert?

When you are an introvert, you may find that it is hard to make friends. It isn't that you don't want to make friends or that you don't like people. But in a world where extroverts—who enjoy being sociable and who expect you to be the same—are everywhere, while you want to be at home relaxing to recharge your batteries, it can be really hard.

This doesn't mean that all is lost if you are an introvert. Introverts can be some of the best types of friends to have, and you will be able to find those who want to spend time with you and won't ask you to change your personality to be with them. But you may have to take a few extra steps in order to make this happen. There are some things that you can do as an introvert to start making more friends and enjoying your social life a little bit more than before.

The challenges of making friends when you are an introvert

There are many challenges that can impact your ability to make friends when you are an introvert. A lot of social situations that include small talk can be hard, and when you are perfectly content to spend a lot of time at home with a good show or reading a good book, it can be difficult to drag yourself away to go be social and do things that physically drain you.

Some of the different challenges that can come in to play when you are trying to make friends as an introvert include:

1. Maintaining too many friends and having too many types of friendships can be overwhelming. As an introvert, you may worry that others will not be willing to put up with your tendency to go off the radar on occasion and take a break.

2. Getting into a group and dealing with a group conversation is intimidating. You are never quite sure when to interject, or how to express yourself without feeling like there is a big spotlight put right on you.

3. In some cases, you can feel a bit of frustration when there is a conversation that goes too fast, and you are not able to fully think about the topic and give your opinion.

4. Small talk is often tedious, or even painful, for a shy introvert. They will sometimes find it difficult to smoothly bridge the gap between deeper conversations and chit chat.

5. Many of the social environments that are needed in order to make friends can be overwhelming to an introvert, and when they do venture out, it can leave them unmotivated to get out there and try it again.

In addition, there are going to be some generic challenges that all adults face when it is time to make friends, even for those who are considered extroverts. Adults tend to be less open to forming new friendships as they get older. They tend to be settled into their own friend groups that they have formed over the years, and it is sometimes hard to break into one of these if you don't already have your own group.

If you have ever gone through the experience of moving churches, cities, or jobs, you know that it is tough to break into some of the friend circles that are already there. As an introvert, you may find that instead of breaking into the whole group and gaining a ton of friends, it can be preferable to have just a few best friends you can rely on, ones who feel like home and will be there for you.

Sometimes you just need one

There is often a misconception out there that you have to juggle a ton of friends, and a non-stop social activity calendar, in order to feel like you are living a good life. Instead of trying to get out of your comfort zone too much, it is often best if you can just find a few people to make a tight-knit friend circle.

Introverts are not hardwired to always be out in social activities, and to maintain a lot of shallow friendships. Instead, they value quality over quantity with all of their relationships. This isn't meant to discourage you from making friends, and if you decide to have a bigger group of friends, that is entirely possible to achieve.

The good news is there are a few things that you can do to help you make friends as an introvert. These include:

Frequent a "friendship goldmine"

Mining a "friendship goldmine" involves participating in any kind of activity that you would naturally plan on doing, regardless of whether you were trying to make friends doing that activity or not. This is something that you can usually tie to a passion, a core value, or a higher goal of yours, like dancing, attending church, or taking French lessons. This is a great idea because you will take the pressure off as you do an activity you enjoy, and you will hopefully also find friends who have the same hobbies, goals, and passions as you.

You can choose to take a pottery class, or go to an exercise group, or spend time in a book club—the possibilities are endless. And you will be able to go to these activities for some time and will see those new people on a regular basis.

This no-pressure approach will help you to get to know someone new, while doing something that you love. If you make new friends at it, that is great, and you can carry those friendships forward into your daily life. But if you don't make a new friend, you can try out something else later, and at least you got to do something that you already enjoy or always wanted to try.

Let things be a little awkward

No one likes to end up in situations that are overly awkward. But when you are a shy introvert who is trying to make some new friends, this is something that is going to happen on occasion. The thing to remember here is that the awkward part is only going to last for the first few minutes. If you are able to accept and even expect this discomfort in the beginning, you will find that this passes quickly and you can often still connect well afterwards.

Once you can power through those few minutes, you will start to form some of the connections that you need. And if the other person isn't able to handle those few minutes of discomfort and decides to move on to talking to someone else, then they weren't the friend for you.

Set realistic friendship goals

The reason that a lot of introverts get discouraged so quickly when they are dating or trying to make new friends is because they hope that they will connect with someone after only one or two outings. If we start to expect that every social event is going to provide us with some friends for the rest of our lives, we will feel very discouraged early on.

The goals that you set for coming up with these new connections need to be more achievable. Realistically, it could take quite a few meetings and social events, spread over a longer period of time so you recharge as needed, before you make any new lifelong friends. In some cases, it may just take one or two interactions to set this solid foundation, but that shouldn't be your goal.

Some of the reasonable goals that you can set yourself include:
> 1. Initiating a conversation with one or two new people each time that you are at a social event.
> 2. Practicing one of the tips that we are talking about in this chapter, such as starting a regular activity that you enjoy, like

pottery classes, and see if you make any connections as the classes unfold.

3. Smiling, in a genuine manner, at a minimum of two or three people when you go out.

If you are able to aim for some of these micro goals, you will find that it is much easier to stay optimistic and motivated when working to make some new friends.

This may seem like a lot to handle—but making friends as an introvert doesn't always have to be a big challenge. If you can take things slowly and really work towards your goals, while making those goals manageable for your personality type, you will be amazed at the results.

Chapter 9: Simple Things You Can Do to Be More Likeable

Are you someone who wants to be able to increase how likable you are? Would you be interested in starting up a conversation with anyone you meet and have them like you instantly?

Everyone wants to make sure that they are liked. Some people care about this more than others, but it is a natural human instinct—we are hardwired to want to fit in and "belong". It makes us uncomfortable or upset to hear that someone doesn't like us, even if we don't know that person all that well.

There are some people who naturally have a personality that makes them more likeable. They know what to say to others, how to act, and how to make other people feel good. Even if you don't have these skills, there are some simple steps that you can follow in order to improve your congeniality to become someone that others are interested in and like as well.

Learn how to treat people better

It's important to make sure that we know the proper way to treat others. To do this, start with a smile. This is a great and simple way to get the attention of another person. Smiling, if it is done in a natural way that doesn't look forced, shows that you are friendly and approachable, and that you are a positive person. Any time that you can, always come prepared with a natural smile. A fake smile can work as well, as long as it doesn't look too forced in the process.

A smile is one of the friendliest greetings out there, and it can work to instantly put people at ease. If you want to start up a conversation with someone else, or you see someone else that you recognize, you should stop for a minute and flash them a smile. This is usually going to make them feel good and can encourage them to like you more.

You should also focus on your body language and the message that you are sending out, to make sure that you are approachable. If you are at an event and you stand back against the wall, keeping your arms crossed with a pout on your face, you will appear to others as unfriendly and annoyed. This will make them think that they should just stay away from you.

Your body language is going to be so important when it comes to showing that you are approachable and that you want to talk to other people. Welcoming others, smiling, and standing with good posture and your arms uncrossed at your sides, can really go a long way in making others feel more comfortable around you.

You may also find that steady eye contact can be a good touch as well. Just make sure that your eye contact is not too intense, and that you remember to blink occasionally so that you don't end up intimidating the other person in the process.

We also need to focus on the importance of being kind. It is sometimes difficult to reach out to everyone you come across with an attitude that is pleasant, particularly if you are feeling drained or annoyed. But if you can do this with as many people as possible, it can go a long way to building up your good reputation. Research has also shown that there are some reward centers of the brain that are more activated if we act generously, like when we help a friend or donate to a charity. Not only does being kind help others to feel good, it will show that you are a caring person, and can also be a good thing when it comes to your own happiness and health.

The way that you make people feel is one of the main things that they will remember about you. Make sure to show respect and try to be polite, for example by holding open the door for others, shaking hands with those that you meet, and treating others the way that you would like to be treated. If you are actually in the wrong for something along the way, make sure that you apologize and act humble in the process.

When you are meeting someone for the first time, a good impression that you can leave with them is remembering their name. Whether it is someone you see at the store on a regular basis, or a business contact, learning the names of these people can be so important and will really make them feel valued and warm towards you in your future interactions. It is easy to forget an acquaintance's name, and just by remembering it you can really get on the good side of that person.

There are different methods that you can use in order to commit someone's name to memory. You can repeat the name a few times in that conversation to get it to stick. You can use your imagination and association to help you to remember the name. The more creative that you can get with these remembering devices, the easier it is going to be to remember that name, and the better impression that you are going to give to that person if you succeed.

If you ever need to express some of your own opinions when you are talking to another person, make sure that you do this in a respectful way. While you don't want to have your views come across as though they are superior to what anyone else thinks, you can still voice your opinion and share your views. It is important to be authentic and just because you might have different views about a certain topic of discussion, it doesn't mean that you are going to lose your likeability in the process.

You can disagree with the opinions of others, but you need to do this in a manner that is polite, one that allows you to talk about your own thoughts but shows that you are fair and also value the opinion of that other person.

If you do both disagree on a point, you can stop the conversation and politely ask the other person to explain why they think the way that they do. This is going to show the other person that you are interested in hearing more about what they think, and then they will be more receptive to the things that you are going to say about your own opinion on the matter.

Refine your appearance

While it may seem a little bit shallow, one of the big things that will determine if someone likes you or not, is your appearance. The way you look will give someone a snap judgement of you, and it might influence how receptive they are to you when you first meet. If you show up in sweat pants or old clothes and don't take a bath or a shower for many days, then this sends the message that you don't care about yourself, and the opinion of a stranger meeting you for the first time you is most likely going to be low. But if you take care with your appearance and work to make yourself look good, then you will find that it is easier to make a good impression that will really make a difference.

There are a few things that you can do to make this happen. First, show some pride in your own personal style. Your clothing is going to be one of the first things that people notice when they see you. Having your own style, one that is unique and that shows that you take pride in your appearance, will prove to others that you have confidence in yourself, and then they will have confidence in you as well.

Next, you need to make sure that you are maintaining your own personal hygiene. You can have the best personality in the world, but if you smell bad or don't look like you maintain your hygiene, others are not going to want to be near you. If your goal is to become more likeable, then you should make it a habit to groom yourself each day.

This can include showering regularly, applying anti-perspirant, and washing your hands.

Oral hygiene is important here as well. To make sure that people are encouraged to talk to you, it is important to take two minutes each day to brush your teeth, two times a day or more, to help remove the bacteria that is there, to make your breath smell better, and to keep those pearly whites looking great when you smile. Take the time to replace your toothbrush at least four times a year to keep it healthy.

Oral hygiene doesn't stop with brushing your teeth. For example, you can also take some time to floss each day, or use some chap stick on dry lips on a regular basis, especially if you are in the colder months.

And finally, make sure that you are careful with the makeup that you are using. You can use it in order to enhance your own appearance and to make sure that the best parts of your face will be highlighted, but you don't want to overdo it. Keep the makeup to a minimum, rather than caking it on, to help you appear more natural and to make others feel more comfortable around you.

You will be amazed at some of the things that you can get to happen, and how much easier it is to feel confident, when you feel that you are more likeable to the other people around you. They are more likely to want to come over and talk to you, more likely to listen to the things that you say and to ask questions, and more likely to want to be your friend, even if you are a very shy introvert. Taking care to follow these tips to be more confident and likeable, can really make a difference in improving small talk and other communication techniques.

Chapter 10: How to Start and Build Up Relationships as an Introvert

As an introvert, you may find that making new friends is not always as easy as it can be for others. Introverts like to go more for quality when picking out their friends, rather than quantity. So, while some people are interested in going all out and having as many friends as possible, introverts tend to be more selective and picky, and will only choose friends that really understand them, who share the same interests, and who are willing to accept them as they are.

If an introvert is not able to share their innermost thoughts, secrets, and dreams with another person, then they are never really going to consider that other person their friend. They may see this person as a nice acquaintance, or someone they like a lot, but not really a true friend. Because of this desire for more depth and quality in their friendships, the introvert is perfectly fine having just one or two friends.

Of course, this doesn't mean that introverts aren't allowed to have a large number of friends if they want. Some introverts are more sociable and thrive with a larger number of friends. But this doesn't mean that they are going to run out and get more friends just to say that they have them.

However, introverts will often find that it is harder for them to develop the high-quality friendships that they are looking for. They have trouble when it comes to reaching out to new people, and even when they do, it is hard for them to find someone they "click" with.

The issue here is that all humans, whether they are introverts or extroverts, are made to be in society and to seek out relationships. In fact, there are many studies out there that show that being social and having close relationships with others increases the mental and physical health of the individual, along with their overall happiness. But a lack of close friendships, and some of the isolation that comes with this, can have the exact opposite effect.

Despite the belief that most introverts don't even like other people, these individuals need human connection, just like everyone else does. But they are going to have some different needs when it comes to their relationships.

A good way to think about the emotional needs of an introvert, compared to an extrovert, is that they are fine having other people around and in the same house, but they don't want a lot of people in the same room as them all the time. They are fine with people, but they get energy from spending time on their own, without other people being on top of them.

However, the world around them is not always going to be the most conducive to this ideal. The world is often going to be loud and in-their-face—and sitting next to someone in silence isn't really going to create much of a lasting friendship. It is important to remember that introverts are just as able to create some of the human connections that they need, but sometimes they need to step away from their own comfort zones in order to make this happen.

There are some things that you can do in order to make it easier to find friends, even when you are an introvert. It actually isn't as hard as you may think.

If you don't have the energy to reach out to others, find ways to draw them to you

As an introvert, there are going to be times when you are too worn out, or too uncomfortable, to go around and try to make small talk to find new friends. You may get into a room full of people, and just want to scurry the other way. This is fine. It is okay to not always have the energy that is needed to be overly social and to be out there chasing down others and trying to do all the work to form the connections you need.

This doesn't mean that you should give up. It just means that you should find other ways to get this done. One method that can be just as effective, if not better, is to find a way to draw others to come to you, rather than you going to them. The idea of a smile can go a long way here too.

No matter what mood you are in, no matter how tired you are, and no matter what circumstances are going on around you ahead of time, make sure that your ultimate goal is to smile as much as possible.

Let's say that you are at a party and you see someone else walk into the room. If you make eye contact with them and smile at them, they are going to notice you, and maybe even come over to talk. That is, if they are interested in making a connection themselves. If they don't come over, then you can just keep going with the things you were doing before. If they do come over, you have created a friendly start to meeting someone new, and all you had to do was smile. You can greet them warmly and they will most likely start a conversation and try to keep it going, and you can just go along for the ride.

It isn't always your job to charm others

Shy introverts can feel a lot of pressure in social settings to be outgoing, vivacious, and charming, fearing that there is no way that another person will ever like them or become their friend. When they try to be charming or outgoing, it usually doesn't go all that well. Often, they will struggle and get their words jumbled, or get lots of nervous laughter, and the situation just gets more uncomfortable for them as it goes on.

The thing to remember here is that there isn't really a rule in place that says you absolutely need to be a charmer to have any hope of making connections. Instead of working so much on charming others, or trying to behave the way that an extrovert would, work on being confident in yourself. Learn how to be self-assured in the things that you appreciate and stand for; for the interests and values that you have; and in who you are.

There is nothing wrong with being "the quiet one" when out in a social setting. Sure, there is a lot of push back in our world against this, where people think that you need to be outgoing and act a certain way, but this just isn't the way that most introverts work.

When you are ready to reach out to another person, then go ahead and do it. If you don't, then don't pressure yourself. If someone does start to approach you, don't feel nervous. If you feel confidence in who you are as a person, and your innate likeability, then it doesn't matter what the other person thinks of you, or if there are awkward moments in your conversation. The more comfortable you are with not being the life of the party, and the less you try to change your personality, the more likely it is that you can actually start to enjoy yourself and attract the kind of people and friendships that will be best for you.

It is fine to be vulnerable on occasion

For many introverts, it is sometimes hard to be vulnerable. Many of these individuals like to keep to themselves, and they strive to showcase a perfect persona to everyone they come across. But when building friendships, think of these words from C.S. Lewis: "Friendship is born at the moment when one person says to another: 'What! You too? I thought I was the only one…'" This moment is not going to happen between you and another person unless you can be courageous enough to open yourself up.

The deeper that you are willing and able to go into these new friendships, the more meaning there is going to be behind them. Building up to revealing a healthy amount of vulnerability is going to need to start somewhere. Why can't it start with you? Showing someone else that you are willing to be honest and open gives them permission to be honest and open as well. You can both feed off each other in this way, in a cycle that will create a deeper bond than before.

There are a lot of ways that you can show some vulnerability to another person. When you are meeting someone new, you can keep it simple. You don't have to introduce yourself and then start talking about all your biggest fears in the first five minutes. Some examples of how to initially show some vulnerability could include the following admissions:

> 1. "I really wish that there were some people I knew at this gathering."
> 2. "Do you know any good ice breakers? I've never been really good at them."
> 3. "I don't know about you, but I really am not a fan of these kinds of big parties."

After you have had a chance to talk with someone for a while, or maybe met up with them more than once, it is time to build up the relationship some more. The way that you show more vulnerability will change as the relationship develops. Some examples of things that you can say to show your vulnerability as you are starting to build up these new relationships, include:

> 1. "I start to feel pretty anxious when I get to a new class."
> 2. "I like hanging out with you."
> 3. "I'm having some trouble with [fill in the problem here]. Can I have a few minutes to vent to you?"
> 4. "I really appreciate the way that you have been supporting me."

It is so important to be vulnerable with another person if you are going to be friends. Friends should be those people who you feel comfortable to share personal life with. If you just want to work on outward appearances forever and never really dig into any of the things that matter to you, then you are just acquaintances. But when you open up and allow yourself to be vulnerable a little bit, then you are going to find that deeper bonds can begin to form.

Seek out other introverts like yourself

There is nothing wrong with picking out an extrovert to be your friend. They may help to get you out more socially and to experience different things in life, and they can be a lot of fun. This piece of advice isn't telling you to completely avoid making friends with extroverts. If you feel a connection with them, go for it.

But if all of your friends are extroverts, then it can sometimes be emotionally draining, since they will want to go out and be social all the time, while you crave some peace and quiet in your own home.

As an introvert, it is sometimes better for most of your friends to be introverts, and for you to look out for other introverts to spend time with. Any time that you do go out in a social setting, whether it is to a party, to a camp, or to school, etc. your goal should be to search out other introverts like yourself, who will likely understand you better and give you the space that you need.

There are a lot of benefits to picking out introverts as your friends. They aren't going to pressure you to change the way that you think or your personality. They won't try to turn you into a vivacious human when you aren't. So, how do you find these people? Look around the room and see if there is anyone who is quietly hanging out along the edges. Then you can make the first move and go and talk to them. It could be the start of a great new friendship.

Figure out the love language of the other person, and then share what yours is

Although the Five Love Languages are often geared towards

relationships that are more romantic, they can be used in many other situations as well. Partners have used them to help understand each other better. Parents have used them to help understand their children and how to better raise them. And you can even use these love languages to deepen the friendships that you have.

There are some simple tests that you can take to figure out what your love language is, and then you can learn a bit more about the others as well. Not everyone is going to have the same love language as you. By assuming that everyone sees things the way that you do, you miss out on appreciating how unique each individual is, which can lead to disagreements and make it harder to form the deep connections that are needed.

There are five of these love languages to watch out for, and they include: physical touch; acts of service; words of affirmation; gifts; and quality time. We often find that we will give out love the same way that we want to receive it. But if the other person we are trying to connect with has a different love language, the desired effect is not going to be received.

For example, if "acts of service" is your love language, you may be more likely to run errands for the other person, help them clean up, or make them dinner. But if their love language is "physical touch", then there can be a disconnect. This doesn't mean that they won't appreciate the things that you do, it just won't lead to a deep connection. You need to meet them where their love language is, and they have to meet you where your love language is, in order to form those great connections.

The first step is to know your love language. Take a look at the five options listed above and see if any of them sticks out for you when it comes to how you react to other people and what behavior you appreciate the most from others. If you are uncertain, you can consider working with an online test to help you out. Once you know what your own love language is, you can then focus on the love language of those around you, making it easier for you to connect in a better and more effective, manner.

Hold out for the true connections, and don't try to settle

This is something that is going to come naturally for a lot of introverts, but it is never something that hurts to be reminded about. There is nothing quite like the moment of two souls meeting. You shouldn't just rush out and make friends with the first person you run across, unless you and that person are really able to click, and you feel a deeper connection with them. Hold out for a bit and see if you can find someone who really completes you, who really "gets" you, rather than just jumping on the first friendship opportunity that you find.

As an introvert, it is a good idea to hold out for a good friend. Hold out for someone who is going to make you feel safe and comfortable right away. Hold out for someone you feel that you can talk to about anything, without having to worry about them judging you. Hold out for someone who is able to make you happy.

It can take many introverts some time to open themselves up to others, because they are already so aware of their own internal lives. The good thing about this is that many times, they are able to get a quick sense about whether they connect with someone or not.

Introverts can get impatient when they aren't able to make those deep connections quickly. But remember that it is always worth it to hold out for that one in a million friend.

Be intentional

As an introvert, you are going to need to take some extra steps and precautions to ensure that you can reach out to other people. Many introverts may find that it is easy to get caught up in their own world, and then not talk to others for a long period of time. It may feel like they are ignoring other people, or that they don't really care, but in reality, they may lose sight of things or not even think about it.

It is important that you don't fall into this trap. You have to check in with your friends often, and this is going to get even more important the older that you get. Of course, it is also something that is going to get quite a bit harder—especially if you keep saying, "We should get together…" but then don't make it a priority as time goes by. Unfortunately, for many friendships, especially when they involve introverts, this can easily happen.

However, you will find that a little effort is going to go a long way. You don't have to make it something big or do a grand gesture each time you catch up. A simple text message to check in with the other person, a Skype or phone call, or a meetup or event planned in advance can all help you to maintain your friendships better, even when you are dealing with being separated by time or space.

It is going to take some work to make your friendships last. You need to make sure that you are intentional in setting up time to prioritize other people, even when it feels impossible or exhausting. When you are able to do this, you will find that it leads to relationships that are deeper and more meaningful, and this can do so much good for your mental, emotional, and physical wellbeing.

Chapter 11: Other Ways to Increase Your Communication Skills

There are so many ways that we can communicate with the world around us. We can write letters, send out emails, send out texts, and talk to others on the phone or in person. There is even a whole part of communication that is nonverbal and doesn't include any words at all. It is so important, whether you are an introvert or an extrovert, to learn how to communicate with those around you, whether by engaging in small talk, business talk, or deeper conversations.

In this chapter, we are going to look at some of the other things that you can do in order to increase your own communication skills. Strong communication skills can benefit you in a wide variety of situations, and some of the things that you can do to increase your communication skills and make them better include the following:

Get rid of any conversation fillers that aren't necessary

The um's and ah's may be a normal part of the way that you talk, but they aren't going to do that much to improve your speech or the way that your everyday conversations go. You need to find ways to cut them out as much as possible. This will help you to become more persuasive, to make you appear and feel more confident, and can really help the flow of the conversation.

But how do you work to break this habit, one that has most likely been formed many years ago? One way that you can do this is to start keeping a rolling tally of when you say any filler words—anything like ah, um, like, or any other word that really has no meaning. Once you see just how many times you are saying these words in each conversation, you will be amazed and motivated to focus on and improve the problem.

There are also a few other things that you can do to help this situation. Sometimes just finding ways to relax when you are in the middle of a conversation can make a difference. When you are tense and nervous, which can often happen when a shy introvert gets out in a public setting and engages in small talk, those filler sounds and words are going to be more likely. Simply taking some steps, like removing your hands from your pockets and taking some pauses before you speak, can really cut down on these.

Often, we will start to rush through some of the sentences and words that we want to say. We are worried about having any pauses in the conversation. The truth is that those silences are always going to seem more awkward to us, but often the other person isn't even going to notice. It is much better to have a few seconds of pause so you can think through what you are going to say next, rather than slowing down your thoughts and making it sound jarring as you add in those unnecessary filler words.

Consider having a script to help with the small talk

Small talk may sound pretty simple in theory, but in reality, it is an art form that a lot of people struggle with. It is important to be as prepared as possible. And for some introverts, having a small script with ideas and suggestions can be the answer to this problem.

The FORD method can be the right option to help you out. FORD stands for family, occupation, recreation, and dreams. This is a good way to remember a few topics that you are able to discuss with another person. Just thinking of those words may be enough to help push you forward to having a new topic to talk about. You can also use these to help you turn awkward small talk into a better conversation as you share information that could help you and the other person find some common ground with each other.

You can also think about a few things that you would say for each topic of family, occupation, recreation and dreams. You don't want to go into any conversation and have the whole thing scripted out. This will be painfully obvious to the other person and is going to turn them off of you pretty early on. But when you do just enough to help you get started, and then you just let the conversation go its natural course, you will be amazed at how much easier it is to talk with anyone, whether you have known them for a long time or just met.

Ask lots of questions, and try repeating what the other person says

This is not a suggestion to just parrot another person and not bring anything to the table conversationally. And it also isn't about just asking question after question without talking about yourself ever. But it is a good way to get the other person talking and to ensure that you keep the conversation going without too many awkward pauses or other issues.

No doubt there have been times that, no matter how hard you tried, you drifted off when someone else was talking and missed out on what they were saying. This has happened to all of us at some point—humans are distractible creatures. Or on other occasions, perhaps you were paying attention, but misheard what another person said.

Asking questions during a conversation, and stopping at times to repeat what that other person has said can help to clarify anything that may seem confusing, and can help you stay in the moment and keep up with the conversation.

Try not to make this seem annoying though, by constantly just repeating everything they are saying and not adding anything yourself. But if you find a way to repeat some of the words in your follow up sentence, this can really help you to remember what was going on during the conversation.

This can also help you to fill up any of the awkward silences that naturally show up when you are using small talk. Instead of trying to stir up a conversation with all of the usual and boring topics, such as how the weather has been, you can ask some interesting questions of the other person to get them talking. Then, when they provide you with some answers, you can work on engaging with those answers. Remember, it is always more important in small talk for you to be interested in the other person, more than being interesting to them.

Find ways to tailor your message to the audience

The best communicators out there are the ones that can adjust how they talk and the message that they are discussing based on who they are talking to.

You may already be doing this without even realizing it. Think about it this way, do you use the same tone, the same communication style, or even the same topics, when you are talking to your co-workers compared to talking to your family? Do you talk to your friends, teachers, boss, and people you just met in the same manner as each other? Probably not.

When you are ready to engage in small talk, try to remember the perspective of the other person, and the best way to approach or get through to them. For example, if you are talking to your boss at work, you will need to keep things professional, so it would not be appropriate to tell them that you are feeling tired and unproductive because you are hungover from the night before. However, if you are with a close friend, you might feel more relaxed, and even hug them, before you ask for an update on a personal matter.

Tailoring your message to your audience can help you to communicate a bit easier. You can keep in mind the context of your relationship, and think of some things that they enjoy, or where they work and what they do in their free time, or even about their personal life if you know them, and you will find plenty of topics that can help you out with this approach.

Be brief and specific

Small talk can sometimes lead to deeper conversations, but often this is just a time to quickly catch up. It is always a good idea to be specific and brief, rather than going on about a topic that no one is interested in.

The acronym BRIEF—background, reason, information, end, and follow up—can be used to help with this. Following this formula helps you to be succinct and to keep conversations relevant, by giving some quick context, or background information, followed by the reason that you've brought up a particular topic now. Then make sure to highlight the key information that you want to share, before wrapping it up. Finally, you can follow up by considering any questions that might crop afterwards. This is great to remember when it comes to sending emails and written correspondence but using BRIEF to be clear and concise can also work to prevent boredom when dealing with verbal communication as well.

Up the level of empathy that you provide

Always remember that communication is a two-way street. You should never be the only one who is talking the whole time, and you should also never just be listening the whole time. There needs to be some talking and some listening on both sides to ensure that the conversation keeps going, and that no one feels like they are either being ignored or doing all the work.

In addition to this, you may find that showing some empathy is going to make a big difference as well. It can help you to relate to the other person and figure out how to connect on a deeper level. It doesn't mean you need to be a people pleaser who only ever says what you think others want to hear, but it does mean that you will have a sense of how a person might be feeling when you discuss a certain topic. This can also help to avoid seeming awkward and insensitive by accidentally bulldozing over the other person's feelings, because you lack the ability to recognize them or to put yourself in the other person's shoes.

You can develop empathy with anyone; you don't have to be close to them. Developing empathy is going to help you to get a better understanding of everything that the other person is saying, even some of the unspoken parts. For example, if your friend tells you that they are excited that their child has gotten his first tooth, you might notice that while they are smiling when they say this, they also look very tired and have low energy. You can empathize with them by saying something like: "Wow, that's great! And you must also be happy to get some more sleep now that he isn't teething and in so much pain." It will be a relief for the proud parent to acknowledge that yes, they are also exhausted and hoping for a more settled night now that their son's tooth is finally out. In addition to forming a deeper connection with that person, empathy can also help you to respond more effectively in all of your communications with others.

Realize the importance of body language

Body language is a big part of communication, and yet it is something that too many people don't even pay conscious attention to in the first place. In many cases, it is going to be more accurate to assess what a person feels and means from their body language, than the words that are used. If someone says: "I am happy", but they are standing up tall and tense, with an angry tone and their fists clenched, then it is likely that they are actually angry rather than happy. But we had to look at the body language to figure this out.

The old saying, "Actions speak louder than words", is true, and sometimes it is possible for individuals to communicate a lot of different things without having to utter a single word. For example, how often have you been able to shrug your shoulders and—without saying a word—convey that you don't know the answer to something? Or, how many times have you simply raised your eyebrows, to convey that you can't believe what the other person has just said? Likewise, how many times have you gestured your hands with the palms up in front of you to suggest: "I don't know what else to say"?

There are also times when body language can be used in order to help reinforce some of the words that we are saying. We might get excited about something and move our hands around to show this. Or we might hunch our shoulders and have a sad tone when we are talking about something that is bringing us down.

In addition, paying attention to the body language that someone else is sending out is going to help us figure out whether that other person is telling us the truth, or if they are outright lying or just leaving something out of the equation. There are quite a few signs that will show when a person is lying. For example, they may clear their throat, stammer or change the pitch of their voice, or stall so that they can think about another plausible explanation. They may tap their foot, put their hands on their face, blush, or even raise their shoulders to show that they are uncomfortable, since they aren't telling the truth.

This is just one example of how you can use body language to figure out what the other person is really thinking or feeling. You can tell when someone is anxious, when they are angry, when they are happy and excited, or even when they are sad, based more on the body language cues that they send out than on the words that they say.

Another example is if an employee tells their boss that they would be more than happy to take on a new account, but their body language cues show that they really aren't happy about taking on that extra work at all, and they would rather be doing something else.

If the management isn't paying attention, they are going to just listen to the words and assume the employee will take on the work with no problems. But when the leadership and the managers really start to pay attention to the nonverbal cues that the employee is sending out, they will realize that they should try to find someone else to handle the assignment. The employee may not want to disappoint their boss, so they choose to say "yes", even though their heart is not really that into it.

Body language can be used in a job interview in many cases. If the body language of a particular application shows that they are really at ease with the subject matter, and they are good at conveying confidence during the interview questions, then there is a higher chance that this individual is going to get the job, especially if the job market is tough. On the other hand, if the applicant goes into the interview with a look of being uncomfortable or appears like they are not in control, these are traits that will turn the interviewer off and can harm your chances of getting the job.

Body language can also be important when it comes to making friendships. No one wants to have a full conversation with another person and feel like they are being blown off or not paid any attention to.

So, how do you know whether or not someone is paying attention or if they really care about what you have to say? If the other person is leaning forward—into that conversation rather than away from it—this indicates an interest in the topic. Listening to the other person and making eye contact can show interest as well. These are signs that you can look for when you are talking to someone else, and that you can use when you are also trying to convey interest.

There are a lot of different types of body language that you can pay attention to in order to figure out whether or not someone is actually saying what the words are saying. Some different aspects of body language that you should pay attention to include:

1. **Eye movement and contact:** When you are trying to work with good communication and you want to make sure that

your body language is saying the things that you want it to, you must make sure to pay attention to eye movement and eye contact. When talking to someone else, maintain eye contact with them, and don't let your eyes wander off. If you let this happen, you are showing the other person that you are bored or that there are other things that are more important and worthy of your attention. This can be seen as rude and can make it hard to create those deeper connections that you are socializing and starting small talk to find.

2. **Posture:** Posture is another determinant that you need to look at to figure out if someone means the words that they are saying, and if you are getting the whole story from them. Someone who is comfortable and confident is going to stand up with good posture. They will stand up straight and tall, have a smile on their face, and will keep good eye contact throughout the whole conversation. Someone who isn't confident—and who maybe isn't enjoying the conversation—will slouch a bit, have trouble keeping eye contact, and will maybe even turn their body away from you in an attempt to walk away.

3. **Where the hands go:** The hands will provide a big clue to how the other person is feeling or what they are thinking. If they have their arms folded across their chest, this can indicate that they are defensive or uncomfortable in the situation. But if their hands are moving around and excited, it could show that they are really animated by the subject at hand.

Hand placement can also indicate whether they are confident, comfortable, or tense. If the other person appears to be tense when they are around you, then it may be a sign that you are doing or saying something that makes them this way, or maybe you both aren't clicking. Sometimes you can figure out why they are so tense based on what they are saying. For example, if they are talking about a bad week at work, that could possibly be why their shoulders are all tense. But in other cases, it may be more of a sign that something is wrong with the conversation or how they feel, and it may be time to give them a break and find someone else to talk with.

4. **Tone of voice:** The tone of voice that the other person uses is going to reveal a lot when it comes to figuring out what they really mean. The words that someone repeats and their tone of voice can reveal completely different ideas in some cases. If you are uncertain about what the other person means, then try to pay attention to their tone of voice and see if this offers some clues.

5. **How close they stand:** You don't want someone to be so close to you that it makes you feel uncomfortable. But you also don't want them so far away that you almost have to scream in order to have a conversation, especially in a crowded space. The body position of the other person can indicate how comfortable they are with you. If you notice that someone is standing further away, or they seem to be inching themselves a bit away from you as you talk, this can indicate that they aren't comfortable being around you at the time, or that they need to be somewhere else. But if the person is faced towards you and keeps a steady distance that is close enough for comfort, then it is a good sign that they enjoy spending time with you and want to keep the conversation going.

There are so many different aspects that can come with good communication when you are talking to another person. You have to worry about how your body language is working, you have to pay attention to the other person and not always be thinking about the things that you are going to say next, and you have to come up with good topics that can keep the conversation going. But if you are able to remember a few of these tips and the other tips we have talked about, you will find that small talk is easier than you think, and it won't take long until you start to make the meaningful connections that you are looking for.

Chapter 12: Tips to Help You Develop Your Social Skills

If you feel like you are always that one awkward guest at social events, or like you consistently struggle to get into new conversations because you are shy, then it is possible that this negative self-talk is affecting your career and social life. By improving your social skills, you will begin to feel more comfortable no matter the social situation, you will make new friends and have more fun when you go out—even when you are an introvert.

Start acting like a social person

This can be hard. You may find that instead of being out and talking to people all the time, you would rather head home instead. But over time, socializing will get easier.

This doesn't mean that you have to go and change your whole personality. There are so many great things about being an introvert, but if you can do a bit of acting and behave a little more social when you go out, even when you don't feel it, you may find that small talk and joining in on conversations can start to feel more natural. Don't allow anxiety or shyness to get in the way and make things more difficult. It is up to you to make the decision to talk to new people, and to start these conversations, even when you feel a bit nervous about it.

It is fine to start out small

As an introvert, you probably don't want to spend all your free time going to parties or putting yourself in a ton of social situations. Introverts can sometimes get nervous just seeing their calendar fill up for the month. They want to be able to sit back and enjoy some things, and sometimes after a long week at work, they would like to have a few nights off at home to be alone and to recharge before hitting the social scene again.

If going out each night to a party or spending a lot of time out in a crowd seems overwhelming to you, it is fine to start out small. You should still work your way up to being more social and going out at least occasionally. But a "slow and steady" approach can definitely get you there as well.

One way to start small, is to just say "Thank you" to the grocery store clerk the next time you go shopping. Then, after a few times of this, start making some small talk by mentioning the weather, or asking about the person's family, or how they are doing in school. This can help you get some more practice with small talk and can make it easier to engage in conversation with others when you do go out in more social settings.

It is easier to get others to talk about themselves

Many introverts find that it is uncomfortable to talk about themselves when they are with others. They feel that doing this makes them seem like they are bragging or puts the spotlight on them. They would much rather let the other person do most of the talking, and let the other person talk about themselves, while they spend the time asking lots of questions.

The good news is that you can easily turn the conversation around.

In fact, you will find that many of the other people that you meet are going to really love talking about themselves. When they find an ear that is ready to listen, they will often just go on and on, and soon you will have made a good ally, and all you needed to do was ask questions and show your interest in that other person.

How do you get this all started? Simply ask a question about the other person. This can be about their family, about their hobbies, or about their career. Just keep asking questions, interjecting with some of your own information when asked, and otherwise just let the other person keep going. Encourage others to talk so that you won't have to be the one who is making all the idle chit-chat all the time.

To help with this, make sure that you are asking open-ended questions, which require more than a yes or a no answer from the other person. If you simply ask closed-ended questions, then you will get very short answers and most likely run out of conversation really quickly.

Also, if the other person does ask you some questions, try to give a full answer. Don't respond with only a "Yes" or "No", even if the question is a little bit closed ended. Doing this will shut down the effort that the other person has made, and they may feel like you don't want to keep the conversation going. Instead, choose to expand on any question that they ask, allowing both you and the other person to feed off each other.

Create goals for yourself

There are many different goals that you can set yourself in order to get the most out of your social improvement. You can choose to open your front door when someone rings the bell and talk with them for a few minutes. You can agree to sign up for a class or a workshop, and then make it your aim to talk to someone at each class. You can start attending a social activity in the community and go to regular meetings, where you will get to know other locals.

When you pick out goals, you must go with ones that will challenge you a bit, that will push you out of your comfort zone, but which won't be so difficult that you aren't able to reach them. Establish a goal and then pick out the right strategies that will help you to attain it, so you end up improving your social life, step-by-step.

Start out with one goal at a time when you are doing this, so that you don't take on too much at once. Pick one of the goals above, or a different social goal that appeals to you, and then build up from there. This way, you can work off the success that you see from achieving the first goal, and build confidence and momentum to attempt the second goal, and so on.

Remember to compliment others

Compliments are going to be your best friend. They don't take long to come up with, and they will make the other person feel amazing. It is such a simple way to get on the good side of another person, and you will find that the conversation will flow much more freely as a result.

Compliments are one of the best ways for you to open the door to a new conversation. You can offer one of your co-workers a compliment on how hard they worked on the presentation they just gave. You can compliment a friend on their new promotion, or a neighbor for getting a new car. There is always something that you can praise another person for, even if it is as simple as pointing out that you like their jacket, and asking where they got it from.

Compliments should show others that you are friendly. Friendly people are willing to give out compliments, whether they know the person well or not, and leading the discussion with a compliment, or finding another natural place to add it in, can go a long way.

Try it the next time that you meet someone new. Take a few seconds while you are being introduced to find something about that person that you can praise them on. You can choose their outfit, their shoes, their handshake, their hair, or something else. The compliment doesn't have to be big, but it shows that you are really noticing the other person and helps draw them to you.

Keep yourself up to date on any current events

One of the hardest things that you have to deal with when working on small talk, is finding topics to discuss with other people. There are many different topics you can discuss with another person, including friends, family, hobbies, career, interests, and current events.

Current events, as long as they are not too controversial, can be a great topic to bring up, and can lead to a longer conversation as you and the other person go back and forth on the different stories in the news that you have read about. The best way to take advantage of this is to keep up to date on all the news stories and current trends that you can find, which will help you to have something to talk about on any occasion. For example, you can look online, watch the news, and read magazines to help you out.

The important thing is to avoid any topic that is too controversial, including religion and politics. You don't want to ruin a potential friendship just because you decided to bring up politics in the first few minutes of meeting someone new. But do take the time to talk about any of the other current events and news stories that may be of interest.

Practice makes perfect

Practice is one of the best ways to help you improve your social skills. If you just read through this guidebook, but never get out in a social situation to use these suggestions, then they are just theories and you will never get better. You have to put yourself in social situations to help you get in some practice to see the progress that you want to make.

Anyone, including a shy introvert, can learn how to improve their social skills. It can take time, and you may make mistakes along the way, but it is going to be so worth it in the long run. The more that you can get out and the longer you practice, the better you will get at this endeavor.

Try getting out just a few times a month, and build up from there

For an introvert, it can sometimes be difficult to get yourself out there and into social situations. Sometimes just going to work and to the store throughout the week is enough to exhaust you. But if you want to work on your social skills, you need to avoid making excuses, and put yourself in social situations.

Likewise, if you are shy, you can also struggle to get out and meet people, but this is because you don't know how to express yourself and are afraid of being embarrassed or rejected. To gain confidence and get around this fear, while learning to communicate effectively, it is also important to get out and expose yourself more socially.

You don't have to go out every night of the week. You just need to get out a little more than usual. Even just adding one or two social events to your calendar a month can make a big difference in how much you work on your social skills. And the more you get out there, the more comfortable you will feel. In fact, you may even find that social activities, when limited and on your own terms, can be more enjoyable.

You get the freedom to pick out what social events you would like to attend, like a reading club at the library, or out with a few friends to get coffee. You can go to a meeting in the civic center of your town or just go out to a restaurant with your partner, instead of getting food delivered to your home. This all helps you to get out of the house, talk to different people, and to expand your comfort zone a little bit. The rest of the nights of the month can be reserved for going home and recharging at your own pace.

Identify and then replace any of the negative thoughts that you have

Many people who struggle with small talk and social interactions may also have a lot of negative thoughts about themselves as a result of this. This is particularly true if the person has difficulty because of intense shyness or social anxiety, and they may assume that no one likes them, that they are going to say something "stupid", or that they will just end up embarrassing themselves. The biggest problem with constantly entertaining these ideas is that they can become a self-fulfilling prophecy.

For example, it is harmful to tell yourself: "I'm so awkward, if I go to the party, no one will want to talk to me or I will just end up embarrassing myself." Because of these negative thoughts and the desire to avoid being embarrassed, you may just sit in the corner alone for the whole party. Then, when you leave, you will think that it must be true that you are too awkward, because no one talked to you all night.

If you want to get better at your social skills and learn how to communicate well with others, you need to learn how to get rid of these unhealthy thinking patterns. Start by identifying the negative thoughts that are dragging you down. Once you have found those, you can work on replacing them with other more positive and realistic thoughts, which will help to build your confidence instead.

By making these changes, you get to control your own destiny. Instead of thinking that you are awkward and certain to make mistakes, you can start out with a little pep talk to get through each social situation. For example, the next time that you go out to a social event, start out by telling yourself "I can make friendly conversation and I can meet new people."

It is so important that you don't allow yourself to dwell on unproductive thoughts that work against you and the change you want to inspire in your life. If a thought makes you feel bad about yourself, or keeps you from socializing with others, then it is destructive and should be challenged.

Having a good set of social skills is so essential when it comes to being an effective communicator. Great social skills are not easy, and everyone experiences awkwardness sometimes. You have to keep trying and keep putting yourself out there, even if you do happen to fail. You will get better over time, and these social skills can serve you well for your whole life. It's never too late to start trying some of these suggestions to help you change the way you see yourself, as you learn to communicate with ease.

Conclusion

Thank you for making it through to the end of *Small Talk: A Shy Introverts Guide to Being More Likeable and Building Better Relationships, Even If You Have Social Anxiety, Including Conversation Starters and Tips for Improving Your Social Skills*. Let's hope it was informative and able to provide you with all of the tools you need to achieve your goals—whatever they may be.

The next step is to start putting some of these tips and tricks to good use and see what a difference they can make in your communication skills with others. As a shy introvert, it can sometimes be difficult to talk with others and form some of the meaningful connections that you are looking for. You may want to make friends, but socializing can exhaust you, which makes it unappealing to go out, and if you are also shy, your fear can hold you hostage when you really want to be out and making friends. You do need to take the time to recharge your batteries before social encounters, which means that any socialization you do participate in needs to count, but you also need to build up the skills and ability to overcome your fears and negative self-talk as well.

Small talk may not be something that introverts really enjoy doing, but it is something that forms a basis for all great relationships. This guidebook has all the tips that you need to really become an expert at small talk, and to get it to work for you. By applying the principles explained in this book, you can take control of your life and learn not only to communicate effectively, but to find joy in social interactions.

By the time that you are done implementing these suggestions, you will be an expert at small talk and be able to wow anyone at your next social gathering, even as a shy introvert.

Part 4: Body Language

Unlocking the Secrets of Nonverbal Communication of an Alpha Male and Female, Including How to Analyze People, Improve Your Social Skills, and Develop Charisma

Introduction

The following chapters will discuss how successful people, specifically those noted as alphas, communicate with body language. What makes people take notice? What is it about them that communicates power? This book will discuss what it means to be an alpha and what makes them winners in whatever they do. It is a description of their characteristics and traits and how they impact others through nonverbal communication--from how they walk, stand, hold their hands, head movements, and facial expressions to what each of their movements means. What an alpha does draws attention, response, and action on the part of others.

Alpha traits and characteristics are not gender-isolated. Men and women both can be alphas. After reading this book, you will be able to identify one. If you desire to become an alpha, this is the book for you. You will learn how to emulate the body language of an alpha. You can change your current direction. How to be a charmer in social situations by using the appropriate actions or expressions is explained. Ever wanted to impress a special someone with charisma? How to be memorable at work? How to get the recognition you deserve?

Build your confidence and learn how to communicate with your presence. Discover the techniques needed to acquire these skills. This book will educate you about the characteristics and traits of alphas and the communication of body language. It will also be informative, and you will learn practical applications of techniques to learn and apply the characteristics and traits outlined in this book.

Chapter 1: What Is An "Alpha" And Why Are They Winners?

What is an alpha in our society (male and female)?

Alpha is the top dog. He is the one who walks in and everyone pays attention. The popular assumption is that an alpha is assertive, a go-getter, no-nonsense, a high achiever, and someone who is well-respected. He is a leader, not a follower. As an alpha, whether male or female, the personality traits are strong and direct.

Ethology is the study of animal behavior. It focuses on an animal's behavior when it is under natural conditions. An ethologist will investigate what behaviors are inherited by natural occurrence versus learned behaviors.

The ethologist's primary focus is to study animals to ascertain what causes their behavior and how they mature and change. They theorize the effects of such behavior on and with other animals and in various settings. The data gained from such studies is used to better understand the biological impact in other circumstances such as the human experience. As the alpha wolf male, dominance theory is the male leadership's role.

"Alphaness" is a term used to describe personality traits which dominate behaviors. It is fundamentally a part of a person's genetics as well as their persona. If you are innately assertive, and it runs in the family, then this, by genetics, is a family attribute. However, if you are not, you can develop these leadership skills by dedicating yourself to learning and incorporating the techniques that are outlined in this book.

Being an alpha does not mean you must possess all the traits, but as an alpha, you may have some variation of them. An alpha may be confident and strong but not very curious. Nor will all aspects of character be of the same strength.

Greater in Some Area and Less in Others

Everyone possesses these traits to a lesser or greater gradation. Dominance is a factor of alphaness. There is not a clear distinction, but rather it's more about the merging of influence and conveyed behaviors.

Okay, so let's get down to business. What are the characteristics of an alpha?

Confident

This is the self-assured, self-reliant, and poised person. They never second-guess themselves.

Competitive

Always in it to win it. Being the best is the main priority. They are driven to be on top.

Presence

When they walk in a room, they draw attention. Their presence causes others to take notice. How they walk, talk, stand, and use other aspects of their body language contribute to their presence.

Dominant

They are in charge and maintain control. They give directions and are straightforward. They assume command whenever needed.

Risk-taker

They understand that you must take a chance to get what you want.

Alphas are a draw for the opposite sex

Alphas are not afraid to communicate their interest in someone.

Vocal

He will speak up and express what he has to say. He has confidence in the knowledge he has.

Strong Eye Contact

He will maintain good eye contact and will be the last to look away. He understands the power of eye contact and how to appropriately use it. He shows confidence and dominance.

Cool Under Pressure

He reacts appropriately under pressure. He does not faint in stressful situations. He recognizes that as a leader, you must show strength even in the most challenging times.

Appearance

Dress the part. The exterior is a validation of who they desire to be.

Prominence

They don't mind being noticed. They will do what they want and do not care what others think. Approval is not necessary.

Ability to Disagree

Alpha doesn't mind saying no. There is no apprehension of possible outcomes or consequences.

They also know how to persevere, are determined and driven. They are resolved to achieve success.

What makes the alpha a winner?

Alphas are winners because of the combination of traits and how they use them to make failure unlikely. Leadership is the ability to control the direction things should go. And because of this trait, others follow instinctively. Most people around them adore them. Personal relationships and acquaintances serve as their fan club. Almost anything needed would be complied with. Their popularity draws in followers.

They have the ability to be innovative. They tend to be creative and resourceful to resolve possible difficulties. Their charm and charisma is attractive and rewarding and makes others feel good and welcomed. Their confidence allows them to accept challenging opportunities. This can-do attitude is what helps them to achieve success. Their confidence allows them to be dominant even in social environments. Their ambitious nature drives them to realize their dreams and desires, and their competitive spirit pushes them to be their best. They also have the ability to maintain control. They do not need someone else's approval to take action. They are able to make hard decisions. Their inner voice is their motivation and sense of what's right or wrong. Confidence within and acceptance that you cannot please everyone give them a free spirit.

What separates them from non-alphas?

They do not back down, they take chances and are not afraid of risks. Whereas, non-alphas look for what is comfortable and generally accepted.

Posture will infer strength, confidence, and position in the pack. 'You know your alphaness.' Standing tall and straight sends a message of confidence and strength. Alphas usually have their heads up, shoulders back, feet slightly apart, and looking forward. This is a strong powerful stance that projects an Alpha attitude. When they are sitting, they sit back and relax, arms apart, and for guys, legs apart (man spreading).

The implications of posture in understanding body language are prodigious. It speaks volumes. You can impact how you are perceived by fine-tuning your physical aspects such as how you stand, sit, and walk. By doing these, you can add power to your presence.

Interestingly, posture has an impact even when someone is not particularly close. A person's posture can be seen or recognized at a distance. Therefore, they can be recognized by others in proximity. Your posture lets everyone know who you are.

It is also an unconscious expression of who we believe we are and our response to the environment we are in. Consider what message your posture is sending.

Alphas smile less. Smiling is considered a subordinate behavior. A person who smiles a lot sends the message of insecurity, nervousness, or subordinate expression. Historically, women were taught that if you are nervous in an uncomfortable situation, just smile. This is recognized as the "peacemakers" behavior, submissive, or passive. Ever noticed when a boss enters a room, everyone smiles at him/her, and the boss is the only one not smiling? An appropriate smile at the right time can be advantageous. Facial expressions are a major factor in body language. Whether a smile or an austere appearance, the appropriate action or response could make the difference and produce amazing results. Body language is the ability to speak without saying a word. And as an alpha, the others pick up on the unspoken language of strength and leadership.

Alphas tend to interrupt others because people naturally quiet down when they begin to speak. It is within. They do not mind interrupting when they feel they have something to say. They have vociferous energy which prompts others to instinctively take heed. They have a base tone of confidence. It is not necessarily the words spoken, but the tone and strength in which the words are spoken. It is in the delivery. Ironically, they may not even know they are doing it. A non-alpha will wait for an opportunity to break-in or approval to speak.

The eye contact of an alpha communicates confidence, power, and strength. It is an important part of body language communication. This is how we communicate with others aside from talking. Body language says more than mere words can and represents a major portion of our ability to communicate. So much is said just with the eyes. An alpha engages in more eye contact when talking to someone. An alpha will maintain persistent eye contact as they exchange communication. This is a sign of strength and confidence. However, they will maintain eye contact less when you are talking to them. They seem distracted or otherwise occupied when someone else is speaking.

It has been said that the eyes are the windows to the soul. It is a general perception that being able to maintain eye contact with someone is an indication of trustworthiness. The lack of good eye contact or the diverting of the eyes is an indication of dishonesty. Have you noticed when watching any of the police or detective programs how when the detective interrogates someone and they divert their eyes and look down to the side, the detective always asks what are they hiding? In the interpretation of body language, eye contact conveys to others trustworthiness. It is very likely for someone to build trust with a person with whom they can maintain eye contact in communication. A non-alpha may struggle with strong visual communication. They are usually the first to look away or down to the side.

Body language is an unconscious delivery and reception communiqué. What you do, how you walk, how you position yourself, the expression on your face, and so many other gestures send a message to others about you. Your body language sends a message to those around you about who you are. As a compilation of gestures, our body language articulates what we think or feel without conscious intent. We do not realize we are doing most of our movements and gestures . Yet, we are sending subliminal messages. Do you wonder what message you are sending? Are you receiving the response you desire when you walk into a room? When you speak, do others listen? Do you maintain eye contact with others? Do they divert their eyes from you when you are speaking? These are a few questions you might consider when determining what message you are sending with your body language. How you move or position your body can accentuate and strengthen what you are saying or draw out the desired response from others.

If you learn to interpret body language, you can understand the unspoken message and be able to distinguish inconsistencies in the actions of others. Have you ever noticed when you ask a person a question and the answer yes, but the head is moving from side to side as if to answer no? This is an inconsistency between the spoken word and their body language. This is a sign that what that person is saying is not how they really feel. So, having the ability to understand the unspoken message through body language will aid you in becoming the person you desire.

When looking at body language, consider the basic types such as facial expression, posture, eye contact, proximity, and gestures. Communication is made without a word spoken through these actions or non-actions. Volumes can be said simply by an expression of the face. In children, when a parent gave that look, the child would freeze in their steps, stop whatever they were doing, and respond without the parent ever saying a word. Many have expressed meeting that special someone by the words "our eyes met across a crowded room." Again, not a word was said, but the message was received. Or what about when someone walks into a room, standing tall, and their presence commanded everyone's attention? The room turns quiet, and all the attention is on that person. Their posture and presence conveyed the message of their importance. Understanding how each of these kinds of expression communicates a message will help to empower you to create the presence you desire.

Having a posture of strength is shown by standing still. Constant movement and fidgeting is a sign of nervousness. This movement is communicated as insecurity, lack of confidence, and inferiority. An alpha tends to stand still. They conserve energy. They move purposefully. Standing still shows power. Stand still with shoulders back and chest out. This signifies that you are confident and in charge. Alternatively, a non-alpha will tend to fidget, move around nervously, and show signs of being uncomfortable.

Nodding is the "bobblehead effect". This is another sign of insecurity. Leaders hold their head still as they speak. The ability to speak without moving your head shows assurance and confidence in the knowledge you are sharing. Be still and proud.

Non-alphas may watch a person of romantic interest from afar, while an alpha will approach without hesitation.

The next question is to how these traits impact you in the workplace, social environments, and your individual relationships. An alpha learns how to modify their characteristics in their day-to-day living.

In Business

Alphas are better in business because of the no-nonsense attitude and the calculated risks they take to achieve what it is they are looking for. Business is of a competitive nature. The alpha is someone who always wants to climb higher. Because of their natural leadership abilities, people tend to be comfortable around them. They have an elevated expectation for themselves and their work production. Business matters are approached from an ethical and profitable manner. Emotions do not interfere in business. Their audacity as risk takers is critical in business decisions. They make the appropriate choices at the right time. A never-give-up attitude drives them to the goal line. They know their faults and accept imperfections, but do not allow them to hinder their progress. They also understand that having a good attitude is important. Their attitude impacts others around them. Maintaining a positive attitude will influence others to do the same. This leadership quality is a magnet for those who desire to excel. Their positive approach emits confidence and causes others around them to perform on an equal level.

In Romance

Communication consists of more than just the words we say. How people see you and what they hear are often more about non-verbal communication. Communication is 55% body language, 7% words, and 38% vocal tones. The major portion of communications are from body language, next is the tone in which we speak, and the least important is the words we say.

When it comes to the interpretation of body language, women have the advantage. Men are less likely to pick up cues than the fairer sex. Studies have shown that it takes approximately 3 interactions or clues before the man recognizes the message that is being sent.

In romance, it is quite similar to the business attitude. The risk taken is seen as a take-charge attitude and a heightened level of confidence. This is attractive and draws the attention of the opposite sex.

They are usually not nervous or anxious in social situations because of their self-awareness and belief in themselves. They possess good qualities and are self-confident. They do not doubt their worthiness for partnership and are attractive to the opposite sex.

In Social life

Alphas are leaders in the pack, and others don't hesitate to follow. This is the decision-maker for the party. The ability to take charge is alluring and draws respect from those around them. They are well-respected, and their opinion is valued. A major part of communication is to be a good listener. As a leader of the group, you must also dress the part. A presentation is an important part of the package. Elegance, flair, and style along with posture and presence send the message of confidence and strength. It sends the right communication through body language. They have earned the respect of others, because they treat the opposite sex fairly. They are confident and do not show fear. They are assertive and engaging with others in social settings

Chapter 2: The Alpha Male: How to Spot One

These are famous alpha men that many will recognize and know their alpha characteristics. You may imagine how it must be to have such presence and power. They are strong, interesting, intelligent, and have command of the room whenever they walk in.

- Barack Obama
- Brad Pitt
- George Clooney
- Bill Clinton
- Denzel Washington
- Clint Eastwood
- Chuck Norris

Everyone is greeting each other and sharing pleasantries. While it is an enjoyable atmosphere, there is nothing exciting. Then, you notice an elevation of voices, greetings with a little more enthusiasm. In walks the alpha male. He has great posture. He stands straight when he walks. Notice how his shoulders are squared. His chest is raised but not puffed out. As he enters, he smiles when he greets someone and tilts his head slightly to show interest when listening. He reaches out and grasps your hand with a firm handshake. He has great eye contact. He knows how to maintain a persistent connection without looking away or downward. He is assertive and has a dominant persona. This guy has natural leadership skills; he just seems to flow without a struggle. He is courageous and appears to be physically strong. He is curious, ambitious, and independent. These are characteristics of someone we all know.

An alpha is aware that he is in command. He is not looking to impress anyone, except that special someone of the opposite sex. How can you identify the alpha in the room?

He is thronged by everyone around him. He is welcomed when he enters the room, and others offer him a seat. He draws attention and respect without utterance of words. Others may feel mediocre in his presence. The opposite sex is attracted to him.

President Barack Obama is an alpha male. When he stands before an audience, he stands with his feet slightly apart, and at times, places his hands on his hip.

This is a posture that's taking up space. With his hands on his hip and his elbows protruding outward, it gives him the appearance of being larger. This posture contributes to him standing erect and tall. His chest is pushed out and proud. His dominant posture is recognized by those around him. His body language says he is in charge, and everyone recognizes him as a leader.

How can you use your hands for nonverbal interaction? Gestures made with the hands can say a lot about you. A strong handshake is a symbol of strength. By extending the hand with the palm facing up sends the message of dominance, because your hand is on top which means you are on top. The palms facing up signify that you are asking for something or that you acknowledge the other person's advantage. When you clasp your hands together, it can be translated in a few different ways. It can mean that you are taking a posture of power or confidence, or it may also indicate nervousness depending on what else is happening at the time.

Hand gestures of leaders include steeple hands, when the fingers touch at the top and form a pyramid shape. Often, with the hand in front of the mouth looking as if in deep thought or concentration. This unspoken action transmits a confident and poised attitude. Ever notice the hands behind the back? This gesture, while it may be used in stressful circumstances when contemplating choices, portrays the authority look.

An Alpha male is assertive, not aggressive. He has a presence of refinement. He seems to be able to manage in any arena. He does not mind not always being right, but failure is not an option. He is very intelligent and knowledgeable. How others see him is not a major concern, because he believes in himself. He is aware of his abilities and is ambitious and a go-getter. As a gentleman, he can disagree without conflict, but he is not afraid of opposition. He is competent in his profession and aims to be the best. He does not have to blow his own horn.

He is admired by many and recognized for his excellence. He understands that much of the communication with him is through his body language. How you interact with others impacts how they respond to you. Your body will communicate things that you do not say in words. Studies have shown that more than 90 percent of communication is through body language. What you are saying is only a part of the communication process. Your expression, your tone, your eyes, and gestures are all just a part of the total conversation.

How do you take on these characteristics of an alpha male when you don't feel like one? You can change your situation and take control of how you are perceived. Here are a few key acts of a confident, poised, and powerful alpha male.

- Take up space
- Set feet about shoulder-width apart
- Stand tall and straight
- Shoulders back, chest forward
- Head held high
- Good eye contact, no looking down
- No fidgeting
- Do not cross arms
- No hands in the pocket
- Do not hold things in front as if to block
- Have an open position
- Face out to the room
- Walk slow and with purpose
- Do not rush or appear anxious

The alpha male is represented sometimes as aggressive and

domineering. However, this is not an alpha male. He is not one who needs to tell others he is the alpha. A true alpha male knows who he is and his ability to influence others. He has a natural following of other males and the attention of females.

Consider the features of body language and how they influence your communication. Eye contact from an alpha male says that he is confident. It also lets the person whom he is looking at know that they have his attention. Their eye contact alone is not the total conversation. The face expresses how he feels or interprets what is being said. The face can say many things and may contradict the words that come from the mouth. As an alpha male showing strength, maintaining good eye contact is a must. Also, facial expressions should also convey the message of confidence and strength.

The posture of the alpha male is tall and erect, with shoulders back and head held high. His gestures should be at a minimum. No erratic movements. He lets every movement have a purpose. All the features of body language, while taken singly, may convey one message, but taken as a whole, make a totally different conversation.

It is normal for a man to desire to be an alpha male. How do you convert this desire into a reality in your life? One of the benefits of this conversion is being the prime focus of others in the group. Having a following of admirers, fans, and devotees is another desired benefit. The alpha male has the ability to draw and influence others. This is a powerful position to be in.

He has a charismatic flair which is influential to both men and women and is a crowd puller for those within and without his social circle. He has an alluring personality. Social preeminence is acknowledged by those in connection to the group and those outside the group. Prestige is associated with his presence.

They show devotion and camaraderie from others who follow. People tend to follow those who possess the in-charge personality. The attitude of devotion and camaraderie is proffered with availability for your desired purpose. He has the privilege of preference. This is the opportunity to be the first to enjoy privileges. Alpha males receive the privilege of having priority over others, being the first to partake.

He is also afforded the power to make decisions on behalf of the group. This includes both making the decision and having the first and final say in what is to be done. Much weight is given to his opinion. Everyone seeks his advice on what should be done, and when all has been discussed, looks for his opinion to finalize what will be done.

Becoming an alpha male does not just happen. There is some labor involved. To be the alpha, you must show that you have what it takes. You must exhibit superior qualities above others. Understand that, as with animal tribes, there is always one to challenge the alpha. He must be able to produce the characteristics that prove he's the alpha male. He cannot be intimidated by others and must show his strength and dominance.

In developing your "alphaness," consider the following suggestions:

Have Confidence: Know that you are the leader. Don't be anxious. If you believe in yourself, others will also. You must project this confidence. Don't wait for permission. Just do it.

Appearance: Be your best self. This is how you look and present yourself. Show your qualities as an alpha male. Be conscientious about your appearance. As a leader, your appearance should stand out as such. This includes how you walk, stand, grooming, body language, and clothes.

Be in Charge: Use your confidence and decision-making skills and take the initiative.

Respect: Be able to disagree and say so, but respect your opponent. You are no-nonsense and command respect from others. You do not withdraw from the encounter.

Boundaries: You know what is important. Making friends is not your first priority. Doing the right thing is the premier.

Listen: Hear what is being said and communicate.

Stand out: Be the life of the party. Be the person that stands out more than the others. Socialize with the gathering; introduce yourself to new people. Introduce those in your group. Participate in events at the function. Be outgoing and involved.

Watch others: If you want to learn how to be an alpha male, watch the actions of other alpha males and learn by example.

Work well with the opposite sex: Be confident and pleasant with women. Know how to interact appropriately without getting out of bounds. Understand the limits and boundaries. Be respectful and courteous.

Alpha doesn't say he's the alpha male. If you have to say you are alpha, you are not an alpha. Your presence will speak for you. Believe that you are and walk in that authority.

Temperament: Maintain control. Be composed. Don't castigate others. Knowing how to disagree and take control of situations are a part of the leadership quality of an alpha. Learn to demonstrate discontentment without being hostile or antagonistic.

An alpha male knows the power position. He knows where to stand and be seated to be in a powerful position. They are the head at the head of the table or the leader in the middle of a group setting.

Take stock of your strengths and weaknesses. Consider what message you are sending. Are you an alpha male, or do you want to be? As you read further, you will learn what it takes to become an alpha and how to do it. Alpha male personality traits include being assertive, dominant, a natural leader, protective, courageous, strong, and curious. Other characteristics include ambition, independence, sensitivity, presence, and being vocal, and competitive.

Chapter 3: The Alpha Female: How to Spot One

How do alpha males and females differ and how are they similar?

The alpha female is similar to male because she is confident in her abilities and takes charge of herself. She is comfortable in her own skin. What others think of her is not a major focus. She knows how to dress to impress and has a commanding presence. She is a leader not a follower and has the expectation that others will follow her. She, like her male counterpart, is intelligent and knowledgeable. As an alpha personality, she projects integrity, principles, and devotion. The competitive nature of an alpha is a part of her character. While confident and self-assured, she is not egocentric. Her opinion is expressed freely even when not solicited. She is not afraid of the possibilities before her; in fact, she welcomes them. Others are captivated by her charm. The male knows what he wants and goes after it and invariably, so does the female.

She is not aggressive but assertive. The alpha male is not a jerk but is confident, masculine and a go-getter, friendly, considerate, and respectful. He attracts females with his sophisticated charm. Physical strength, prowess, and social intelligence epitomize his gracefulness. He is a lover, not a fighter. He demonstrates his alphaness through inner confidence and how he handles himself. These attributes are shared both in male and females.

They differ, however, in how their body language is interpreted and how well they can interpret the body language of the opposite sex. Men are less likely to catch body language clues than women.

Because women have been conditioned over time to be responsive to the needs of others, they tend to be more attentive to nonverbal messages. So, women are 3 times more likely to pick up on nonverbal messages given than their male counterpart.

The Traits of an Alpha Female and What to Look for When Trying to Spot One

Oprah Winfrey is the ultimate alpha female. She is a take-charge woman who knows what she wants. Making a mistake is not her fear. She is not apologetic for seeking what she desires. Some may feel threatened by her no-nonsense attitude. She has the attention and respect of other women and they look to her for leadership. These are some of the characteristics of an alpha female.

She is usually highly successful, self-reliant, and self-confident. She is often referred to as a queen. Beyoncé is a perfect example. She is referred to as Queen Bee and she has such a following that they refer to themselves as the hive.

This emphatic nature is the power behind her push. She is driven and comfortable in negotiations. Her motivation is to achieve her desire. She has an assigned destiny and she is determined to accomplish it.

Equivalent To Male Counterpart

Her abilities are not conditioned based on anything other than her own actions. She is intelligent, strong, and confident. She is not intimidated by the opinions of others. She does not accept the limitation of gender and believes that her success does not inhibit others, but rather encourages or inspires them. She does not put men on a higher pedestal, but as equal co-conspirators. She is not the persecuted princess or the maiden in jeopardy, nor is she a helpless female who needs a man to rescue her.

Decisive not Passive

She can and will make decisions based on her evaluation of the circumstances, whether it is a business decision or one of a personal nature. Just because she is female does not diminish her proficiency. She takes the initiative and is a risk-taker.

Knows Who She Is

She knows her assets and deficits. She knows how to accentuate her strengths. She is not afraid of being herself. She is independent, authoritative, and open-minded. She has the freedom to express her femininity or not. She is not pigeon-holed by stereotypes.

Famous women who personify female "alphaness" are Oprah Winfrey, Michelle Obama, Hillary Clinton, Mariska Hargitay, and Beyoncé. These women are alpha females . They are admired, respected, solicited for advice, and have leadership. When they enter a room, they command attention. Other women replicate their style and mimic their attitude and tone. Even with other women, the attentive look and subtle touch make others feel noticed and appreciated.

The most prominent person in a grouping is often referenced as an alpha personality. This could be male or female.

Female alphas are "social conductors" and non-alphas are "her orchestra". She is the leader and the others follow. A behaviorist will note that women will point their feet in the direction of the person they are most interested in or that they feel is leading the group whether the person is talking or not, even if in a circle.

Olivia Pope is a female alpha. She is strong, intelligent, deliberate, and successful. Her followers look to her for direction. She is the "fixer." Alpha men also respect her decisions. Olivia does not care what others think about her or her choices. Even in romance, she draws attention and is sought after. And her decision in romance is hers and hers alone. She is comfortable in her own skin. She knows what she wants and does not mind going after it.

When in the company of other women, the non-alphas all follow the alpha's social cues. They imitate or mimic her actions. Non-alpha women will join the grouping with the alpha female. They will alter their posture and position their body to be more like her. When she laughs, they will imitate her laugh in tone and length. Whenever the female alpha exits the scene, a "social vacuum effect" takes place.

There is a noticeable absence of her presence. Non-alpha women are at a loss until someone else takes her place. There, however, can only be one female alpha in a grouping. When there is more than one, there may be uproar in an attempt to be on top. This may bring to mind an episode of "Housewives", but don't be confused. That diva attitude is not a part of her personality. An alpha female is not a diva. She is distinguished in her independence. She does not have time for nonsense and does not show a negative attitude. And she is absolutely not a damsel in distress. Whereas there cannot be more than one alpha in one grouping, there must be at least one. With an alpha female, there is some gaucheness in her absence. In a business setting, she is the facilitator, and in a social setting, she is the one who puts everyone at ease. She makes whatever setting she is in flow. She is the social butterfly, a great communicator, has humor, and is a problem solver. She knows how to take charge.

Understanding her also means being able to pick up on her nonverbal cues. This begins with her gaze. How she looks at you will help you interpret the unspoken communication she gives with her eyes. In a business environment, eye contact conveys confidence and trust. In a social setting, she is engaged and interested in the conversation. And in a romantic setting, her eye contact or lack of it is an indication whether she likes you or is disinterested.

A simple smile and lifting of the eyebrow while looking says she is interested and there are possibilities. Or, if she licks her lip while looking, this is also a sign of interest. Other signs of interest include playing with her hair while engaged in conversation, or that "come hither" look. That is accomplished by looking back over the shoulder. The body speaks subconsciously when we are happy, interested, disappointed, and aroused. Without thought, she will, when interested in someone, move closer to them. On a date, she reaches out and touches. This is a sign of attraction. But if she crosses her arms and legs or moves away, this is a sign of disinterest. Interestingly, she will imitate the actions of the person she is interested in.

More Nonverbal Expressions of Interest

If a woman repositions herself closer, she's indicating that she is welcoming your touch.

- Rubs her legs
- Reaches out to touch you
- Nodding her head 3 times while listening
- Pushes glass close to yours
- Confident posture
- Face-to-face position

- Tone of voice – pitch slightly elevated

These are all nonverbal clues that she is interested. This is an indication of a desire to know someone better. If a woman looks temptingly at your drink and she is without, this means she desires one. There are many silent indicators that we are attentive and we can better communicate and understand others.

First impressions

> Availability–smiling, uncrossed arms, uncrossed legs, and upward gazing (not looking down or at shoes)

Fertility

> Men - standing up straight, squaring the shoulders, planting feet slightly more than shoulder-width apart and displaying hands are signs of fertility

> Women- keeping hair down, tilting her head to expose pheromones, and keeping hands and wrists visible to display the soft skin of the wrist are highly attractive for men.

Attraction

> Lean in--nonverbal way of telling they are interested. Subconsciously pulls them toward you

> Head tilting--shows interest and engagement

The signs of body language

- Flushed and blushed
- The redder the lips and whiter the eyes, the more fertile and attractive someone is.

Power of the purse

> A purse is an interesting indicator of nonverbal behavior

> She holds on tightly to her purse when not interested.

Feet pointed towards a person

> This is an indicator of attraction.

Make eye contact

> Shows you are interested and confident.

Good posture

>Stand tall, be confident, but at ease.

Be Cool

>Display a "cool, calm, and collected" attitude. Be confident.

Heads up

>Look up; do not move around looking down.

No hands in pocket

>Don't put your hands in your pockets

Converse

>Be smooth in conversation. Talk at a natural pace and tone. Don't talk in a rushed manner, too loud, or a lot of nonsense.

Facial expression

>Smile. This is a welcoming expression.

Are you an Alpha female?

Do you feel like you are always in the limelight? You are confident and everyone wants your advice and direction. You are the go-to person. At work and social settings, you keep things going. You are driven with determination and perseverance. You are goal-oriented and live a purpose-driven life. You are an overcomer and overachiever. You stand alone many times and do not fear this isolation. You are not afraid of romance but not defined by it as well.

Balance is important to you, so you try to maintain it in all facets of your existence. You choose to be your best self. Your fulfillment is in your accomplishments. Physical, spiritual, and mental health is important in order to be superior. Intellectual greatness is achieved, because you continue to learn and seek wisdom and knowledge. You are admired because of your tenacity, that never-give-up attitude.

Do you welcome change? While others tend to resist and become anxious at the thought of change, you welcome it. The change represents growth and advancement. You can recognize opportunity when it does not appear transparent. Sacrifice is a part of your growth and an investment in your future. While many admire you, you are also misconstrued. But you are a strong woman, and able to move forward.

Are you unapologetic about what you believe? Your confidence and integrity make it possible for you to be strong and courageous. You are not motivated to fit the mold created by others. Nor are you motivated by the opinions of others. You are a risk-taker and believe you can achieve only if you are willing to take the risks.

If these qualities describe you, you are an alpha female. If they do not, you can adopt them as a part of your character, and you can become that alpha woman.

Chapter 4: Body Language in Social Situations: How to Charm

In a social gathering with colleagues and senior executives, introduce yourself or get to know them better. Be careful not to get too relaxed. Limit drinks to one. Try to embody the message you want to deliver. Let your body speak for you. Be pleasant, welcoming, and at ease. By standing tall with your shoulders back and your head high, your body language is one of confidence and strong self-esteem. Keep in mind that your posture sends the message of strength or weakness, confidence, or intimidation and self-esteem or self-doubt.

Greet party guests with a handshake and a smile. Your posture should show that you are at ease and comfortable. Show that you are accessible by adopting an open position. Your legs should be slightly apart roughly equivalent to your shoulders. Your arms should be relaxed at your side. Avoid crossed arms and legs. You are sending a closed off message.

Look at the person you are speaking to. Eye contact is essential in both nonverbal and verbal communication. It helps to send the message you desire. It shows that you are interested, paying attention, and listening. Leaning in also enhances engagement. When leaning in, be careful not to invade another's personal space. If when you lean in and they lean back, you have moved in too close. In a social setting, you should not get closer than 18 inches. Your arm movements should be kept at or below shoulders. Your gestures should not look as though you do not have control.

Remember, your posture, how you stand, and how you walk is extremely important. When you enter a room, check yourself first. Be well-groomed. Hygiene is imperative. This is your hair, teeth, breath, and clothes. Dress nicely and appropriately for the occasion. Next, gather your thoughts and have the right mindset. Know where you are going and why. Ok, you are groomed, dressed, and have your thoughts together. Breathe and relax. Stand up straight, shoulders back, and relaxed stride. Don't walk too fast but be confident. You are in control. Move as though you are the center of attention.

Now, how do you introduce yourself?

- Make eye contact - interested and engaged
- Smile - welcoming and friendly
- Good posture - body language should convey confidence.
- Handshake - firm but not gripping
- Greet others and shake hands and move around the room.

How do you become the alpha you desire to be? As the old saying goes, "practice makes perfect". Recognize alpha qualities in others. If there is an alpha that you admire, study their actions and how they move. Also, recognize how others respond to them. If you want to be an alpha, act like an alpha. Take on these characteristics. Fake it till you make it.

At home, rehearse the characteristics you desire to incorporate. Use the mirror to practice your facial expressions and your posture. Let famous alphas such as George Clooney and Mariska Hargitay be your inspiration. Make different facial expressions and tweak them to convey the look you are aiming for. Looking in the mirror, stand straight, shoulders back, and head high. Imagine yourself as the alpha. At the same time, make positive affirmations. Take on the attitude and believe that you are. Envision yourself as an alpha-- strong, confident, and the center of attention.

Below are some affirmations to practice for males and females. Recite these affirmations daily. Say them while standing at the mirror practicing your stand, posture, and facial expressions. You can also recite these affirmations throughout your day. It is a boost of confidence if you repeat them just before entering a room, meeting, or situation where you want to shine.

I am an alpha.

I am strong.

I am dominant.

I am a leader.

I am always at ease and calm.

I am assertive and powerful.

Others perceive I am powerful and self-assured.

I am confident.

The opposite sex is very attracted to me.

I can take the lead in any social situation.

I am totally secure in myself.

I speak with power and influence.

I am attractive to the opposite sex.

Make an entrance

    Be well-groomed, bathe, shave, brush your teeth, use a deodorant, apply makeup or not, hair cut or styled, and clean nails.

Dress appropriately.

    Don't be too trendy, be comfortable in your choice, and pick a statement piece.

Enter with confidence

    Stand straight, smile, and avoid looking down or slumping or fidgeting

Bring a gift for the host

    Shows appreciation and others will notice your thoughtfulness

Greet people you recognize

    Greet the host.

    If you don't know anyone, introduce yourself.

Be confident

    Use positive affirmations

Make a good impression with body language

    Firm handshake

    Lean in or point legs and feet toward the person you are talking to

    Relaxed posture

    Widen stance to show confidence

    No crossing arms or fidgeting

    No fiddling with the phone

    No looking bored

    Make good eye contact

    Smile not nervously, but genuinely

    Breathe deep

Don't be a space invader

    The proximity of your body when you are standing near someone can express more than just your level of confidence. Proxemics is defined as the study of how space is interpreted by people in terms of distance, nature, and impact and the relational bearing on the environment and culture. The allocation and tolerance of spatial distance are unique to each person depending on their personal history.

However, there is a general consensus based on basic relationship statuses. The variations of relationships which are impacted by proxemics are intimate, personal, social, and public. Each has an acceptable distance which allows a certain amount of space or closeness. Also, these variations may differ from one culture to another. Because of cultural differences, sometimes body language can be misunderstood.

In today's culturally diverse society, it is critical to take into consideration the scope of nonverbal signals as expressed in different ethnic groups. When someone infringes upon a proper spatial distance, others may feel awkward or uneasy. Their actions may well be open to misinterpretation.

The Four Major Classifications of Proxemics

- Intimate space (touching – 18 inches)
- Personal space (18 inches -48 inches)
- Social space (4 ft-12ft)
- Public space (12ft - 15ft)

These four distances are in coordination to the four types of relationships namely intimate, personal, social, and the public.

Intimate space:

This is the space between those of close personal relationships. It ranges from touching to 18 inches. This is the utmost intimate region because it is reserved for those of the closest relation. This is dedicated to special people such as the beloved, familiar, and adored.

Personal space:

This is conversation space, usually from 18 inches to 48 inches. This is the distance where it is comfortable to communicate, make eye contact, and observe facial expressions. This is close enough to shake hands and reflect on other body languages. This is also the friend zone, which is acceptable for social gatherings such as parties and friendly exchanges.

Social Space:

This is an impersonal business space. This is the normal distance for working in the same room or during social gatherings. The appropriate distance is 4 feet to 12 feet. This is also appropriate for acquaintances and people you may have recently met. If you do not have an established relationship with someone, this is the appropriate space.

Public Space:

This is a speaker's space. The room allowance is 12 feet to 15 feet. This is the spatial distance suitable for teachers, public speakers, or group presentations. Nonverbal communications are used such as extreme gestures to ensure they can be seen at a distance. Facial expressions cannot be seen or interpreted in this arena. There is usually an audience such as a large group of people at this distance.

Utilizing the proper spatial distance is complimentary to the other forms of body language and helps to improve communications. Also, understanding these parameters will help in interpreting nonverbal communications when someone stands closely or at a distance.

Chapter 5: Body Language in Dating: How to Impress with Charisma

You have just met an interesting woman, and it seems as though you may have some things in common. You have never gone out before, and you want to make a good impression.

George Clooney is the ultimate alpha male. He makes no excuses for being himself. He is handsome, dresses well, has a presence when he stands or walks, and he makes eye contact that makes the girls swoon. He was chosen twice as People magazine's cover as the sexiest man alive. Do you want to be an alpha like George? You know, the one who gets the girl and the one who every girl wished she had?

How do you get there?

George Clooney presents himself in a cool, relaxed, confident, and graceful manner. You have an expectation of greatness. If you are in his inner circle, you feel privileged. How do you achieve this status?

Analyze his body language. What is it that he does that makes people, both male and female, recognize him as the alpha in the room? What is it that you can do to model this attitude? If you desire to be the alpha in the room and attract that girl, there are a few things you must do.

First, you must take on and accept the posture and presence that says you are relaxed and confident. As stated previously, how you stand

and how you walk is important. Be tall and erect, shoulders back, and chest out. But don't overdo it; you don't want to look stiff or uncomfortable. Be relaxed and comfortable in your own skin. Know in your own mind that you can do this. Your walk should say that you are the guy to get to know. Be graceful in your movements. Look forward when walking. Do not walk with your head down. Walking with your head down is a passive or docile posture. It does not send the message of confidence or an alpha attitude.

You are out to make the right first impression. This first impression is what women see before they even hear your voice. From across the room, they see this "sexy guy," but the only thing they know about you is what they see. So, make yourself interesting. A quick first impression is made in roughly three seconds. When a person meets you for the first time, within about three seconds, they assess who you are, and their impression of you is based on how you present yourself, your appearance, nonverbal communiqué, your actions, presence, and how you dress. Ironically, first impressions are lasting impressions and difficult to change.

One way to lose the interest of a lady is to talk too fast. Slow down and get her attention. Don't rush through your words. Your excitement is a sign of insecurity and nervousness. When you speak slowly and at ease, it relaxes the conversation, and she is drawn in more. Show her you are interested when you lean in and lightly touch her on her arm, near the elbow but not too high up.

Facial expression should be a slight smile which is welcoming and conveys self-confidence. Eye contact is irresistible to women. Make eye contact and give the look of a man in charge who knows it. Not the jerky one, but the man of confidence and power. When George looks at women, he activates their interest and desire for him. If you want to interest women, maintain strong eye contact. Don't be intimidated or afraid to look her in the eye. Don't look away or look down. Be interested and look into her eyes deeply. Your gaze should say you are interested.

Recognize your posture. Are you slouching and making fast, jerking movements? Do you fidget or twiddle with your hands? If you do, stop it! Calm down and breathe. Take it slow. Don't move nervously or in quick movements. These actions demonstrate that you are not stable. But when you have it together and show slow, easy, and confident movements, this says to the lady that you are the man and you know it. Women will identify this masculine quality in you right away.

Another thing to mention about George Clooney is his voice. I know his voice is not body language, but what is important about it is his tone. It is not the words he uses, but rather the tone of the voice that makes women drop.

He has a deep soothing tone that is strong and commanding. By talking in a low, deep tone and speaking slowly, he creates sexual tension. You can set the mood by your tone, speaking slowly and at ease, taking pauses as you speak and in a low voice. Imagine George as he speaks and the reaction he receives. Try it! You can do it. Don't talk too fast and don't stammer when you talk. And please do not go to the extreme and sound like you are fake or pretending. Watch your pitch--go low not high.

Other alpha males who make the girls swoon are Pierce Brosnan, Idris Elba, and Brad Pitt. Idris Elba is an alpha male who attracts women with ease. He utilizes his skills of charm, confidence, and seductive eye contact to reach women.

He is attractive to women because he exudes confidence in the way he walks, talks, and maintains alluring eye contact. He has such a cool, calm, and collected demeanor. When he looks at someone, his gaze is intense. He is interesting yet mysterious. You know enough to like, but not so much to prevent you from wanting to know more. He has exhilarating energy that excites the ladies. He is competent, and his sexy voice with its deep tone is enhanced as he speaks slowly. You don't have to worry about him looking nervous, because he doesn't fidget. And with a great body and a rationed smile, the women are drawn in. He knows how to project the right impression.

Studies have shown that men with higher self-esteem are more desirable and attractive than those without it.

His sense of confidence and self-esteem are sexy, no question. In six studies from the journal, *Evolutionary Psychology*, men with ostensibly higher levels of self-esteem were rated as more attractive and as more desirable relationship partners than those with lower levels of self-esteem.

So, when you walk into your date, enter with strength and presence.

Approach a woman from an angle, not from behind or head on. Establish eye contact and maintain the connection and also have a friendly facial expression. Be open and welcoming with your body. Don't fold your arms and cross your legs. Be relaxed and calm. Be solid with a confident posture. While engaged in conversation, a light touch is just enough to let her know you are really interested. Masculine body language directed toward a woman is very alluring. This masculinity is presented in the traits of walking with purpose and having that relaxed and open posture. Take up space and keep your gaze of interest. And only smile on occasion. Your expression should draw mystery and curiosity. These characteristics, when mimicked, will be an attraction for women. This is swagger and confidence. Know that women are more observant of one's actions than one's words.

An alpha woman, out for the evening, notices on the other side of the room, a man whom she is interested in. She pauses just long enough until he notices her. When he does, she maintains eye contact long enough to connect. This should be about five seconds. She then looks away. Because it takes men a little longer to recognize the nonverbal message, she will have to repeat this three times before he recognizes her interest. She knows what she likes. After that, she gives a slight smile. This is a signal that it's okay.

A subconscious response should become evident, such as a change in posture that accentuates attributes like arching the back, tilting the hips, and playing with the hair. All of these are done when a woman finds a man whom she is interested in. If the interest is reciprocated, he responds with changes in a posture like standing with his chest push out and touching his hair. Face-to-face interaction says they are into each other. Face-to-face and feet pointed in the other's direction.

Sitting across from each other at a table encourages conversation, establishes good eye contact, releases tension, and makes each more comfortable. This is a good arrangement when sitting. If standing, the gentleman is positioned at a 45-degree angle initially and face-to-face as the interest increases.

Your body language tells others how you feel, your motivations, concerns, things you are partial to, and those things that you loathe. Your presentation, no matter what the setting is, must be the best presentation of yourself. Your charisma is what connects you to those around you. And as an alpha, you must be able to draw the attention and interest of those around you. Your presentation must be that you are the alpha and in charge. Your presence, attitude, posture, and walk must all agree that you are the alpha in the room. As a charismatic leader, you use many nonverbal cues.

You become extremely likable when you use appropriate body language indicators. A sincere smile at the right time, optimistic eye contact, and a slightly raised brow will generate a sanguine response. A variation of gestures and opposite body adjustments are indicators of interest as well as nonverbal communications such as turning their bodies toward each other during colloquy or moving one's drink closer to another's. These are movements that are interpreted as having an interest in the person you are interacting with.

Chapter 6: Body Language at Work: How to Be Memorable

Do you get nervous when preparing for an interview? How do you make the right impression and hopefully get the job? You can make a notable mark by incorporating a few techniques in your regime. The first impression that you give is important. An impression is made in the first seven seconds after someone meets you. So, your appearance, presence, and body language will have an immediate impact. You must have positive body language during an interview.

According to Sheryl Sandberg, it is important to lean in during an interview because it sends the message of interest. You want to send the right message. Hopefully, you show confidence and ambitions nonverbally as well through your conversation. Your body language should be a confirmation of who you say you are in your interview. As stated before, the majority of communication happens through body language and tone of voice as opposed to the actual words used. The study of human behavior and body movements has been used to investigate the influence and impact of such movement on others.

So when you interview:

Make eye contact

By making eye contact, you send the message that you are confident (even when you are not). Maintaining good eye contact shows strength and confidence. Be careful not to be awkward and stare but communicate with your eyes that you are focused and listening. If it is difficult for you to maintain eye contact, try to focus on the space between the eyes.

Give a firm handshake

Shaking hands firmly expresses that you are confident and sure of yourself--firm handshake, neither weak nor squeezing. You don't want a wispy handshake which screams insecurity--neither do you want to cause pain. So, grasp the hand and hold firmly while making eye contact. If you have sweaty hands, wipe them discreetly before shaking hands.

Breathe

Before you enter, take a deep breath, expand your chest, and exhale slowly. Andrew Weil, MD, author of *Breathing: The Master Key to Self-Healing,* suggests breathing exercises "since breathing is something we can control and regulate. It is a useful tool for achieving a relaxed and clear state of mind." While doing breathing exercises, release the stress and focus on the mission ahead. Clear your thoughts. And be positive.

Avoid restlessness

Excessive movement is a sign of nervousness and uncertainty. This is the point where many suffer--the uncontrollable, unconscious movement, and reaction. Place the feet squarely on the ground and put hands on your lap. Do not cross your body. Do not cross your arms across your chest or your legs. You are closing yourself off from others.

Do not ramble

Answer carefully and only what was asked. Don't ramble on about other things that were not part of the topic. Your speech should not be aimless but rather a purposeful and intelligent conversation. Be interesting.

Body Language in Business Meetings

They say actions speak louder than words, and in a business meeting, your body language speaks volumes. There is a proper and effective way to communicate in this manner that garners the attention of those around you to get the message across. According to various research studies, more than 90 percent of what we say is made through our body movements, tone of voice, facial expressions, and gestures. You want to leave a lasting impression in a business meeting.

Walk like an alpha

Make an impression when you walk in. Use good posture. Walk in tall and erect. To make that great first impression, your entrance should tell others that an alpha has arrived. As you enter, be sure you are standing erect and your shoulders are back. Your posture is important; it expresses your level of confidence. Remember: Tall and Proud. This is what you should feel and what your posture should communicate.

Greet with a handshake

As stated previously, a firm not wispy or crushing handshake is preferred. You want them to respect you and not see you as weak or unsure nor aggressive or overconfident. The handshake is also an indicator of personalities. The person whose hand is on top and palm facing down usually has the advantage.

Sit Up Straight

Sit up! Do not slump, hunch, or droop. This is an attitude of disinterest and laziness. Carol Kinsey Goman, Ph.D., a body language expert, says. "It makes you look submissive and like you don't have much to offer, and that's not a good look for anybody — particularly if you're trying to have leadership presence in your organization." Your feet should be planted squarely on the floor. Do not cross your legs, and if you do, only at the ankles. If you are standing, stand erect, head up, shoulders back, and chest forward. You are sending the message of confidence.

Stop crossing your arms; stop showing your attitude or insecurities. (Goman) "Most people are going to interpret that gesture as being resistant or closed off."

Don't be distracted

No texting or emails or playing games on the phone, tablet, or computer during an interview. Pay attention, know what's going on, and make eye contact with the speaker. Your distractions are disrespectful and distracting to others. You are leaving an impression by your actions. Any form of fidgeting shows boredom.

Maintain Eye Contact

Whether you are meeting one-on-one or in a group, eye contact is imperative. Do not look from side to side or downward. It is interpreted as you are not one that can be trusted nor should you look up as if lost in space. This truly transmits that you are lost.

Don't be Dismissive

Be engaged, be a part of the meeting. Speak up! "Say something early. Just get your voice out there, even if it's something that's not crucial to the conversation. You need to be vocal and jump in because it's often more difficult to interject as the meeting goes on."(Goman) You want to be memorable.

Presentations

How do I make a good impression in my presentation? What body movements do I use to convey the message I need to give? While portraying a vision of strength, you also want to appear comfortable and at ease. Being an alpha in any environment should send the message that you are comfortable in your own skin. This is who you are and not what you are trying to be. So, relax. Use hand gestures in moderation. The fewer the gestures, the more impact they will have.

You are a leader, and as the presenter, use the room as if it was yours. Maximize the space walking around and project yourself. The ability to move around and utilize the room gives presence and shows that you are the leader and are in charge. Take command of your space and be at ease. Be careful. Again, use moderation, don't go overboard, and run around aimlessly. Be purposeful and utilize it to your advantage.

Your Face Says So Much

Facial expressions say the things that your mouth does not. Whether you smile at the appropriate points or raise your brow to question a response, your expression is a confirmation of the message sent. Onlookers view your expression and internalize the meaning.

Being alpha is a part of the entire person. The body language of an alpha commands attention and respect. While some aspects may change in different circumstances, it is much the same most of the time. You carry your confidence into every situation whether in a social setting, a business meeting, or even in your personal interactions. How people perceive you is based on all the same activities.

While you may alter your expressions to be more serious in a professional setting, your expressions reflect your nature as a person. A smile at the right time gives a welcoming sign without a word being said. A raised eyebrow with a smile from a woman who is gazing into your eyes says I am interested.

The true alpha understands the implication of body language and also is an expert in business etiquette. He understands that body language is so important that it could have a major impact on business. This is also a part of business etiquette. How one acts during professional interactions has implications in the culmination of dealings. If you understand body language and its impact, it will help you navigate through difficult transactions.

It is understood that your posture while standing and walking is one of strength and dominance, but what about when you are sitting? While there are many different ways to position oneself, what is the most powerful or the most advantageous? A strong posture, even when sitting, is important. In business meetings, be attentive with an erect and observant pose. This means sitting with your back straight. Your legs should be squared on the floor. Do not fidget or be antsy during a meeting. This is a sign of nervousness or anxiety. There is some allowance for crossing the legs at the ankle. Do not cross legs at the knee.

Also, the hands are communicators and speak even when we do not want them to, so keep them on your lap unless in a controlled effort of expression. Avoid making erratic or jerky motions with your hands. No talking with your hands or pointing. Avoid distracting motions. Your hands should not be headrests or hip supports. Don't cross your arms or put hands in your pockets. This is a position recognized as being closed off. Your hands should be in a position that is open. Otherwise, keep your hands folded on your lap.

When standing, do not hold hands in front of your genitals and do not hold objects in front of the body. Both of these stances are distracting. One gives the appearance of weakness because it prevents one from standing erect and pushes the shoulders to the front rather than back. The other indicates that you have something to hide or that you are hiding behind the article to divide you and others.

Recognizing spatial restraints and spatial etiquette during business meetings is required. Social space limitations are appropriate here. This is the 48-inch or 4-feet of space immediately surrounding a person. When a person's space has been violated, they may back away or lean away. This is an indication that spatial comfort has been disturbed.

Stand tall and erect. Your posture should send the message of confidence, power, and respect. When you walk, it should be slow and with purpose, not too fast or erratic. When sitting, sit up straight and erect. Be attentive. Know where to put your arms and not let them move aimlessly. Your demeanor should be one of ease and relaxation. You have the power so embrace it.

Conclusion

Thank you for making it through to the end of *Body Language: Unlocking the Secrets of Nonverbal Communication in an Alpha Male and Female, Including How to Analyze People, Improve Your Social Skills, and Develop Charisma*. Let's hope it was informative and able to provide you with all of the tools you need to achieve your goals whatever they may be.

The next step is to make these traits and characteristics of an alpha a part of you. Build your confidence. Fake it till you make it. Practice your posture, walk with confidence, and believe inside that you are an alpha. Dress to impress and not to be trendy. Take care of your physical appearance. Practice daily being the alpha you desire to be. Recite affirmations and believe you are an alpha. When you can see yourself as an alpha and believe you are, others will see you that way as well. Remember, it is in the eye contact, presence, stance, posture, ease, facial expression, and a handshake that you speak.

Finally, if you found this book useful in any way, a review on Amazon is always appreciated!

www.ingramcontent.com/pod-product-compliance
Lightning Source LLC
Chambersburg PA
CBHW030106100526
44591CB00009B/291